GW01064095

Fiona Kidman has published more than 30 books, including novels, poetry, non-fiction and a play. She has worked as a librarian, radio producer and critic, and as a scriptwriter for radio, television and film. *The New Zealand Listener* wrote: 'In her craft and her storytelling and in her compassionate gutsy tough expression of female experience, she is the best we have.'

She has been the recipient of numerous awards and fellowships; in more recent years, *The Captive Wife* was runner-up for the Deutz Medal for Fiction and was joint-winner of the Readers' Choice Award in the 2006 Montana New Zealand Book Awards, and her short story collection *The Trouble with Fire* was shortlisted for both the NZ Post Book Awards and the Frank O'Connor Short Story Award. Her novel *This Mortal Boy* won the 2019 Ockham New Zealand Book Awards Acorn Foundation Fiction Prize, the NZ Booklovers Award, the NZSA Heritage Book Award for Fiction and the Ngaio Marsh Crime Writing Award for Best Novel.

She was created a Dame (DNZM) in 1998 in recognition of her contribution to literature, and more recently a Chevalier de l'Ordre des Arts et des Lettres and a Chevalier of the French Legion of Honour. 'We cannot talk about writing in New Zealand without acknowledging her,' wrote *New Zealand Books*. 'Kidman's accessible prose and the way she shows (mainly) women grappling to escape from restricting social pressures has guaranteed her a permanent place in our fiction.'

Also by Fiona Kidman

Novels
—

A Breed of Women, 1979
Mandarin Summer, 1981
Paddy's Puzzle, 1983
The Book of Secrets, 1987
True Stars, 1990
Ricochet Baby, 1996
Songs from the Violet Café, 2003
The Captive Wife, 2005
The Infinite Air, 2013
All Day at the Movies, 2016
This Mortal Boy, 2018

Short story collections (as author)
—

Mrs Dixon and Friend, 1982
Unsuitable Friends, 1988
The Foreign Woman, 1993
The House Within, 1997
The Best of Fiona Kidman's Short Stories, 1998
A Needle in the Heart, 2002
The Trouble with Fire, 2011
All the Way to Summer, 2020

Short story collections (as editor)
—

*New Zealand Love Stories: An Oxford
Anthology*, 1999
The Best New Zealand Fiction 1, 2004
The Best New Zealand Fiction 2, 2005
The Best New Zealand Fiction 3, 2006

Non-fiction

—

Gone North, 1984
Wellington, 1989
Palm Prints, 1994
At the End of Darwin Road, 2008
Beside the Dark Pool, 2009

Poetry

—

Honey and Bitters, 1975
On the Tightrope, 1978
Going to the Chathams, 1985
Wakeful Nights, 1991
Where Your Left Hand Rests, 2010
This Change in the Light, 2016

Play

—

Search for Sister Blue, 1975

So far, for now

*On journeys, widowhood and stories
that are never over*

Fiona Kidman

VINTAGE

VINTAGE

UK | USA | Canada | Ireland | Australia
India | New Zealand | South Africa | China

Vintage is an imprint of the Penguin Random House
group of companies, whose addresses can be found at
global.penguinrandomhouse.com.

Penguin
Random House
New Zealand

First published by Penguin Random House
New Zealand, 2022

13 5 7 9 10 8 6 4 2

Text © Fiona Kidman, 2022

The moral right of the author has been asserted.

All rights reserved. Without limiting the rights under
copyright reserved above, no part of this publication
may be reproduced, stored in or introduced into a retrieval
system, or transmitted, in any form or by any means
(electronic, mechanical, photocopying, recording or
otherwise), without the prior written permission of both
the copyright owner and the above publisher of this book.

Design by Carla Sy © Penguin Random House New Zealand
Cover photographs by TCrowePhoto (top) from iStock
and Ilnur Kalimullin (middle) and Kishan Modi
(bottom) from Unsplash
Other photographs courtesy of the author,
except where indicated
Author photograph by Robert Cross
Prepress by Image Centre Group
Printed and bound in Australia by Griffin Press,
an Accredited ISO AS/NZS 14001 Environmental
Management Systems Printer

A catalogue record for this book is available
from the National Library of New Zealand.

ISBN 978-0-14-377580-5
eISBN 978-0-14-377581-2

The assistance of Creative New Zealand
towards the production of this book is gratefully
acknowledged by the publisher.

penguin.co.nz

ARTS COUNCIL OF NEW ZEALAND TOI AOTEAROA

For Max, Darcie and
Josephine & Isabel and Hugo

———————

Contents

Preface 11

Mine alone 15
So far, for now 17
About grandparents 24
Finding home 42
North River 49
On writing memoir 63

The outsiders 83
Albert Black 85
Pure Duras 117
Quardling around Glover 128
Some other girl: the case for Jean Batten 135
Flying places 150

The body's sweet ache 167
On being massaged 169
Playing with fire 183
In the time of Covid 192

Going south 197
At Pike River 199
99 Albany Street 225

This new condition 237
Truffles 239
The blue room 245
On widowhood 247

Acknowledgements 265
Sources 267

Preface

More than a decade ago, I finished my second book of memoir, *Beside the Dark Pool*. My life seemed to have been rich, interesting and fortunate. As I confronted getting old, it seemed that nothing much more would happen, that the story was over. I would like to reassure readers that old age isn't dull. Things keep on happening. It's true that we lose more and more friends and family who have been significant, and this means learning new ways of coping with what we have left, to find our inner resilience. I can't deny that grief doesn't stalk us as we grow old. But there are pleasures all around. I find them in new friendships, books, my garden, the endless connections we make with one another.

These autobiographical essays are not in themselves a memoir, not a 'what happened next in my life' - or not exactly - but they reflect the progress through a time of change, and what has interested me over these years.

For those who have read my two memoirs - the first was *At the End of Darwin Road* - there will be echoes of some stories I have told before. Every author has their own voice. The essential past doesn't change, but how we look at it can. I have different perspectives now on some events. Perhaps that is one of the gifts of age - a softening around the edges, an acceptance of how things have gone.

I hasten to say, however, that, as a writer and a human being, I am as resistant to injustice as I have ever been. In a panel discussion some months ago, I commented that writing is a political act. That is not perhaps the case for all writers, but it remains so for me. I don't believe that justice is always meted out fairly and it seems to me that governments will often try to take the easy way out of their dilemmas. In these essays I have challenged perceived wisdoms about issues both past and ongoing. I have also examined the role of people who might be regarded as outsiders. They are all individuals who, in one way or another, have contributed to the way I see the world, even if I haven't met all of them in the flesh.

Every life is extraordinary if you allow it to be. I am grateful for mine.

Mine alone

So far, for now

How this new condition
changes language, not we
or us or ours
but I and me
and mine, mine alone
the hollow hours.

'Sleep a little longer,' my husband said, that morning. 'You have a long day ahead of you.'

'It will be the last time I go,' I said. 'No more travel. I'm going to be at home with you. Summer's coming and we'll spend it together.'

'I know,' he said.

We had always been on the move, that is how we were, but always, too, homing in, back to our house on the hill. I had kept going here and there longer than Ian, but then I was younger. I knew how he waited for me to return each time I jumped on a plane to go somewhere - to Europe, to a festival or just away for a day, like this trip to Auckland for a reading, some book sales.

His frailty was increasing. What was more important? I asked myself. The public life of a writer, or spending precious time with the person with whom I had shared my life? When I said that the travel was over, this was the last trip, I knew Ian was happy, although he had never tried to hold me back. This was another thing about us: we gave each other freedom to be who we were, to go where we pleased, to share the company of others. But, of late, I had sensed that my absences had become harder for him. Two weeks earlier I had finished writing my novel, *This Mortal Boy*. It had been an all-encompassing process, consuming my thoughts day and night.

'Thank you for coming back to me,' he said, a few days after I announced that I had arrived at the end of the book.

'I never left you,' I said. 'I was there all the time.'

He had shaken his head. And I suppose in a sense I was away when I wrote. As I suppose I am now, although there is nobody here to notice one way or another.

The reading went well. In the taxi back to the airport I rang and told him all about it. But I was tired that night. At the airport I learned that the plane was running late. I left my phone in the tray when I went through security. I was called on the PA system to collect it. That meant going back and through security again, and then proving that it was my phone. And then the plane was delayed again. At home, we were due to watch *The Brokenwood Mysteries*, our favourite-of-the-moment Sunday night programme. Just watch it, I told Ian. You don't have to wait for me. But he said he would record it so we could watch it together when I got home, or the next night, it didn't matter.

For the next hour or so, until we finally got under way, I read Diana Wichtel's fine memoir, *Driving to Treblinka*, about her search for her missing father. I rang Ian again when we got into Wellington, around 11 p.m., and told him I'd be there in a few minutes. I had taken up the offer of a taxi chit because I didn't want him driving out in the dark. He was due to give up his beloved old Mercedes sports car in the next week or two. He'd accepted that.

He was there waiting for me when the taxi drew up.

There is a long flight of stairs up to our house. The cable car wasn't working that night. Ian had come down, torch in hand. I berated him for doing so.

'Hurry on up,' he said. 'It's cold and I've got the house nice and warm and all the lights are on. Keep going.'

So hurry I did. I passed him and then, two steps ahead, I heard Ian fall. The thud. That sound will stay with me always.

There are some writers who would tell you the last detail. I'm not one of them. I thought I was, but I'm not.

The ambulance drove slowly through the deserted streets. I recalled Ian saying once that when an ambulance was going slowly it was a bad sign; there was nothing to hurry for, like the night my father was taken to hospital for the last time. The ambulance stopped while Ian's oxygen was adjusted. I remember that we were taken through a side door to Accident and Emergency but the next hour became a dream time. There was a CAT scan and a neurosurgeon. My family had begun to arrive: my daughter and her husband and my granddaughter.

I think it was the neurosurgeon who suggested that my husband's life support be turned off. There was irreversible brain damage. It could be a few minutes, perhaps a couple of hours, before Ian died. We needed to make the way easier for him.

Yes, I said. I guess so. Whatever is best. I suppose people say no. The situation was explained to me, the x-rays shown, demonstrating the extent of the injuries. So, yes, I said again. What else could I have done?

We told the rest of the family. My son was in Australia. He rang all his five sons and, in turn, they each called my mobile and asked that it be held to Ian's ear so they could say their goodbyes. One of the boys was already at the hospital with his mother. One was in Australia, another in London. When they had all spoken to their grandfather, they told me they were on their way home. All of them.

A nurse asked if there was anyone else I wanted to call. The monks, I said. For Ian was a Buddhist. His whakapapa stretched back to Ngāti Maniapoto and Ngāti Raukawa, but over the last thirty or so years, he had identified strongly with the Cambodian community, seen himself as a part of it. It had begun when he was a schoolteacher in a catchment area for refugees, and a tide of people who had escaped the Khmer Rouge regime came into his care. Two or three times a year, until age caught up with him, he had travelled to Cambodia as a volunteer worker with landmine victims. A part of his life was devoted to the local community that worshipped at Buddhachayamahanath Temple, overlooking the sea at Island Bay; the senior monk was one of Ian's closest friends.

So, as the night turned into morning, saffron-robed men appeared and started to chant. The steady rhythm of their voices began to calm us.

Ian, not yet ready to die, breathed steadily on.

A nurse said she thought it would be best to move him to a ward where we could all be more private. They were not happy about taking him through the corridors, because he might die in transit, and they didn't like this to happen. Still, she could see that the swelling crowd and the chanting would be better 'upstairs'.

As we made our way through the hospital, I realised I was still wearing the clothes I'd had on at the literary gathering in Auckland. The vigil began, the monks chanting intermittently until dawn broke, when they had to leave for prayers at the temple.

I asked the family to go home and sleep. I wanted to spend some time alone with my husband, just to hold his hand and talk to him about all our life together. I had met him when I was nineteen. We had been a couple for fifty-eight years. I believed he could hear me, although the nurses said that he couldn't.

The family, risen although I don't believe anyone had slept, called by to bring me food and a change of clothes. I'd rung people, close friends, Ian's sister. A little boy brought by his father unfurled a kite Ian had given him and raced it around the room.

I talked to Ian about the children and how they had made us happy and how things had turned out all right in the long run. I was talking to him about the River Kwai, where we once spent days in a green jungle retreat, and about the Hokianga, where we took holidays every other summer, when a nurse came in.

The staff had been good and kind and gentle. This nurse said, 'It's all right, it *was* an accident.' It was only days later that I turned this comment over more thoroughly. At the time, I thought, Well, yes, of course it was an accident. How could it have been anything else? Why did I need to be reassured?

When later came, I thought, Well, it happens, I suppose. You read about these things in the newspaper. I wondered how it had been determined as an accident, as opposed to not being one.

What I actually said, by way of reply, was that Ian had squeezed my hand when I was talking to him.

She said that that wasn't possible, it would have been a reflex.

'So I'll never hear his voice again?' I said.

'It's very unlikely,' she said, and I knew I was backing her into a corner. I have a friend who is a scientist. He has reminded me of Einstein's theory that all matter is vibrations, even objects that appear to be stationary. A bust of Einstein stands in our garden; it's been there for decades. When I look out the window from where I'm writing, I see his blind concrete eyes, his bristling moustache. He was our touchstone. We would refer to Einstein to resolve our problems. I couldn't believe, that morning, that Ian did not hear me, was not conscious, in some area of his still breathing form, of the things I had told him.

By the early afternoon a crowd had gathered, all the family who could get there now assembled. Our son was on his way from Australia. At the temple, the monks had told worshippers the news and word had spread. The corridors of the hospital had filled with Cambodians. There were people everywhere. The chanting rose and rose.

So my husband died.

I turned to my family and said, in disbelief, 'I'm a widow now, aren't I?'

Some forty hours had passed since I had woken the previous day for the trip to Auckland. Now I slept for fourteen hours straight. Before I went to sleep, I found Ian's old brown woollen jersey and held it in my arms, his scent still fresh on it.

When I woke, the house had been taken over. The family had moved in. I noticed the change as soon as I entered the kitchen. Ian had a fondness for cheap electrical goods. The toaster and the jug and other items had all been replaced with shiny new ones. Every room was dusted and immaculate; flowers sat on all the tables.

We brought Ian home the next day, to lie in this room overlooking the garden and the sea and the birds he fed every day. He loved everything that flew. Planes pass the window, lifting off from the airport, or coming into land, depending on which way the wind is blowing; he had been a pilot once when he was a young man. He stayed with us for nearly a week, never left by himself. Each night around five, the monks would come to chant, and Cambodian people to kneel in my house.

Ian had always said that he wanted to be carried feet first from this place that, in life, he never wanted to leave. The cable car was working again. On the day, when it came time to go, our son arranged for the pall bearers to lift the coffin onto it, standing straight up. Feet first, we said, and were overtaken by wild hilarity.

––––––––––

We buried Ian on a lovely spring day in the first week of November. Before the service, I placed a sheaf of sunflowers on his coffin, and the fisherman's cap that he'd bought in Greece and wore every day. In front of it, I stood a painting of him by the artist Ken Hunt; he painted it when Ian retired from fifty years of teaching. In the painting, Ian is dark-skinned, silver-haired, a handsome man with the trace of a smile hovering on his lips. The expression is, in some way, a touch wistful, and there was that about him in moments of reflection. I recognised that. The sun shone, hundreds of people came. When the undertaker had asked me how many people they should cater for after the service, I'd said, a couple of hundred. He had shaken his head and observed that people always thought more would come than actually turned up. Perhaps a hundred and twenty, he suggested.

He had got most things right but not this. People had come from far and wide, from London and Australia and all parts of the country. They spilled out of All Saints Church in our local village, and into the adjacent hall, and across the lawn, and onto the pavement. One of my granddaughters-in-law sang 'Without You' to open the service. All the family spoke. The monks chanted. A former student read a poem. The eulogy was given by Annette King, a former Cabinet minister, who had been a close friend. Our daughter gave a haunting reading from a short story of mine called 'Silks', about the time when Ian had nearly died while we were in Hanoi, and the way it brought us all so close. Our son talked about his father's unconditional love.

Many of the Cambodian community are taxi drivers from the same company. Ian had once said, in a joking moment, that when he died he wanted all the taxis to stop the traffic in Wellington. They had taken him at his word. As we left the church, a long cavalcade of white taxis with blue lights on their roofs snaked through the city behind the cortège, leaving chaos in its wake. The taxis peeled off at the gates to the cemetery, and then it was just us, thirty or so family with our great-grandchildren, plus all the nieces and nephews.

Ian had chosen the spot where he would lie – in a small dip in the cemetery, surrounded by trees where birds rest and sing. Our daughter led a waiata; although he was being buried here, in our hearts it was time to take my husband back to his roots, for the final farewells from the place he had come, the marae of his childhood.

I knelt beside him.

All the lights are on, he had said that night. Keep going.

We had come so far, he and I; for now, I had the rest of my life to consider how I was going to do it.

About grandparents

1

Every day the sea
     grandmother
the last fringe of light lies
beneath a banner of storm
clouds the burden of hills
presses against air from out
of my window I touch the leaves of kowhai we planted
a whole quarter of a century
ago such an accumulation
of years how we guarded those saplings
from hurricanes
     nothing much changes
lights aeroplanes a tangle of cable wire
but the outlines of the place
we've both called home
are still here
I know you through
these hills, this horizon, tonight's
wild dark, our summer
          days
because you are my grandmother

Grandparents, they are the history that lies beneath our skins.

For much of my life I chose not to pursue my ancestry. And yet it was there, lying at my feet and all around me. All the time. I live on a hill that overlooks land occupied by my forebears two hundred years ago.

On 31 January each year, two distant cousins and I set off for the Seashore Cabaret on the foreshore of Petone, a satellite district of Wellington. The café, its dancing glory days now in the past, is up a steep flight of steps and crowded with what you might call a cross-section of people, some eating large meals: women in head scarves, Māori and Pacific Island families, young mothers with wriggling shouty children. The walls are crowded with retro posters and there is an advertisement for tarot readings on Sunday afternoons at five.

My cousins, the Sutherlands, and I are all of Celtic descent, but we are not here to look for mystical meanings, or the power of the Celtic Cross, although that's not to say we're uninterested in the past. We have a number of things in common. Melody and Bess are sisters; one was previously a trademark executive, one a librarian. When I was very young, I was a librarian too. I feel it's a sign that we're intrinsically connected by books and ideas. Every time we meet, I find myself searching their faces for clues to my own identity. Do I look like them? Melody has auburn hair, Bess has curls, mine was once heavy and dark. It's the eyes, we say, it's something about them that's distinctive, that sets us apart, though in my heart of hearts I know that's not exactly true. If I resemble any of the women who went before me, it is most likely my Irish grandmother, whom I never knew. Never mind, there is a sense of kinship. And, given how few close relatives I have, Melody and Bess have designated me their honorary second cousin and I like so much that they have. It's more like fourth or fifth; it's always hard to stitch up the generations. What we recognise is our forebears in common, Alexander and Elizabeth Sutherland, who arrived on the appointed date of our meetings, in 1840. We gather to spend time together and to remember, to look at the sea, at the heads that the *Oriental* sailed through before reaching safe harbour, to consider the beach below us where the emigrants landed; to marvel that our great-great-grandmother had given birth not long before – it is said while the ship was hove-to at the Wellington Heads, although the dates are a little cloudy. We laugh over the fact that if Elizabeth could have made it to land, the little girl, whose name was Kathrean, would have qualified for a bounty as the first European baby to be born in our town.

In the north, six days after the *Oriental* made landfall, the Treaty of Waitangi was signed.

On my mother's side, this is my whakapapa. We remind each other, Melody, Bess and I, that our ancestors are not called pioneers today but settler colonists, the takers of the land; it seems to ill behove that we celebrate their heroism. Yet we can only salute the fortitude, the sheer will to live, that Elizabeth, our great-great-grandmother, exemplified on that journey. Without her, we would not be here.

Those forebears were settlers in the land-hungry migration organised by Edward Gibbon Wakefield, an Englishman with a shady past and a penchant for kidnapping young heiresses, who set up the New Zealand Company to buy land from Māori for much too little and sell it at a profit. My Sutherland great-great-grandparents came on one of his five ships. We may acknowledge this troubled past to each other, but we have become part of this land and there is no returning, any more than there was for that birthing woman on the *Oriental*. We have no other place to call home; we are prisoners to our history but also its celebrants.

I think of Elizabeth on the pitching sea, tended in childbirth by women who had come from the same village of Badbea (pronounced bad-bay), in the Highlands of Scotland, and how she somehow survived her ordeal.

We don't know much about her at that stage of her life, although there is a legend with the power of myth that I come back to over and again, and if I have told it before, it is because it never leaves me. It is a metaphor for what mothers do when their children are at risk, or they are likely to be separated from them.

That village of Badbea was occupied by tenant farmers. Most of us who are descendants of this line know the story of the Clearances, the way the landed gentry turfed tenant farmers off the land, burning the roofs of their crofts so that they could not live in their houses, leaving families homeless and poverty stricken. They were sent to small farms on the coast where farming was unsustainable, expected to take up fishing or the collection of kelp from the seas. The weather in Badbea is said to be so harsh that, as the people worked, they had to tether their livestock and their children to rocks or posts to prevent them being blown over the cliffs. My great-great-grandfather, Alexander Sutherland, raised by the local preacher (so there is that in my line too), was an opponent of the Clearances and one of the first in the village to depart for New Zealand, joining the mass migrations to the 'colonies' that was taking place all over the Highlands.

Elizabeth's family didn't want them to leave, and she didn't want to go either. She already had a little girl, Christy, and she was recently pregnant. With great reluctance, Elizabeth travelled to the eastern coastal village of Brora, where a ship was waiting to take the travellers to London to join the migration. They had with them an assortment of possessions that included a Bible, some willow pattern jugs and a mahogany table. But when it came time to board the ship, Elizabeth held back, holding Christy in her arms. I can hear the keening rising in the air, the laments and the farewells; I can see her refusal, see her mother's anguish, yearning for her daughter and grandchild to stay.

At that moment, her husband came down the gangplank, snatched Christy from her mother's arms and left Elizabeth standing there. So that was her choice, to follow her child, her first born, or give her up forever. She followed.

I would have done this too. I would follow my children to the ends of the earth. But it doesn't always work like that, as it did not for the mother of Elizabeth, and that is the lesson you learn, I suppose, that there is only so far you can go with your children. And then, when there are grandchildren, they might be anywhere in the world, scattered in foreign countries. But they are always kin, they are part of who we are.

Later, after this migration, my great-grandmother, Margaret, was born, here in this town.

We point to the heads, Melody and Bess and I, and wonder aloud how Elizabeth did it. The sea is sometimes sunlit, but the last day we went it was sullen, clouds hovering overhead. The records do not say what the weather was like by the time the ship reached the shore in 1840, but we believe it rained for days afterwards. There is a touching story about a young wife who sat on an upturned boat, soon afterwards, and remarked quietly that it was 'a long journey to make just to see some rain'. We don't know the exact spot on the sandy beach beneath the Cabaret where the new settlers first set foot but we understand they made their way ashore along a rough, newly erected jetty. They would live in tents for some time to come. What we do know is that we are sitting here in the Cabaret, exploring the ties of blood, because our great-great-grandmother made it that day.

Survival. There are two sides to most stories. One displacement sets the scene for another. I know that my great-great-grandmother flourished in this country. A cow had been carried on the *Oriental* from London to Wellington, and Elizabeth was the only woman who knew how to milk it. She got more cows and made butter, which she sold for five shillings a pound. She and Alexander grew wealthy on a farm that spanned the bay below where I live now; they added sheep to their holdings and grazed them on land that, coincidentally, borders the house where I have lived for the past fifty years. When the great earthquake of 1855 occurred and the land was displaced, they picked up their sheep and carried them around the coastline to new pastures to the north.

I let none of this touch me for decades.

My grandparents, my mother's parents, disapproved of her marriage to an Irishman who was not Presbyterian. We moved away from them when I was a child. I turned my back on my mother's history. But there are certain things I know without being told, and I found myself increasingly unsure of where they came from. In 1986, I wrote a novel called *The Book of Secrets*. It was about a charismatic preacher called Norman McLeod who led a migration from the Highlands of Scotland to Nova Scotia, and from there to Waipu in the north of New Zealand, where my own parents owned a farm. I considered Waipu and its history the sole inspiration for that book, but I don't know any more whether that's true, especially as I sit with my kin remembering the *Oriental*'s landing. Who am I? One part of me is from the Irish grandparents I never knew, the other part from a Scotswoman. When I was nine years old, I knew, like her, how to milk a cow, I called a fictional character in *The Book of Secrets* Christy and I am, I have learned, the descendant of a preacher who drew hundreds to him. The same keening that farewelled McLeod and his followers followed mine. A part of me is undone by this knowledge.

In the passageway of my house, I have an old wood-framed photograph of my great-grandmother, and one of her husband, Neil Small. She stands in front of a velvet curtain looped back by braid, her fingers trailing over the back of a chair. Her eyes appear fierce and direct, although my informants tell me she had dementia by the time the picture was taken, so that stare is hard to interpret. She wears a hat like a guardsman's helmet tilted over her brow, and there is a ruffle of lace at her wrists. This is Margaret, grown old and rich, bringing with her a variety of legacies. Above my bookshelves stand fluted silver vases, and on the middle finger of my left hand I wear a mother of pearl ring. The vases and the ring came from her.

Later, all that money would be gone. She lies in death in a country cemetery, surrounded by Neil and several of her descendants. Their son, another Alexander, married my grandmother, Elizabeth Stewart, from Dumfries. In a drawer, I have the paisley crinoline cover that Elizabeth's mother wore on the ship out (it actually belongs to my daughter but I am caring for it at the moment), and in family lore there is a wealth of 'good connections'. The Stewarts went all the way back to Robert the Bruce, fierce battles and murderous times, to the Sinclairs and the Kirkpatricks and the Mackays and the Camerons, names borne by my mother and her siblings. I am one of their two surviving remnants. The clans speak across centuries. My uncle Robert, my mother's brother, bought a length of Royal Stewart tartan to be made into a skirt for me when I was a child. I failed to learn the Highland fling.

because you are my grandmother
I wear old fine gold and mother-of-pearl
because, because of this,
I wear this hair shirt of guilt
the settlers' shame

There was that too. In the years that I spent on farms, there in the Waikato, and later in the Far North, it did not occur to me that I was occupying what has been termed 'debatable land', that in time to come the entire country would be contested. Now I understand the concept better with each passing day. Just recently, while talking to a woman I had newly met, I described my house on the hill as my tūrangawaewae.

'Not in a Māori sense,' she said, with some acidity. She was talking about spirituality and connection with the land.

It stung. Looking at my history, my whakapapa as we say now in Aotearoa New Zealand, and where it stretches to that Petone beach, I know that in a sense what she said was true.

'It's my place to stand,' I answered, uneasily. 'It's the place where I know who I am.'

And that is true too. I have no other.

'The Emigrants' by Gerald Laing, situated at Helmsdale near Badbea, in Sutherlandshire, depicting a crofting family looking back to the home they have been forced to leave.

HEATHER HOURIGAN

2

If my maternal grandparents left a trail of belongings that revealed their journey from the poverty of the Highlands to the rich, hilly expanses of New Zealand, there is little of my Irish grandmother to be found, except a handful of letters and the photograph my father kept, the one in which he likened my eyes to hers. I'm sure there is some truth in that. Hers are large and direct beneath the straight dark brim of her hat, and my optician has remarked more than once on the expanse of my eyes, a problem for those who suffer, as I do, from dry eyes. So much more blinking to be done. These are my grandmother's eyes, the imprint she has left on me and, as I have got older, I feel the Irish in me in an astonishing way. It seems that what Ann O'Hara of Bandon, County Cork, bequeathed me was her gene pool. Her husband, Henry Eakin, was born in County Leitrim, but I know even less of him.

Ann died years before I was born. She is buried in a cemetery off Tees Road in Middlesbrough, the Yorkshire town where my father was born. In her death notice, the text read: 'And they shall be mine saith the Lord of Hostes, in that day when I make up my

Jewels.' Writing to my father, her sister described her as 'that most unselfish of women'. Probably true. She had given her childless sisters her eldest boy, my father's brother, to raise in Ireland.

I have nothing of hers but there is a letter that she wrote to my father in 1934, from Granville Road in Middlesbrough where she and my grandfather were then living. Calling my father Lofty, and further on Nip, she asks whether he received the suit and a cash draft she had sent. In a sense he was her only child. His sister had died shortly after birth. His brother had been frail when he was relinquished to his aunts. There is longing in her tone: 'This has to be a short letter till I know what or where you are likely to be, you see at present I do not know.'

A month or two later my grandmother died of bowel cancer. My grandfather had gone for a walk in the afternoon. While he was away she was overtaken with dreadful pain and knocked on the wall of her terraced house to alert her neighbour, but by the time she reached hospital, it was too late. She had had some discomfort, my grandfather wrote in another letter, but she had been treating it with a bottle of stuff from Pedlow, the doctor – a tablespoonful three times a day. During the autumn she had got two or three bottles of something else from the chemist and thought that suited her better. Just before Christmas she complained of indigestion and decided not to have a roast fowl, but managed some lamb and plum pudding instead.

After she died, my grandfather took up with a widow called Mrs Murphy, who had nine children. She was supposed to be taking care of him but there are a number of photos of the pair of them at Redcar, where they had gone to live. I suppose that my grandfather must have had a late, last love. He left her what money he had.

My knowledge of his early life is scanty, except that he was born in County Leitrim, near the ruins of fifteenth-century Fenagh Abbey, once a place of worship for the Church of Ireland, and a place my father would recall from time to time. My grandfather was Protestant; his family was connected with the Royal Irish Constabulary and, for someone seeking their Irish roots, that's not a good look. But if I don't tell that truth, sooner or later, somebody may well do it for me. Our history is never as shiny as we would want, our folklore often clouded.

Despite that deep conservatism in my father's background, my Scots grandparents disapproved of my mother's marriage simply because he was Irish.

3

During the Second World War, my mother and I lived with her
parents, my maternal grandparents, the Smalls, on a Waikato
farm, and several of her siblings, my aunts and an uncle. At
night, my mother and I slept in a tiny cottage at the bottom of
the garden, heated by a wood stove as the winter fogs swirled
outside. In season, calves bleated against the walls. Alongside
my uncle, my mother milked cows when they 'came in' after their
calving; my father came and went on his leaves, wearing his air
force uniform. My uncle played his bagpipes on the hills at night
when milking was over. One of my aunts was a pale beautiful
invalid and had breakfast taken into her on a tray, complete with
her daily senna pod juice to help with her constipation. Another
aunt was brisk and accepted no nonsense. Yet another visited
and flashed an engagement ring, long after the time for marriage
seemed over. I was the tearful flower girl at her wedding when she
became the third wife of a man who would adore her always. I
was supremely happy there on the farm, ensconced in this broad
nest of family. At its heart were Sandy and Lizzie: Alexander,

descended from the Sutherlands, and Elizabeth from the Stewart line.

My grandmother was already old and floury faced. By the time I was born she was almost past hoping her barren children would provide her with grandchildren. I threw a stone at her one day when she grew irritable and, in the fuss that ensued, I ran for my life, straight between the legs of a horse that stood still and allowed me to pass. In the terror of what might have been the consequences, the way I could have been *killed*, how fortunate they all were that I had been spared, I was forgiven. Of course I was.

As for the story of my grandfather, that is a familiar one too. My parting from him was the central drama of my childhood, the trauma that I would endure for years to come, the one that makes me fear separations and partings. I will hold on like someone clinging to the edge of the precipice with their fingernails rather than let anyone leave my life. I've fallen off a few times; there are slippages and surrenders and goodbyes and the moment when it is impossible to remember the phone number of a beloved person. The wounds aren't fatal but that one, that wrenching and tearing apart, felt close to it. We would sit, my grandfather and I, in long slanting sunlight at the breakfast table and his stories would begin, always the stories. He had a trim moustache and a shining bald head. He would spread his porridge with honey and butter while he talked, his attention always fixed on me. But naturally, for I was the only child, the whole of the next generation, as near perfect as it was possible for a round girl with a pudding basin haircut to be. Our conversation would go on, long after everyone else had left the table and gone their way for the day's work.

Alongside of us, filling the length of a wall, stood a tall dresser, ceiling high and ornately carved. I would know it anywhere. It was a family heirloom, and I understood it came on a ship, although which one is a mystery. It wasn't on the *Oriental*, so possibly it was on a later sailing, the Stewart migration perhaps. Sometimes when I climbed down from my chair I would trace the whorls in the wood, the intricacies of each groove, as high as I could reach, the dark stain polished to a satin finish by my grandmother and the aunts.

My grandfather and I would set off to the hills then and he would go on talking and I would ask for more and more about the old days, the horses, journeys around a long-gone sheep station that took days, about how he cut out his rotten tooth with his pen knife once when he couldn't wait to get attention for it, about how to slit the throat of a sick sheep, about the word of God when it came to him, about where the hens might have laid their eggs today. I was like a bell hung round his neck, the voice that told the watchers and minders where we were. My grandfather had dementia, as his mother had, but I didn't know this. I know only that when my father came back from his wartime service, my parents and I packed up and left. The last time I saw my grandfather was on the railway station at Frankton Junction, his old, old face leaking with tears. That's the opening scene of my second novel, *Mandarin Summer*; a child leaving behind those she loved, the bitter aftermath of that farewell, that sense of loss, for me, and for him. Whenever I think of him, I recall the family story that, after I was gone, he would scour the hills looking and calling for me.

And far away in the north I would be asking myself why I was there and how I could get back to him. So here I go, weeping about it all over again. He died soon after and that was that, but *that* never really is. It's a word which means nothing and covers pretty well everything, if you let it.

The dresser slipped from the family's grasp, and I realised after a time that though it represented those years, it was an object, not the person I loved. By the time I found it again, it had assumed a different place in my history.

Besides, I have many things. As well as Margaret Sutherland's mother of pearl ring, which I wear most days, I have Lizzie Stewart's wedding ring and my mother's, and sometimes I wear all of them, though I'm not given to rings in a general sense. I have in my possession the black lace collar that was worn on a mourning dress of another great-grandmother. I have family china, which is unfashionable now, and my grandmother's clock. And so on. That accumulation of the past. You could create a museum if you allowed yourself, and that is not something I want to do.

Yet there are nights when I say to my grandmothers, as I look towards the same sea they sailed across, do not abandon me.

4

I was forty-three when my first grandchild came along, and another five would follow. Each child seemed like a miracle. I would hold these new-born babies, sometimes within minutes of their arrival, with such a profound sense of wonder, as if they were an extension of myself. Which, in a manner of speaking, they are. They stopped coming a long time ago, but now they are reproducing themselves. I have five great-grandchildren already. I have to remind myself that they already have grandparents - my children. I have learned to cede some rights. But they are still part of that great life cycle to which we all belong.

I have a saying that I pass on to friends who are becoming grandparents for the first time. I tell them: 'Becoming a grandparent is nature's way of reminding us when we are old what it is like to fall in love again.' And they agree.

Grandparents, it has to be said, can be crashing bores, thrusting photographs in front of their friends, or even people they meet on buses and trains, demanding that these children be admired. They are the smartest kids, they will tell you, cute and funny and endearing, and given the slightest chance they will launch into a story that demonstrates the truth of their assertion. I have done it myself, waited for the murmur of approval, the polite nod of the head, the obligatory smile. But it's true, there is some deep level of response, almost hormonal, primeval, a triumphant inner shout that says I endure, I am now, and I am the future. We see it in these children.

My own parents were fine grandparents, their home the perfect holiday destination for our children until they moved close to us. My father and I had had an uneasy relationship, as he did with most people, and remembering that makes me sad for all sorts of reasons. He had an inner loneliness but, in his grandchildren, he discovered a love that tumbled out unrehearsed. There were times when I envied the closeness between him and my daughter. He blew blue smoke rings around his grandchildren until the last painful week of his life, when he left behind an unexpected legacy. As he lay in hospital, he repeatedly asked my son, then eighteen, for a cigarette, which he refused, as he was bound to. Afterwards, my son told me that he had made a resolution, stubbed out his last cigarette because he couldn't bear to be in that dreadful position himself. He never smoked another. A day or so later, my father died in an infectious-chest ward, while down the corridor lay his newly born first great-grandchild, unmet though he had longed to survive long enough to see her.

What sort of a grandparent have I been? Or, were Ian and I, because it was a joint endeavour from the beginning.

In my view, Ian was a model grandfather. When he set eyes on his first grandchild, a girl, a fierce protective bond was forged between them that lasted until the day he died; he never stopped loving her, he never failed her. And when he was old and growing frail, she looked after him. Neither, so far as I could see, did he fail the boys who followed. In their memory, he is the person who made them laugh, who performed tricks, who made sure they got home safely, who put his hand in his pocket if they needed things, who stood and cheered Saturday after cold Saturday at sports grounds, who muttered curses to himself if the referee called against them. When the chips were really down, he'd speak his mind to his grandsons and they would listen. He was Grandpa; his was the word.

For my part, I cooked often for my grandchildren, and food is as good a persuasion, a honey pot, if you will, as any. They swarmed all over many meals. But I was also the Grannie who was hopeless at board games, timid at cards, couldn't kick a ball, but decided they should have experiences, like going to the theatre. The girl and I did a lot together, the experiments with the boys were more spasmodic, but instilled in all of them is an acknowledgement of the arts and a real love of music and drama and painting. I'm proud of that.

In return they would bring small treasures and finds, and these are scattered around my house still. I used to think I should explain the odd assortment of mementoes: they're not connected, they don't have a theme and most of them have little value, except to me. A visitor once remarked that our house was 'comfortably cluttered'. Well. So? There are shells collected at beaches, toby jugs from second-hand shops, pen knives, a chipped vase, stones painted in rainbow colours, a model fishing boat built to scale. I know where each item came from. There is, as well, a beautiful art installation painted by the grandchild who is now an artist in London. And, tucked alongside my grandmother's silver teapot, there is a souvenir Arc de Triomphe, about the width of my closed fingers, coated with a dull bronze-coloured patina that is soft and silky to the touch. When I look at it, I see a fifteen-year-old boy with a dagwood haircut, wearing the baggy trousers that were fashionable twenty years ago, boarding a plane.

At school this boy had a best friend whose English parents decided to relocate to their hometown, taking their son with them. As they left, they said blithely to my grandson, Come and see us in England. He took it seriously; he was that kind of person, still is. He scrimped and saved by stacking shelves at the supermarket after school and family threw in money as Christmas presents. When he had the fare together, he bought his ticket and off he went, all by himself, an unaccompanied minor.

'Darling,' I said, at the airport, 'you can't go all the way to London without going to Paris.'

What on earth was I thinking? This boy, my son's child, looked at me with the typical quizzical gaze that he has carried from childhood, through medical school and into marriage and parenthood. I could see what he was thinking: How do I afford that? And, it occurred to me afterwards, What a mad grandmother I have. I popped a roll of notes into his hand.

'For Paris,' I said. 'You get on the Eurostar.'

He went, and to Amsterdam too. On the way there and back he was searched for drugs, this blond, clean as a whistle child. Well, of course he was. What *was* I thinking, *really*? When he arrived back in New Zealand, his parents had to sign to get their child back off the plane.

The Arc de Triomphe is what he brought me back, his trophy and mine.

I have been that sort of grandmother.

My children didn't know their paternal grandmother until they were at school. I had been married to Ian for ten years. There had been an estrangement within the family. I loved Ruby, real name Amelia, when I met her, and it was mutual. She knitted for the children and crocheted a bed jacket for me and gave me treasured items of jewellery that she wanted me to pass on. Her story, a hard life, is reflected in my short fiction, 'A Needle in the Heart'. Her lineage, Ngāti Maniapoto and Ngāti Raukawa, runs through some but not all of my descendants. My son, who came to me as an infant, is of Greek origin: he is Papou rather than Grandpa to his grandchildren and they call their grandmother Yiayia. So I have grandchildren and great-grandchildren who are Greek. And Ngāi Tahu. And Spanish and French, and Chinese and Dalmatian, not to mention that blend of Irish and Scottish that runs through my veins and our story and song lines.

Although it is true that I come from settler stock, what I see in my descendants are people far removed from that constraint, that perception of themselves. They are both of and at one with the land and, at the same time, bring new dimensions to what it is to be a citizen of Aotearoa New Zealand. They have set me free from the uneasy past.

Everyone has grandparents. Not everyone has grandchildren. I have been fortunate.

There are things I could go on and on saying. Like the names. We hand them down too, treasures to keep memory alive. My granddaughter shares the names of two great-grandmothers, and also of my mother, Flora. My son bears the name of his adopted great-grandfather, stretching back generations and carried forward to his children and *his* grandchildren.

I can tell you about the olive trees that grow outside my kitchen window. Each one was planted by a grandson, each one sturdy and brave against the winds that blow here on this hill where I live.

I can tell you that, at Ian's funeral, he was carried from the church by his six grandchildren, who had hurried from here and there, around the world.

I can tell you that the one who came from London slept beside his grandfather's coffin for five nights, here in this room where I am writing now.

I can tell you that my granddaughter slept beside me on some of those nights.

And that is enough.

Finding home

It occurred to me one day that I did not know where my first home was, where I had lived immediately after my birth. I know the town. It is Hāwera, which lies within sight of Mount Taranaki, the name translating more or less as 'shining peak', as it surely is, a glorious snow-topped cone. For a while it was called Mount Egmont, and briefly, in the eighteenth century, Pic Mascarin. I am awestruck by its presence, its thunderous, presiding beauty. But although my mother had left an account of her life for me, she hadn't included the address of the house where I spent the first nine months of my life. I had never thought to ask her. It felt as if a void had opened up before me. I think now that she needed to forget that place.

Over the years I had accumulated a sense of the town, although I visited only once or twice, on the way to somewhere else. In the days when I worked as a radio producer, the head of my department was Helen Young, known as Hennie, an elegant and wholly delightful woman who had come from Hāwera. As it happened, her father had delivered me, in his role as a doctor. Her cousin worked in our department too, and one or two other people on the same floor had connections to the town. Sometimes I wondered if I had got the job because, in a sense, I was one of the 'family'. I understood the network but was never really part of it.

Much later, I wrote a novel called *The Captive Wife*. It concerns a woman called Betty Guard, who was kidnapped on the Taranaki coastline in 1831, and one of the two pā sites where she was held is Orangi Tuapeka, near the end of the road that runs past what was once Mount View Hospital, where I was born. During a research trip, I found that building, now a large house sitting in a pretty garden; it seemed like enough at the time.

My parents left Hāwera because the town hadn't worked for them. This was at the end of the Great Depression, the beginning of the Second World War. They had returned to New Zealand from a couple of years working in Australia, because my mother wanted her children to be born in her home country. My father took a job as a door-to-door insurance salesman. Born the night Michael Joseph Savage died, I was a sickly child from the outset. When I was near death, my mother was referred to a visiting specialist who told her she was a bad mother and that her child needed to go to Karitane Hospital in Whanganui and to stay put until she was sent for to collect me. In the meanwhile, she was not to go near me. Thus, I was separated from her for several of those early months.

As she would tell it, she went nearly crazy with despair. She paced the floors of the house she and my father rented and took up smoking, lighting one cigarette after another. She could have taken to drink but she was never a drinking woman. Or, she could have taken her life, but she needed to stay alive because she had to believe I would survive. Of course, my mother's faith was not misplaced. I did survive, in rude good health, seemingly unharmed by the experience, though I think my mother never entirely got over it. I was her only child and, except when I travelled, I was rarely far from her sight for the rest of her life. In fact, some intense mutual attachment must have been forged: I needed her to be near me in order to feel safe.

After my mother died, I wrote a poem in which I imagined the house as narrow and quite dark:

> . . . *watching their cigarettes drift*
> *curling smoke through the nights, listening*
> *to pounding seas on Taranaki's wild*
> *coast and the wail of the sickly child.*

But soon I realised that the house was nowhere near the sea, even if the hospital was.

In 2019 I was invited to tour South Taranaki for a week, giving talks and visiting schools. My base would be a motel in Hāwera, in Princes Street, which runs off the main South Road. I had been invited to talk about *This Mortal Boy*, published the year before, and the first event was in the library, by which I was immediately charmed. It had matchwood ceilings and stained-glass windows and I could imagine my mother there, finding some kind of comfort from the elements. She had worked at a small-town library in Western Australia. There was an authors' board on the wall too. My name was on it, as if I belonged here, and, alongside it, that of my loved friend, children's writer Jennifer Beck. We had been to school together in the north, and now, however much by chance, we were being hailed in what some might describe as my hometown.

Not that I could really frame my parents in Hāwera. I couldn't see them walking on the footpaths. Would my lanky father, the insurance salesman, with his carefully polished accent have fitted into the White Hart Hotel on the corner of High and Main streets? Perhaps. He would have loved the hotel's name, echoing the places he called home – England and County Cork. I thought he might have gone in and talked to the men at the bar as he sought prospective buyers of insurance policies. But he was shy and a little awkward around strangers and he stammered when under pressure. Besides, buying a round would have stretched what I later understood were the near non-existent finances.

When I visited, the hotel was one of the few original wooden buildings left, besides the library and the old wooden courthouse, crouching nearby under a spreading pōhutukawa tree. There are several square solid concrete buildings, decorated with arches and curlicues. The translation of the word Hāwera is, I believe, 'breath of fire', dating back to a quarrel between tribes in which the village was razed (although I have also seen it referred to as 'burnt place'). Owing to some devastating fires in the town since European settlement, the locals had taken to building in durable materials they hoped would be fire resistant. Because a lack of water had hampered early firefighting efforts, they had erected a 54-metre concrete water tower. It stands sentinel, dominating the townscape, the tallest building in Taranaki. Inside, there are 215 steps to the top. I haven't climbed them, but then I never climbed to the top of Florence's Duomo either.

I ranged around Taranaki, that sliver of land on the western edge of the country, speaking in all the little places: Manaia, Waverley, Stratford, Eltham, Ōpunake, Pātea. For the school sessions, kids were bused in from Waitara and other outlying districts, red brick and concrete towns, home to meat works and dairy farming. At some venues there would be a crowd, in others perhaps four or five people. I like small audiences, the feeling of connection, of simply sitting down and having conversations and learning about those who make their lives in a particular place. There was one library where we sat around a table and had morning tea, laid out with beautiful china and food: I learned a lot that morning about horse breeding. In another, there were four people, two a young couple who lived in a car at the edge of the university campus where they studied. And, one morning, there were eight people in a library, five of them older men. They listened intently as I spoke about Albert Black, the boy who had been hanged in the now decommissioned Mount Eden Prison. One of the men waited until question time to speak. He had been in Mount Eden, he told us, and it was just as bad as I painted it. He launched into some painful memories. One of them was being watched in the shower by female prison officers. They used to walk around the decks above, all the time, every day. That couldn't have been right, surely? Somebody laughed. I didn't. I agreed with him, it wasn't right.

Some evenings, I would eat at a café on High Street. The walk back to the motel seemed longer at night, dark alleyways, green fluorescent lights showering from the recesses, shadowy doorways. I thought about Ronald Hugh Morrieson, the author in whose name I was touring. Morrieson is something of a cult figure, whose novels, which include *Came a Hot Friday*, *Predicament* and *The Scarecrow*, all made into movies, are preoccupied with 'sex, death, mateship, voyeurism, violence, booze and mayhem in bleak small town New Zealand' but also filled with 'his irreverent black humour'. The writer cum dance band player and music teacher had left a legacy that I can't imagine has always been welcome in the town, yet he and his work are honoured still, and I admire that. He died from alcohol-related causes in 1972, when he was fifty. I felt his footsteps behind me, as I walked the night-dark streets.

For those who prospered, the town had much to offer, as I knew from Hennie, who gave me such support when I was younger. I know of Hāwera's history of music, and there is a sense that the place is steeped in words and song. It is the birthplace of other poets, near contemporaries of mine.

This was not my parents' experience there. My mother had left Australia with a trunkful of pretty dresses - pale green silk, red and navy stripes - and strapped shoes. She never wore them again. As a teenager, I wore some of them until I realised I was seen as ridiculous, and the clothes were disposed of. She had been alone at the worst time of her life, divided by family rifts, too proud to call for help. My travelling father perhaps still carried his dreams.

After that tour, I began a serious hunt for the house. I turned first to the electoral rolls but there was no sign of my parents there. I realised that their return to New Zealand would have been too recent to be recorded, and before long they would have left, my mother and I to join her family further north, my father to disappear into the air force. I knew I had been baptised, and because I was sickly it had been very early on so that my infant soul would not be condemned to purgatory. The kind people at the church where I thought this must have taken place had a gap in their records, something to do with the war. They were so sorry, they said, but 1940, that year of my birth, was not there. I tried Karitane. Surely, the contact details for parents of their charges must be recorded. Alas, their records did not go back that far. I began to feel like a missing person.

I had one last inspiration. It was in this town that my father, heading towards forty, made the desperate decision to go to war. When he enlisted, there must surely have been a home address. My next call, then, was the Defence Force. And yes, there it was, that first house where I had so briefly lived. I learned some other interesting facts too, about where my Irish father had gone to school in Middlesbrough, and afterwards to a technical college where he had excelled in physics and mathematics, that he had a whole range of skills he never talked about and never employed in New Zealand, except in the air force, where he was an armourer. (He never served overseas; he had flat feet.) In a photograph taken the year of his enlistment, my father looks handsome and confident in his uniform, as if he had come into his own. It didn't last, but I see, in that captured instant, what might have been, the person I never really knew.

I have been to see the house. It is white and plain, set back from the street. Among more modern houses it looks a bit like the *Little House on the Prairie*. There was nobody home when I called, so I couldn't go inside. But the neat, comfortable room that I glimpsed through a window did look quite narrow and, yes, perhaps a bit dark in the afternoon. Maybe it gets the morning sun. I hope so, for the sake of whoever lives there, and for my mother. She never said. The mountain was clearly visible at the end of the street and, in the back garden, there was a lemon tree groaning with ripe fruit, windfalls beneath.

This house is someone's home. I won't say where it is because I would be betraying them; their history in that house is their own. But I know where it is. And in this discovery of mine, I discovered so much more than I anticipated.

The house. My father's story. My beginnings.

The house at Hāwera.

ROBERT CROSS

North River

1

During my teens, I lived in Waipu, the Nova Scotian settlement to the south of Whangārei. Many years later I was invited to contribute to a book of essays that accompanied the diaries of the local Presbyterian clergyman, who lived there at the same time. The book, published in 2018, under the imprint of the Waipu 150 Trust, was called *A Conscientious Bloody Clergyman: The Diaries of Reverend William Levack 1952-1964*. This is an adaptation of the essay I wrote on the year I was allocated: 1954.

A particular day in mid-December of 1953 is etched forever in my memory. In a caravan of small trucks and trailers, my family moved to a farm in Waipu. We had come from the north, so we travelled along the back road that veers off from State Highway One and down along to what we then called North River, followed by clouds of dust. These vehicles carried all our belongings, our cows, dogs and ourselves, my mother, my father and me.

Like a lot of families, we had known some bad times after the Second World War, and money was scarce. Looking back, the whole farming endeavour seems whimsical and could have been doomed to failure from the start. My father, a bookish man, had a delicate constitution that wartime service hadn't helped. The farm we moved to, like the one we had left, was very small, we had no machinery and none of the vehicles belonged to us. Although we would live some 8 kilometres from the Centre, as the township was known, we never owned a car or truck, or farm machinery except milking machines. It turned out to be near subsistence farming as it had been when we lived further north.

What's more, people had said, 'Oh, you'll never fit in there. The Novies keep to themselves', an off-hand reference to the early Nova Scotian settlers who had arrived in the 1850s. We hadn't really fitted in where we'd come from either, for reasons that are now neither here nor there, but had a lot to do with class and money. But it's important to say these things because this is an account of how good neighbours can change lives, and this is what happened to us in Waipu. We found them, or perhaps it was more a case of them finding us. It may have helped that my mother was of old Scots stock, true crofting Highlanders on her father's side, Lowland on her mother's, Sutherlands and Stewarts.

Of course, nobody knew this, that hot December day. The neighbours would get to know more about us later. But that evening, as the trucks moved off and left us with our unpacked bundles and hungry animals, there was a knock on the door. It was Laurel McAulay from across the road and over the paddock. She had brought a billy of soup and a loaf of bread. Laurel was a direct, no-nonsense woman who never seemed to make small talk. But in her own blunt way, she said, 'I thought you might be in need of some tucker.'

The profuse thanks offered by my parents – my father, the Irishman, suddenly full of blarney – were brushed aside.

'Just call out if you need anything,' Laurel said, her eyes travelling over the situation. And then she was off.

This was a practical demonstration of a lesson the Reverend Norman McLeod, who led his followers across seas and continents to settle in Waipu, had instilled in his flock: to love your neighbour as you love yourself. It's the second commandment, the book of Mark, Chapter 12, verse 31. In the years to come, I didn't like everything I heard about McLeod, and thought his views on a range of topics harsh, but with this I was, and remain, in total accord. It's a basic tenet of survival. We need one another if we are to live in this world. I never once felt like an outsider in Waipu. I would live there for only two years but they are among the truly significant years of my life.

We haven't quite got to 1954 yet. It's still a couple of weeks away, with the arrival of Queen Elizabeth II on her first visit to New Zealand, the Tangiwai rail disaster and Christmas to come, in between. But there was also the small matter of hay that needed to be cut, and this is partly how we became connected with the community. The farm was bounded on one side by a river. A wide green paddock swept from the little square farmhouse down to its edge. The grass hadn't been cut for a couple of years. I believe it was brown top, brought to New Zealand in a mattress by James Fraser from the North Channel of St Anns in Cape Breton, Nova Scotia. Deep and lush, more than was needed by the tiny herd we had brought with us, it was, in fact, a cash crop waiting to be harvested. But, of course, we had no machinery, and I still remember my father looking across that paddock, his shoulders lifting, then drooping in despair.

He needn't have worried. The next morning, a group of swarthy, black-singleted men arrived. These were the McAulay men, described by the Presbyterian minister, the Reverend William Levack, in his diaries as 'the men with jutting jaws'. They were Murdoch, the husband of Laurel, and Ken and Harold, their two sons. I don't quite know what happened next, except that by the end of the day some arrangement had been made whereby tractors and haymaking machinery would be acquired, and a posse of helpers brought in to cut and bale the hay. I remember that week as a daze of sunlight and excitement, as more and more people arrived, baskets of food were unloaded beside the river and a sudden happiness descended on my family, in a way that had been missing. In late afternoon, before milking on other farms began, there would be a round of beers for the men. In Waipu there were those who drank not at all, or those who did so with gusto. The North River men fell into the latter category. The McAulay family had a large herd by the standards of the day, nearly a hundred cows, perhaps too many for Murdoch; I could hear him in full voice some evenings, roaring across the paddocks as milking approached and the cows were bolshie. 'You might as well speak to Jesus,' he would shout.

Just two days before the New Year was upon us, I found myself on the side of the street, wearing my new uniform for Waipu District High School, even though school was some weeks away. Her Majesty the Queen was being driven through the town, from Whangārei to the south. It was a hot dry day, the beginning of a drought that would last until early March. I can barely recall my sight of the Queen, just the flash of a white-gloved hand inside a black car. But what I do remember is my first meeting with a group of people with whom I would share the next two years of my school life. There was tall, fair Jennifer Baildon, daughter of the headmaster, Jennifer Gates (later Jennifer Beck), who became a lifelong friend, Alison Foote, Marina Markotich, Hector Ewen, with his halo of golden curls, Barry Connell. We would all be in the same class. In that first year at Waipu DHS, Mr Baildon taught French to the two Jennifers and me, and two boys, in the primary school cloakroom.

I saw the recently opened museum; the six-sided monument topped with the Lion of Scotland, commemorating the six ships that brought the Nova Scotian settlers to New Zealand; the white-painted Presbyterian church; the church hall, where the following year I would sit my School Certificate exams; and the manse. The hall was shaded by a huge magnolia tree, its creamy flowers shedding a lingering scent. The manse was home to the Reverend Levack, the prodigious diarist, who had come from Mauritius to preach in Waipu, with his wife Deborah, whom he called Doof, and their three young sons. Alexander, the eldest, was a year behind me at school, a dark, vivid boy with a quick sense of humour.

Just a week later, as the Queen continued on her tour and the country continued to grieve the victims of the rail disaster, Waipu had to contend with its own massive sorrow. News came through that Douglas McAulay (another branch of the McAulay clan), a popular young family man, had fallen into the sea while fishing. Four days passed before his body was found. On 13 January, the Reverend Levack conducted his funeral service. He wrote in his diary that 'the funeral of Douglas McAulay at 1 p.m. was the largest of its kind I have ever officiated at. His wife attended at both the church and the grave. Which was very brave, but to my mind not quite right. Women, as in Scotland, should not be at the grave. Perhaps it is different in New Zealand.' Although we were newcomers, the sense of sorrow throughout the neighbourhood was palpable and lasting.

On the farm plenty of work awaited. Mad as it sounds, there wasn't even a cowshed on this place my parents had acquired, so building one was an early task. A slab of concrete had to be laid, all of it on the same day. My father looked morose. My mother and I stood at the ready, as he explained how we must hold the ends of a long flat board to screed the mixture as he poured it. Once again, as if they had been watching for something like this to happen, the helpers arrived. Nobody had asked them, they just came.

So we got to know the McKays and the McKenzies, whose farm shared a boundary with ours, Elliot Brown and his brother Ray, and all their families. Being neighbours in the Waipu sense was not just about hot scones and cool beers. It was about trust too; little things like leaving doors unlocked so that neighbours could pop in and borrow a cup of flour or an aspirin if they ran out, and bigger things like watching out for one another's children and being on call if there was sickness. There was also the small matter of listening in on the party line, which many did shamelessly; the code was not to repeat overheard secrets.

My father and Elliot became friends; Elliot had a puckish sense of fun, and the pair of them bellowed at each other's stories, some fantastical. On one occasion when the Reverend Levack visited the Browns, whom he described as 'a complicated family', he wrote that 'Elliot has seen a flying saucer and is quite convinced it is a man-made thing, but what men, and from where?' The reverend seems to have been open to a bit of leg pull. Meanwhile, my mother had been invited for a cup of tea with Julie, Elliot's wife. She recalled the pleasure of just being able to sit in the farm kitchen with the children running about and having a relaxed and affable conversation. My mother was a naturally shy woman and it took a lot to get her to talk about herself, but there she felt at ease.

In March, on St Patrick's Day, there was a commotion in the village. I witnessed the evidence as the school bus was turning into St Marys Road to school. In Levack's words, 'the lion on the top of the Waipu memorial is discovered to be draped in green and placarded "a touch of green for the blue-noses". The children are most excited about it.' Indeed we were and the rumour soon swirled around that the miscreant was one of the school staff who lived near the women teachers' hostel. The finger was pointed at tall, bespectacled Fred Larkin, although so far as I know it was never proven. It's perhaps no coincidence that the Reverend Levack refers to a teacher throughout his 1954 diary as Mr Larrikin. Mr Baildon called a school assembly and told us it was no laughing matter. None of us laughed out loud. Fred went on to marry my favourite English teacher, Eileen O'Shea, who lived at the hostel then and inspired in me a love of poetry. When I met Eileen again many years later she and Fred had had four children and good and happy lives. My history teacher, Judith Bird, lived at the hostel too. She would feature for many years in my Wellington life.

I never got to talk to the popular, ever busy Reverend Levack, although I remember him visiting the school to provide religious instruction for the primary students. I wish I had met this seemingly tireless man. His remarkable diaries list not only preaching sermons and conducting weddings and funerals, but a range of activities including dancing, singing (often), milking cows, joining the Masons, giving speeches, playing bowls, judging hat-making competitions and sailing his boat *Phoebe*. But, Scots Presbyterian though my mother was, my father was Church of Ireland and I had been brought up an Anglican. Despite differences in interpreting the scripture, my father and the Reverend Levack seem to have had entertaining conversations at the saleyards, and perhaps, too, at the library, which they both frequented. The minister recorded joining the library and that he paid fifteen shillings for the privilege. The library opened on Saturdays and was run by Bertha Gates, the mother of my Gates friends. 'The country library has been staying overnight at Miss Gordon's so there should be some new books at last,' the minister writes. As it happened, my father helped choose books from the Country Library Service van, which was a great place to get to know the locals.

William Levack was a good sort, my father would say, adding that the man was 'no wowser' and seemed to like a drop. Apparently that was right, given the reverend's accounts of his home brew consumption, and of taking his sons to help him dump 'four dozen empty wine bottles out on the boat on the river'. Later in the year a group of us who were Anglicans went to confirmation classes. I used to go with the Hardie girls, Glenda and Barbara. We were instructed by Father Fisher, as he liked to be called, an Anglo-Catholic or High Church Anglican priest. After a meeting with him, the Reverend Levack remarks, with some acidity: 'He was an hour late. Fellow with a head like an enormous pumpkin. I addressed him as Father Fisher, just to show these boys what's what in the Holy Catholic church.' I'm not sure whether he is the same 'Father' he had met earlier in the year, who 'claimed to live on oysters and stout'. I wasn't much taken with the man myself. However, my mother made a beautiful white pleated dress for my confirmation service, held in Maungatoroto in November. She toiled over that dress, hoping that it was something I would wear in the future. Of course I never did.

One of the two biggest events of 1954 was when Don 'Gussie' McKay (so named because his father's name was Gus) won the seat for National in Marsden, our local electorate, a seat he would hold for the next eighteen years, later becoming Sir Donald McKay. Waipu was, and I imagine still is, true blue, as were my parents then. Don Gussie was not part of the volunteer brigades who arrived at our farm but certainly we had met him and his wife Miri (short for Miriam) at gatherings along North River. The Reverend Levack wrote: 'Election day. Don Gussie won, and the cat had four kittens called Hill, Hosking, McKay and Vallance Independent, so we drowned Hill, Hosking and Vallance and kept McKay.' But he hadn't been at the McKay farm the evening before, and I had. The McAulays held an election night party and we all gathered around the radio every few minutes waiting for the results to come through. It was very late when the winner was finally announced. Someone decided that we should all go to the farmhouse and wait for Don Gussie and his wife to return from party headquarters in Whangārei. We were bundled into a car and off we went, with much tooting of horns as we drove in procession around the winding road. But winning is one thing, and talking to reporters another. It was four o'clock in the morning before the triumphant member of parliament arrived. Everyone went very quiet, and then as the car drove through the gates, all the lights were turned on and the gathered farmers sat on the car horns with siren blasts that surely must have put the cows off their morning milking.

As usual, we had gone in someone else's car. Transport always was a problem for our unmechanised family. I was picked up every day by the school bus, chock a block with exuberant little Brown and McKay kids. Rod McKay, the youngest of Don Gussie's four children, and Craig Brown were six-year-olds when I started travelling with them, and I could have sworn they brought a boxful of tricks every morning. Rod would become a leading figure in the community and clan chieftain, while Craig grew up and became mayor of Whangārei.

We had rural delivery for our mail, and our meat and groceries were also delivered. But as for getting around, my parents and I biked to most places. If I visited friends, or went to basketball practice at the weekend, I pedalled many miles over metalled roads fraught with corrugations. The neighbours offered rides but they must have thought us unusual. The McAulays were unfailingly kind. The brothers noticed that I had a fairly restricted social life and once they got to know me would ask if I'd like a lift into dances in the Centre or a square dancing evening. The Reverend Levack writes of monthly Scottish country dancing, apparently held in the church hall and 'much appreciated', but I think the square dances, in the community hall in the main street, were different, although invariably we concluded the evening with a set of Lancers. Still, I can never hear 'Red River Valley' without my feet beginning to twitch. I loved the calling, the circling to my left and to my right.

As the year drew towards its close, another big event was looming, the visit of Dame Flora McLeod of McLeod, twenty-eighth clan chief of the McLeods. The Reverend Levack reports months before on finding groups of neighbours gathered together arranging for the visit. As early as August, after planting '200 onions under [his] bedroom window', he had, at the Caledonian committee, 'proposed the banning of kilts, jackets and sporrans for women. The Dame Flora McLeod of McLeod is coming and I propose to put an ear-chopping display on behalf of the local McLeod.' (This last a dig at Norman McLeod, who reputedly had a boy's ear cut off for stealing.) Perhaps there was a hint of unease in this entry, for when Dame Flora did arrive, he nearly 'committed the gaffe of bursting into a party which I only realised in time was specially reserved for McLeods only', a reminder perhaps that, friendly as the locals were, Waipu came about because of McLeod and his followers, and certain boundaries had to be observed.

There was something else my father and I did with the neighbours in those two enchanted years. Some evenings one of them, usually a McAulay, would call by and suggest a trip to Ruakākā to collect scallops. This was in the days before the oil refinery, when the beach was just a long shining curve of sand, and the scallops so plentiful we would pick them up by the bucketful, enough to feed the farm dogs as well as ourselves for as long as the feast would last. I see us now, ankle deep in water, the blue skeins of twilight winding around us, and the ride home in the deepening evening, and we would all be singing.

2

Waipu is still part of my life. The town has fuelled several of my works. The river comes back to me in dreams. It stands like a mysterious presence, the deep swirling waters where thousands of eels swam, the banks thick with hawthorn and willows. I don't know who planted them. When I was young, I didn't have the kind of curiosity that asked who had been before. The farm was ours and I was happy, that's what I knew. I left it at the age of sixteen because there was no work up there, and I wasn't ready to be married, though some of the girls I went to school with already were. I stood at the farm gate with my parents on the day I departed and felt that my heart was breaking. Theirs were too. My father dragged himself to the cowshed each day. My mother carried on as if all were well. The farm had been her dream, the place that gave her a presence in the world. But it went up for sale a few months after I had gone and was sold within weeks of the notice going on the gate. My mother hid in the hills that day, hoping that the buyers would go away, but it was all over. A month later she was working in a Rotorua clothing factory sewing working men's pants, and my father had taken up work in an office. I see this as my parents' tragedy. If I had been a son it might have been different. Not that my mother stayed in the factory for long:

> After the farms she came into herself,
> expert in china, the best saleswoman
> for miles around, the past a good omen,
> that homestead of her birth with shelf
> and cupboard crammed with fine crockery
> she knew by rote: Doulton decorated
> with pansies (her favourite), the encrusted
> Moorcroft, the eastern chinoiserie,
> that jardinière enamelled with prunus
> standing in the hallway. She chuckled, how
> easily the names rolled off her tongue. Now
> it seemed she had made some grand entrance
> of her own. Her husband wore a collar
> and tie to work, life a different colour.

My father retired from his office job when he was sixty because he was sure he would die young. He lived for nearly another twenty years.

The square dances and how I came to leave the farm are reflected in my short story 'Circling to Your Left', which opens my collection, *All the Way to Summer*. It is about what might have been, for them, for me. I could have been in that town still, but you know when it's right to leave and there are times when your life hangs in the balance, depending on what you decide.

'Flower Man', my first story to be published in the literary journal *Landfall*, arose from something that happened in the last of my school days, the death of a much-loved local figure, an elderly man who supervised the end of year exams in the local church hall. He was known as Danny 'Ferry'. He died under the magnolia tree outside the hall, after telling his students that he 'could not go on that day'. In the story, a group of his students, in their grief, run amok and cut down the magnolia tree. This is not what happened; the tree still stands in Waipu. Nor was I present when Danny 'Ferry' made his exit, although a day or so before, I had sat and inhaled the scent of a flower he had placed on my desk, as he did for each student taking part in the exam. I was trying so hard back then to turn every inspiration into total fiction, rather than let the story take me where it would. I suppose, in its own way, it speaks of the breaking out of youth facing the future, tearing up the familiar behind them.

When I came to write *The Book of Secrets*, things changed again. It was all about research and making things as true as I could, alongside an invented story. I went to Nova Scotia, pored over documents, read everything I could lay hands on. It took me years. Tucked away in all of this was the memory of an old woman who lived alone in a rickety house that I passed each day on the school bus. She was known as Kitty Slick, although that wasn't her real name, and some called her a 'witch', which wasn't true either. I made her the central character in my novel and called her Maria, a descendant of the migration. Unseemly things happen to her, including the birth of a child who dies.

This offended her relatives and the community, and although the book sold in its thousands, and continues to sell fitfully thirty-five years later, I was asked not to come back to Waipu. That was deeply painful. I was restored to the town several years later, when locals Lachie McLean, both a farmer and a theatre director, and Patsy Montgomery, the director of the local museum, reached out to me. Lachie, a slight man with weathered outdoor skin and an elfin grin, has directed musicals in the area for five decades. His home, Birdgrove, is the oldest surviving farmhouse in Waipu, surrounded by an exquisite garden. It's situated on the Braigh, a plain that runs between the Brynderwyn Hills and Bream Bay. Old settler territory. Patsy has been a potter; in my kitchen I have tiles she has made showing the school bus I used to travel in, the old Four Square on the corner where our groceries used to be delivered; she still sings folk songs. I was welcomed 'home' in a large public gathering on a clifftop one moonlit night, after I had made a conciliatory speech, in which I talked about the way fiction and reality blended together, and the way that I put myself into the heads of my characters. If there was a witch, I said that night, then it was me.

It was through Lachie that I came to play a role in the Waipu pageant, which he produces every ten years. He jokes that it is the local Oberammergau. The Waihoihoi River runs along behind the town, winding its way through banks that form a natural amphitheatre behind the old manse, with plateaux on either side. It is here that the migration story is re-enacted, at exactly the place where the settlers are understood to have stepped ashore. Waka paddled by Patuharakeke, the local hapū, come sweeping down under the floodlights, as do almost life-sized ships; on the banks straw houses are burned down in emulation of the crofts that were destroyed during the Highland Clearances. The flames light up the sky. The Highlanders leave amid keening and the music of bagpipes, as the story crosses the ocean with the crofters aboard the ship, led by Norman McLeod, then landing in Nova Scotia. All of this is in the pageant, all the way to New Zealand's shores by which time, forty years after the migration began, the number of ships required to get from Canada to New Zealand had risen to six. They were built by the Nova Scotians themselves, in their own backyards: they were called *Margaret, Highland Lassie, Gertrude, Spray, Breadalbane* and *Ellen Lewis*.

This story is narrated and dramatised by performers on floodlit platform stages. I was one of the two narrators in 2013; the other was a man called George Mutch and our voices were thrown from either side of the river. I also played a role in the drama. In my first scene, I was walking along the main street of the town when a high school girl approached me. We introduced ourselves. 'So you're Dame Fiona Kidman?' I agreed that I was. 'So you're the woman who made all the trouble in this town.'

I didn't make the greatest actor. I've always had a secret yearning to act but when it comes to the point I freeze. Perhaps writing is an act of performance in itself and trying to do both may not work. On the night of dress rehearsal, I stood up, stared around at the assembled cast, and said, 'Oh shit, I can't remember all of this.' The show was being filmed for television; the cameras stopped rolling. It came more or less right on the two nights that we played, each time to an audience of three thousand on the riverbank.

This is how I came to play myself playing myself.

In that crowd, among the music, and the fires lighting the sky, and people I had known since I was growing up, I felt an immense sense of belonging. The words of the old psalm, number twenty-three, which I was required to read at my first school assembly in the town, and which is read also at my mother's family's funerals, came back to me: 'He leadeth me beside the still waters.' If this seems too biblical a conclusion, Waipu is a town that is biblical in its beginnings. The quiet and unquiet place.

This is the other place I call home.

On writing memoir

It's like this. I face a group of people who have come to learn about writing their memoirs. More and more people want to do this as they get older. They have a story to tell, evidence to leave for those who come behind, their children and their grandchildren, something that says, I was here, and this is who I was, and these are the things that I have done. Remember me.

Writing down the story is one way of creating a record, and it's more enduring than Hansel and Gretel's trail of crumbs in the forest. It can be read and reread and made sense of time and again. My mother left me a precious gift. In the last years of her life she wrote her own story, in crabbed handwriting, her hands buckled by arthritis, clenched around a triangular rubber aid on her pen. Here and there in her narrative, there is a crossover between what she had told me and what she had been prepared to put on the record. There were some things she wanted to leave out but crept their way into the story anyway. A bare accounting of events, none of the pain, but something of the joy. I feature in that joy. I keep the exercise book in a drawer beside my bed. It is, as they say, the thing I would reach for if the house burned down. If I could escape, I'd take the family history with me.

For nearly a decade, I met with people wanting to record their stories. We would gather once a fortnight over the winter months at the Thistle Inn in Wellington. One of the oldest surviving pubs left in the country, it was built in 1840 by a Scotsman called William Couper and rebuilt in the 1860s, with an extra storey, after a fire. The white wooden building stands at an angle on the corner of Mulgrave and Aitken streets, near Old St Paul's, and a stone's throw by a strong arm in the other direction from Parliament. Originally it was over the road from the beach and whalers used to pull their long boats up outside and tie them to a hitching post while they went in for an ale. It's said that the chief Te Rauparaha drank there, and certainly the whaler Jacky Guard, the husband of Betty, was a customer. The sea is now further away, since a massive earthquake in 1855 altered the shoreline.

Inside, there are original wooden floorboards and wide sash windows. A steep staircase leads to the upper rooms, and it is in one of these, the Katherine Mansfield Room, that the memoir writers met. In 1907 Mansfield wrote a story called 'Leves Amores'. This is how it begins:

> I can never forget the Thistle Hotel. I can never forget that strange winter night.
> I had asked her to dine with me, and then go to the Opera. My room was opposite hers. She said she would come but – could I lace up her evening bodice, it had hooks at her back. Very well.
> It was still daylight when I knocked at the door and entered. In her petticoat bodice and a full silk petticoat she was washing, sponging her face and her neck. She said she was finished, and I might sit

on the bed and wait for her. So I looked round at the dreary room.

Mansfield goes on to describe the ugliness and drabness of her surroundings – the piece of cracked mirror, the torn wallpaper, although she can trace a pattern of faded rose buds and flowers. Yet, before the night is out, the building will yield up its own delights, as we suspect will happen as the narrator tells us that, after the opera, 'we came out into the crowded night street, late and cold. She gathered up her long skirts. Silently we walked back to the Thistle Hotel, down the white pathway fringed with beautiful golden lilies, up the amethyst-shadowed staircase.' We readers are not surprised by the passionate embraces that follow: the atmosphere is there, the place, with its own history, is described to us. Was this Mansfield writing from memory or imagination? Not our business, really, because the work is presented as a fiction. But we do know the building exists, and its possibilities. We know because we have climbed that 'amethyst-shadowed staircase'; we are open to our own pasts in this place where the embraces happened. We know, somehow, that Mansfield has been here.

It's a polished place now, after renovations and refurbishments, all gleaming wood and modern comforts. In the room where we gathered, there was space for fourteen people to sit in a half-circle, while I sat by the whiteboard at the front. Down below is a classy well-appointed restaurant and bar, with a big television screen so that patrons can watch rugby games in comfort; in winter there are roaring fires. In the floor lies a cutaway scene beneath glass (or something akin to it) showing a ship's hold complete with large faux rats. A corridor to the side of the bar leads along to a private sexy dining room, full of red velvet curtains.

At morning tea, we had warm muffins, a choice of blueberry or savoury. At lunchtime, we descended to the restaurant, where we gathered at long tables, and the noise levels rose and slowly, slowly we were at one with each other.

On the first morning, some of the group may say, Oh, my life is so extraordinary that I don't know where to begin, there's so much to tell. Or at least they're saying it to themselves. You don't want to be too boastful among strangers. Others may say, and possibly out loud, that their lives have been so dull, so *uninteresting*, that really there is nothing to tell. Only they don't believe that. Somewhere, deep inside, they're waiting for the moment when they dare to reveal themselves. They're waiting for that axe that breaks the frozen sea within, as Kafka famously said – or something like that. And they have dared to dream of writing it all down.

These fourteen expectant people are waiting for some magic tools. But this day is not about style, or about how to write a bestseller, it's about letting go of the future and re-entering the past. And that requires stamina.

There's nothing for it but to plunge them straight in at the deep end. To help them through the inevitable round of introductions, I've given them each a note asking them, while waiting to begin, to jot down five interesting things about themselves. They're already uneasy, although there are some who will want to tell you twenty-five things. I'm not sure at this stage whether this means that oral history is really their forte, or whether it means that their stories will pour forth once they start writing. It's the ones who say they can think of only two slightly interesting things that will be the challenge. For me and them.

But at least their brains are loosening up and, better still, for the moment, their tongues. What I like in this early round is that they're also having to listen to one another's stories, and start responding to them. When I was a journalist I learned early on that the people I interviewed loved to tell me about their lives, even the parts that had nothing to do with the subject at hand. Off the record, they would often add, and I've said that myself, hoping for the best, but it's the way one thing leads to another: it can be irresistible to hold back on some detail that illuminates the whole narrative.

As the tales begin to spill among the group, I tell them that what's said in the room must stay inside it, that only the person who owns the story is entitled to share it. Establishing trust is important because it's only by opening up to yourself that what really happened in a life begins to emerge. One of the first questions I'm asked is what to leave in and what to leave out. The only way I can answer that is by saying, Tell everything but only tell yourself. Then decide what you want to tell the rest of the world.

Where to begin?

The best place to begin is at the beginning, I say.

And the question flies back. How to begin?

Where did you come from? I ask. Where were you born? Jot down your parents' names, if you know them (not everybody does). If you don't, write down the first people associated with you after your birth. Put down where your first home was, and find out what it tells you about you and your circumstances, or those of the people you called family.

I have written about memory and how I connect it with images of water in *Beside the Dark Pool*, but these are continuing refrains in my life, so bear with me.

One of my early memories is the reservoir my parents built on the land in the Far North. They toiled over it, but the water was always brackish and full of frogs. Or how I learned to swim beneath a waterfall, taught by a famous pianist, whose method was to go to the centre of the pool and tell me that I must fling myself from its edge in order to reach her. Then there was the lake in Rotorua I lived beside with my husband when we were first married, its blueness on summer evenings as we sat on the steps outside our apartment, the dark purple it turned in the winter. And now I live above a bay, and beyond that Cook Strait, sometimes calm, often wild and unknowable.

And this is where the surface of water comes into it. Once it's broken, there's no knowing what lies beneath. It can be potentially dangerous, but also a place for exploration, to be free and unafraid. It requires a moment of oblivion before you take that step, before you risk yourself to its depths.

But once you're in, you're in.

All right, I say. Now write down a secret in the family.

This is where things start to get really interesting and a bit tricky.

Although we mightn't want to own all our secrets, it's possible to enter speculative places, to imagine what might and might not be true. Keep writing, don't stop, write down *everything*. Remember, you're in charge of what will be read.

At this point, some of the group may decide to leave. They have that fragile hunted look I've seen before. This course was supposed to be fun, a hobby perhaps, a new skill. Well, there are some side-splitting stories told in a memoir group; sometimes we fall about laughing. Life is funny.

And dreadful.

And looking into the darkness, into the underworld, can be agonising. No wonder some have to leave; they're just not ready to go there.

Even what's funny can kill us.

––––––––––

There's another gentler exercise that I sometimes do with a group. I provide some topics – a piece of jewellery, a dance, playing a joke, the first day at a new school, a problem with a car – and then ask them to divide into pairs and choose one of the stories to tell the other person. After ten minutes they must reverse the process. When that's done, I say, Pick up your pens. Write down your own story, the one you've just told, write for fifteen minutes, and I'll tell you when to stop. Almost to a person they write freely, their stories fresh in their minds. When I stop them, they look at me with astonishment. I've written three hundred words, they may say. Or, I didn't remember that story at all, but now I want to write more about it, it's so clear in my mind.

That's the power of storytelling. When a story is told, externalised, if you like, it has a life of its own, and it becomes so much easier to write. So when the interrogation of memory begins, we discover there are so many things we thought we knew but don't. We often have to look for clues about family. I understand some people in the group don't want to write about family at all. They've come because they've had amazing careers, or extraordinary travels, or endured some harrowing trauma, and left family far behind. They may already have excellent records, diaries and journals and, these days, jottings on their phones. But still, here they are, not knowing how to begin. So this first day is devoted to what they might discover in their early lives, and this can be a trigger for remembering the decisions made later on.

Sooner or later comes the moment when I have to do the work, tell them something about the process of writing your life, how to identify its various guises. I tell them there are several ways to look at what is also called, voguishly, life writing. There is auto-biography, and biography, and, yes, memoir. That's not all, but it will do for a start and perhaps it's enough.

Autobiography is what you do when you set out to tell the whole story of your life. At least, that's what the reader expects. They want to know it all, every last little detail. As well as your successes they want to know about your foibles and your failures and your fears. They want to know both who you've hated and who you've loved and, even more, they will likely want to know who you've made love to - although sometimes if there are too many lovers, they may find that tiresome and excessive; I can recall any number of these books where I've thought, Oh God, not another bonk. Please. In short, an autobiography is a revealing document and writing it may well be a confronting exercise and an even harder experience to live with once it's published. Not that I seriously believe many people do write their entire story. Why on earth would you?

Biography is when another person writes the story of a life, whether the subject be living or dead. This is a much more selective process. You, the writer, gather up material you've researched about your subject and deliver it up, framed by your own interpretation. Your subject may have agreed to have their biography written, or it may be an unauthorised version, or the person may already be dead and so it may seem not to matter whether what you've written about them is true or kind. I've read any number of biographies, some of them about the same person, and in each of them the subject looks different. And, just sometimes, you may disagree with the author's interpretation. I know I did when I read a biography of the famous woman aviator, Jean Batten. She was such a hero of mine yet the only known biography of her read like a sustained attack. So I wrote a novel that isn't a biography, but a translation, as nearly as I can make it, of what it was like to be her. So yes, there is all of that.

And a word of warning for those who plan to write biographies of living people: it's difficult to capture something they will agree with, so you may well end up writing an unauthorised version. I withdrew my permission for a biography before the first words were written. I couldn't lay myself so bare that another person was able to pick over the bones of my past; a bit of the flesh perhaps, but not that skeleton of disaster and turmoil that lies beneath the skin of most lives. I felt guilty about changing my mind, but I believed I had no other choice, and I still do.

Well, this isn't very encouraging so far. But there's another way, the disreputable third way so beloved by politicians but so damned helpful when it comes to writing the story of the self. There is, as I've said, memoir. It's just what the word implies – a selection of memories and stories about your life, shaped and crafted, the important things said, the disagreeable possibly left out. (Don't leave all of it out; after all, you're human.) What you can bear, what you can live with, what is, above all, *interesting* to the future reader. Not, of course, that you'll think about the reader as you write, for that's one of the great inhibitions – the idea that this will be read by others. What will people think of me, of the writing? What judgements will be made?

I always recommend that, as you begin the journey into memoir writing, you don't think too much about publication. That may or may not come later. When you write about your life, you're writing first and foremost for yourself. Look, I say, this is only a beginning, a first draft, not a last will and testament. Real writers will face many drafts – and make many discoveries – but until they choose to release their memoir into the world, it belongs to them and nobody else. The decision about what to leave in and what to take out will come later, after that essential first draft is written.

There is a fourth way, one that I've practised, in a sense, with Jean Batten. My novel about her is a fiction based on fact, with scenes and incidents imagined. As well, there are fictions about people's real lives that are simply told in the third person, as if the writer is no more than a character. One of the best examples I've read is Margaret Atwood's *Moral Disorder*. It is, she has said, the nearest she will come to telling her story, so it can be read as a kind of memoir. And, in the telling it is simply enchanting, the love story between her and the late Graham Gibson, how they met, how they set up house. It's Atwood at her most tender, and her most funny. The characters, Tig and Nell, have maintained their noms de plume since Gibson's death. I come across stories in magazines in which their story continues, the name Nell a signal that Atwood has again assumed the mantle of her past life. So fiction can play a part in telling your story and it shouldn't be dismissed. You don't *have* to tell it all. Or you can, then take a step back and let the reader do the work.

If we're talking about family, the group asks, how do we look for the records? Where will we find them?

So here are a couple of ideas. Genealogical records are often helpful for those wanting to explore the distant past. In the digital age, they're much easier to access than they once were. And for those who aren't handy with technology, there are museums and libraries where you can get help.

There are letters, although that's where the new age fails us. People don't keep things the way they used to. I have a friend who is trying to revive the art of letter writing. It's his mission, he says, to single-handedly save the postal service from extinction. He has a beautiful fountain pen that a collector gave him in exchange for a favour. He has found a supply of elegant notepaper. Every now and then, one of his letters drops into my letterbox, four pages of news about this and that, not necessarily important but chatty and keeping in touch – the way he might in an email (and technically, he is a very able person). The difference is that I will store his letter away in a box marked 'Correspondence', instead of deleting it after a suitable interval, and eventually it will land in my collection of papers at the Alexander Turnbull Library. It was, after all, through letters my father kept from his aunts in Ireland that I discovered the house where my never known Irish grandmother lived as a girl, the house that, when it was sold, allowed us to buy the farm in Waipu, that farm with a river that curled through the bottom paddock, and where my father and I sang to each other as we milked cows in the evenings. From a letter I know how my grandmother, Ann Eakin, née O'Hara, died, in Middlesbrough in the mid-1930s – and, through it, I know it's important to have regular colonoscopies. 'My Lofty,' she had written to my father, 'a ten-shilling note to help you out, but there isn't much more right now.' My Lofty - it breaks my heart. He called her the Mater. I found the letters in a suitcase long after he had died. Why hadn't I listened more to him while he was alive? That is such a trite question. It's the one half the group asked as they introduced themselves at the beginning of the day.

For a while, when email was first available, I used to dutifully print out ones I thought interesting and add them to my files. But they accumulate so quickly and, besides, there can be something oddly intimate about emails, rapid outpourings that more-considered strokes of the pen don't deliver. I stopped when I looked at some of my own. Emails are a betrayal of sorts; we put too much or too little into them. They're so often about feelings, rather than the details of a life. It's so easy to be romantic or angry or simply indifferent in those fluid movements on the keys, when there's no envelope to be sealed, no stamp to be licked, no walk to the post box, just that dangerous send button.

Do look for the suitcases in the attic, prise open their rusted locks. They've been kept for a reason. An aunt left me a suitcase of used spectacles and half-full needles of morphine. As a young woman she was a nurse but her life had been lonely. She was a beautiful woman. There weren't any letters, but I discovered a lot anyway.

Talk to your friends and siblings. I was an only child and although my mother was the youngest of six, I had just one first cousin, and so I've depended on friends. Their versions of events, though, can be surprisingly different. When I went to Menton on a Katherine Mansfield fellowship in 2006, my friend Madeleine came to visit. We have been friends since childhood but we hadn't seen each other for a long time when we were reunited in the south of France. Time is such an enigmatic concept. It doesn't exist once it's passed. There's no way of reading it in the future. It's just there, ruled by the passing of the seasons, the turning of the earth each day. Perhaps that's why a person is said to have lived for so many summers. Anyway, many summers ago, Madeleine and I lived across the road from each other in a little country town with a dusty avenue leading up to it, rimmed with hakea hedges, which have pale green leaves that end in pale pink tips, and banana passion fruit vines with their pendulous, yellow-skinned fruit full, inside, of greenish seeds in watery sacs that have a cloudy taste like custard. We were children abandoned to the heat of the north while our mothers worked in orchards. Both of us created stories, which Madeleine wrote up in her copperplate hand and illustrated. Her mother was alone, which was hard straight after the Second World War, while my mother had worked in a serving position in the town when we first went there. We didn't fit into the local social scene, a group of jitterbugging gin-drinking people who had escaped the Raj. Well, I go on writing about this, and thinking about it. Some things shape who you are.

I was planning to write a memoir while I was in France and I had Madeleine lined up to 'interview', to verify, if you like, my memories of that time. Soon after her arrival we found ourselves sitting on the balcony of the Palais Lutetia, home to the fellows during their sojourn in Menton, the town near the Italian border where the famous writer lived and wrote in her dying days. As we looked out over the Mediterranean, I learned that Madeleine and I had a different understanding of those years up north. I could go on for pages about those differences - in the way we saw our parents, our circumstances - but they are between us. Enough, maybe, to say that she saw me as fortunate because I had two parents, and I saw her in the same way because her grandparents lived with her - and they had a swimming pool, which meant that they had visitors. My parents and I lived in a small army hut, with not a lot of room for extras, and the truth was, we were ashamed.

It was spring when Ian and I arrived in Menton. As we stepped off the train in the late afternoon sunlight, I smelled it, the heavy, languorous scent of citrus flowers. And in an instant I was transported back to my childhood on the other side of the world, where the main local industry was growing oranges and lemons. And here that same wall of perfume was waiting for me, unexpected, intense, disturbing.

I lay down that night in the Palais Lutetia and dreamed of my mother. I saw her working in the orchards, harvesting lemons, along with a team of pickers, mostly women. Unlike my mother, who would climb the ladders and strip the trees down, in the right way, some of the others stuck to the lower branches. But then, my mother was Scots Presbyterian, a woman of great conscience. Little and light, she would climb those trees, even when it was wet and cold, because we needed the money – one shilling and sixpence for every wooden case filled. Her dark hair was covered with a beret; she wore trousers and my father's shirts, rolled up at the sleeves. A pouch was strapped around her waist, to hold the lemons until she came down. When I was little, before Madeleine came along, I would often go to the orchard and sit under a hedge. I was supposed to be reading a book, but I could never take my eyes off my mother for long.

And there she was again in my dream, clippers in hand, high above me, dropping one golden orb after another into her pouch, her hands flying among the leaves. When I woke I was in tears. And yet, as the scent rose to meet me again, sharper after the night's dew, I was at home. There, and in that other place. I had gone to Menton to find my way into writing memoir, but there it was, the whole map of my childhood laid out before me. I breathed in and out again. I surrendered.

Perhaps I should add that the next day, when Ian and I walked down the main street of Menton, I discovered that it, too, was a town inhabited by Raj refugees, living their dream. On the beach, they lay in polished ranks, the crisp old leather of their skins shining, as they baked under the blistering sun, their cut-crystal voices rising as they ordered another drink from the waiters at the kiosks on the street above.

Something else happened on our way back from that first walk into town. Roses grow on trellises beside the long avenue that runs from the town centre to the Palais Lutetia. They were coming into bloom. A gardener returned our greeting when we called 'Bonjour', then cut off a dark pink bud on a long stem and handed it to Ian to give to me. For love, he said. Be happy.

We were, in that town.

The bud opened and stayed fresh for a week. I have a photo of it in a vase on a windowsill.

Timelines are important. Again, that idea of beginning at the beginning, of setting events against dates – when you lost your milk teeth, started at a new school, menstruated, shifted house. When you first noticed that your parents weren't getting along so well, or they were getting along very well and had a new baby and how your life changed. Open up your senses, your ability to see and hear, to smell and touch and taste. Savour the world.

One of the guest tutors at the memoir groups was Mary, a writer and publisher. In one of her exercises she asked everyone to close their eyes while she produced objects out of a bag. They were then asked to identify these, by touch and smell. There would be bunches of lavender, some spices, a piece of the rug from her dog's basket, a fur collar. And then she would ask them to write something that the scent or feel evoked.

There are photograph albums. But don't get me started here or I might cry. The children when they were little, their faces full of trust: at water play, and on their trikes, wobbling along a stretch of the concrete driveway you laid with your husband. The girl in the tutu, not wanting to be a ballerina after all, the woman along the street who made her dress because you were no good at sewing. (No, the woman is not in the picture at all, but you had forgotten about her, and how she saved the day as the other mothers excelled at running up nifty outfits.) There's me, looking out of a picture taken in Menton when my hair has just been cut and my eyes are alight with pleasure because it's the most beautiful style I've ever had and the woman, Marinella, who created it, sang to me in Italian as she worked. Just ignore the picture of me with an Afro perm taken years earlier; none of us seemed to have much taste at the time – it was the eighties. How could we have done that to ourselves? And here are the great-aunts and uncles who could have been forgotten by now, except that they loved you and their names are engraved on your heart – but the person in the next generation looking at the picture may not remember them at all, unless there's a name attached. Didn't I go to her ninetieth birthday? a puzzled relative might say. When I was quite small? And yes, and it was out in the country, and afterwards we all stayed in a motel together, and the pizza place was closed but we made do, found food and you all swam in the pool. Then one of you fell over and we had to take you all to the emergency clinic late at night, which was a trauma, but no great harm done. Yes, all those faces from long ago, but they mean something. They mean that this is your history.

———

The first day is drawing to a close, but I have a last exercise to present before they pack up. I've selected a group of poems, each one different but roughly based on an aspect of family. I hand these out without looking to see whether I think they will suit or not, so men might get poems by women and vice versa, young and old, all mixed up. After a few minutes, while they read the poems and some of them hiss, I *hated* poetry at school and I thought we were here to learn about writing memoir, I ask them, one by one, to read the poem I have given them.

Here are two that I often included. The first is by Lauris Edmond, who was my great friend for twenty-eight years, between the time we both arrived in Wellington, and her sudden death in January 2000.

Red nightgown
(for Stephanie)

I lie still, hardly breathing.
I must certainly not laugh or
she will wake, and we have had
enough of that for one night . . .
why else are we here in this
absurd nesting of mothers
and daughters? – I in my black
nightgown, curled round your
smaller blue, you round that
morsel in red, unfledged little
dreamer soaring in sleep
across adventuring heavens,
sure beyond all surmise
that tired and fallible women
will wait for her awaking.

And the grandmothers in the group breathe in, and out. They know what this is about.

And then there is this, which is funny and sad and deftly reveals two characters in the flick of a phrase. It's by the American poet Billy Collins, who was the poet laureate in the States a few years ago. I met him at a publishers' party one night in Wellington and thought him shy, or perhaps he was tired. There was a long wait for dinner and the evening was ragged round the edges. His demeanour said, I'm done and when will we ever eat, so I left him to it, the imagined conversation never taking place. But I love his work, the way it hits the nerve.

No Time

In a rush this weekday morning
I tap the horn as I speed past the cemetery
where my parents are buried
side by side under a smooth slab of granite.

Then all day long, I think of him rising up
to give me that look
of knowing disapproval
while my mother calmly tells him to lie back down.

There are others in the mix - Alistair Campbell's elegiac short poem, 'My Grandfather', in which he remembers his Rarotongan ancestors who ate human flesh, or a couple of lovely poems by American writer Sharon Olds, one of the great sensualists of my era. Her 'Making Love' shakes the group with its candour and sideways allusions to sex, the heaviness of the body, the aftermath in the room of a passionate consummation. Perhaps I'm a little careful who I give that one to; even at the beginning, you can tell some people are more resilient than others. A poem I especially love, by Elizabeth Pierson Friend, called 'Steam Reassures Him', concerns a woman being watched by her husband as she does the ironing. He is lulled by the sound of steam and the hiss of starch, the iron's slide around the buttons of his shirt. It says so much about domesticity, and about how women's roles are seen within it (so it could be a feminist poem), yet it carries a certain comfort with it.

I read a poem too, just to be part of the group, and it might be one of my own, one of the really hard ones, just to let everyone know that this isn't an easy exercise for me either.

The last time I did this, I read 'The Garden at Sainte-Agnès'. It's for Ian, about the year we spent in France, about one of our favourite hill towns that we used to visit, one euro each way on a bus that whirled us up from Menton. I wrote it on the last day we were there, before starting the journey home to Wellington on the other side of the world. The poem starts out with a small geography lesson, reminding the reader that Sainte-Agnès is the highest coastal village in Europe, so it's a long climb to reach the ruins of the castle perched at the top of the mountain. But on the way up, the climbers reach a medieval garden tended by two women. It continues:

There were days when we needed
to go to the hills, to sit in the garden
beside the low parterres

shaped in crosses and stars
around the apple trees, to simply
watch the small orange butterflies
losing themselves in the spent
tiger lilies, inhale the thyme
and chives and potted sage

and watch the sheep of Sainte-Agnès
grazing in all the dim sweet
green world down below. If it was
never more perfect than this
it would be enough and more. Dear,
there is so much to remember.

The poem has become part of my own personal memoir. Written with immediacy, the detail as exact as I could make it, it evokes not just that particular afternoon but some moments in a life that can never be repeated. The poem transports me back to that place, the word 'remember' at the end signalling that this is how the last day in the south of France was to be staked in memory. I think the scene setting helps, and I recommend to would-be memoirists, or writers of any genre, that the observation of an environment and recording of detail can enrich any account.

At this point, I say to the group, Right, now pick up your pens and write a poem about someone in your family or circle of friends. There's a momentary silence, but the mood is upon them now, and nobody says anything much, not even, Does it have to rhyme? They begin. One or two people may cry as they write. It's not my intention to make them cry, but if a memory has been dammed up and bursts the flood banks then something big has started. And everyone has to respect that. We are sharing our memories with kindness and good humour and we are building trust.

The trust is important if people are going to read their work aloud. But there's an out in the next part of the exercise when I ask who will read their poems aloud. I have only one rule in the group and that is the pass rule. If it's too hard, you can say 'Pass' and everyone must respect that. Some will read, and some will pass. But everyone in the room is now alert, listening to their own heartbeats.

That's the first day. Time to make our way down the wooden stairs into the gathering up of the day. These are the survivors. They have begun opening themselves up to the dark, to memory. They are ready to write.

There is yet another suitcase in this story. It's one I read about in a series of essays in the *London Review of Books* by a woman called Frances Stonor Saunders, whose Jewish parents had fled Romania during the Second World War and later led quiet domesticated lives in England. Her father had a suitcase of documents which she was still finding the courage to open, years after his death. She writes this, at the end of a long search for the truth of her origins: 'It's said that a myth is a story about the way things never were but always are. Truth is not an event but a process.'

I like that. It rings true.

The outsiders

Albert Black

1

Albert Black.

A young Irishman from Belfast.

His story would break your heart. It broke mine.

He came to New Zealand when he was just eighteen, full of the vigour and expectations of youth. It was 1953. He was an emigrant, what was known as a ten-pound Pom. He travelled aboard the SS *Captain Cook* on a cheap government-sponsored fare to find work and a future in a new country. My dad did that too. The bargain was that you worked for two years in your new country before you could change your mind and leave. Albert's grandmother had given him the money, the ten quid he needed.

Albert Black, who came to be known as Paddy, never left. He is buried in an Auckland cemetery. I was given to understand that his body was placed in a makeshift grave in the corner of Mount Eden Prison, where hanged men were buried, before being despatched to Waikumete Cemetery.

My father never went home to Ireland either; he lived on and on into old age but in the end I think he died of a broken heart, of homesickness and longing. Isn't that the immigrant story?

I think it is part of Albert's story.

It was part of the story, too, of Alan Jacques, whom Albert was accused of murdering. He was a migrant youth too, an unwilling deportee from Britain, where orphanages were emptying out their premises after the Second World War. Except Jacques wasn't an orphan; as it turned out, he just wasn't wanted. Not wanted on the voyage, not valued on his arrival. A bitter young man who got into a brawl in a milk bar in Auckland's Queen Street. The knife that killed him was wielded by Albert Black, but Jacques carried one too. The case came to be known as the 'juke box murder'.

Two foolish fallen boys. There were girls in the story as well, but then there often are.

The more I looked into the matter, the more I became convinced that the verdict should have been manslaughter. I am still convinced of this. At the heart of the verdict lies deep prejudice. Prejudice against the outsider, the 'foreigner'. I ended up writing a novel called *This Mortal Boy*, which addresses my conviction as well as I can.

I hadn't planned to write this book. But it arose out of a number of preoccupations. I have a son and grandsons. As they grew up, I was beset by the fear that one of them would make a dreadful mistake. Even the best young people are capable of these - like being in the wrong place at the wrong time, getting into a fight, one terrifying party, drinking and driving or getting in a car with someone who is, taking an accidental overdose, jumping off a pier into shallow water at midnight. These young men who so absorbed me made it through. But I'm still drawn to reports of others who have not made it. I look at the gaunt, lost faces of their parents, hear the warnings that have come too late for their own children.

For as long as I can remember I've been opposed to the death penalty. I can't say how my opposition began, but it has mattered since I was in my teens. Perhaps it was conversations overheard about the hangings that happened with grim regularity in the 1950s. Or perhaps it was the time, the year after Albert Black's hanging, that I spent working as a clerk in a courthouse, where justice often seemed scant. Anyway, one day about five years ago, I picked up a newspaper and read an article about Albert's long-ago case. I was fifteen back then, and he was twenty. It all came together – the boy who made a mistake, the loving mother trying to save his life, my own Irish connections through my father and that whole era of the 1950s of which I was a part. There was a rustling in my brain that said, *This is the story*. It said: *I know this boy*.

––––––

Recently, I was invited to begin a public conversation about Albert Black by describing what 1950s New Zealand was like for me. I did my best. At first, I said that the era was by and large pretty good for me, that although it had a reputation for being a dour, grim, post-war decade without colour, I didn't find that. After an early childhood beset by the usual angst – a miserable back story is always an advantage for a writer – the next part wasn't a bad life at all. In my early teens I lived on a farm, milked cows morning and night, loving the heaving flanks of the beautiful animals, had friends, was part of a caring community in the Far North. From there, I moved to Rotorua. It was a teenagers' playground, with a carnival at New Year and an abundance of dance halls and milk bars. I wore my cardigans back to front with the sleeves pushed up in a flirtation with widgie culture, hung out at a notorious but wonderful dance hall called Tamatekapua, where there was a blind saxophonist called Tai Paul and a crooning young singer called Howard Morrison, who swayed his hips. There was flickering electricity that went on and off, and at half-time we were treated to a cooked supper. My 1950s ended with a marriage proposal, which I accepted, and that marriage survived until I became a widow four years ago.

At this point, I hesitated because, by then, there were a few raised eyebrows. And so I found myself reflecting on what I had said.

As a librarian, in those days, I was in charge of the banned book section at the public library where I worked. There, in the stack room, reached by way of a ladder, sat *Madame Bovary* and *Peyton Place* plus *Ideal Marriage*, which described the mechanics of sex. A useful thing for a girl to get her hands on, especially if she faced the terrors of unprotected sex from time to time and an unexpected pregnancy. I was spared that disaster but I knew the fear, the tyranny of the late period, and how a family, and the girl (but not the boy) could be brought to their knees by the shame.

There were book burnings too, if police happened upon banned literature in shops, so my guardianship of the titles on the library's mezzanine floor was particularly acute. The death penalty swam in and out of sight, depending on whether a right- or left-wing government was in power, meaning that it was administered on a political basis. I loved and was loved in return by my mother's rural relatives, but I knew better than to question their values. In short, the price of my unruly weekend freedoms, when I cast aside my librarian's grey tailored suit, was learning to walk on eggshells pretty well every day of my life, not just for what I *did* but what I *said*.

In other words, I remembered the dark side of 1950s New Zealand.

I am first and foremost a writer of fiction, meaning I make things up. These days, I write historical novels that require research. It doesn't mean that facts, the things we know really happened, are not facts. As nearly as I can, I shadow the truth of what the record tells me. The invented parts are unrecorded interactions between characters, the parts we can never really know: who said what in every conversation, what dreams our characters have had, who slept with whom at any given time, the secrets of the heart. But it's possible to draw certain conclusions from those things that history says are true and, drawing on all our experience, to dramatise the action and bring the characters closer to us and our own truths.

Albert's parents were Albert and Kathleen Black. They were married in St Anne's Cathedral, Belfast, in 1932. Albert junior was the second of three sons, born in July 1935. The first child, William, had died in infancy; Daniel, the third, was ten years younger than his surviving brother. After the death of the first child, who appears to have been the impetus for his parents' marriage, Albert was a much longed for boy. His mother surrounded him with a fierce protective love. By all accounts, from surviving relatives I have traced since *This Mortal Boy* was published, he was a gentle kid and, as it happens, that is how I had portrayed him. They were a Protestant family in that beleaguered and divided city. His da was profoundly deaf. I wasn't aware of this when I wrote the book and I don't know the cause of it. I surmised that it was a war injury. Certainly, his grandfather came from a regimental background. At the time of Albert's birth the family lived in Tate Avenue, about which Seamus Heaney wrote a poem that includes this stanza:

> *Instead, again, it's locked-park Sunday Belfast,*
> *A walled back yard, the dust bins high and silent*
> *As a page is turned, a finger twirls warm hair*
> *And nothing gives on the rug or the ground beneath it.*

It is an unremarkable-looking street, as those first two lines suggest. But see how the third and fourth lines pick up and project life, tenderness and an alertness to an inner existence behind the curtained windows. That is how it appeared to me, on the day when I went looking for the house where Albert first lived. It was modest and two-storeyed, brick like all the others, standing at the end of a path with a neat floral border. There was nobody home that day I knocked on the door.

The second Black home was off Sandy Row, in Gay Street, which no longer exists in name, for reasons that are perhaps predictably unsurprising – though I have always thought gay a lovely word, evocative and sprightly, and one that still belongs to all of us. The change meant that this second house was untraceable, but it would have been close to Blythe Street Public Elementary School, which Albert attended until he was fourteen. He was, as we shall see, literate, and wrote in a strong sweeping hand, but jobs were not easy to come by. He was a slight youth, five feet eight in his stockinged feet, with a head of luxuriant dark hair and fine features. That's as I see him in three of the four photographs I have, good looking with that blackbird on the wing kind of Irish charm. In the fourth photograph, perhaps near the end, he looks child-like and exhausted. His first job was in a linen mill, and after that he worked on and off as a plumber's helper for the Belfast Corporation Gas Department. When he was seventeen he took up labouring. It was around then that his grandmother, who lived round the corner in Sandy Row, gave him the money to start a new life.

On board the *Captain Cook*, where he was renamed Paddy, he quickly made friends. In particular, he became close to a lad from Liverpool called Peter Simpson, and another couple who settled in Christchurch. It was Peter Simpson who would keep Albert's last letters, written from Mount Eden.

———

Albert and Peter, indentured for two years to a government department, were sent to work in the Hutt Valley, north of Wellington, for Post and Telegraph. At first, they were housed in a transit camp but, soon tiring of that, sought accommodation with a widow in the local suburb of Naenae. This woman, called Rose in the book, provided a stable home for the two young men. She had a garden with roses and taught music; there were home-cooked meals and friendly cats. Albert and Peter became part of the family. One of the children, a small girl at the time, remembers Albert singing, helping to build a playhouse, keeping a pet hedgehog and crying when it died, and a Christmas when she stood on his feet while he waltzed her around the living room. She remembers his gentleness.

The land in the Hutt Valley, once covered in a forest dense with nikau palms and rimu, had been disputed land, fought over by Ngāti Tama and Ngāti Rangatahi tribes, before successive waves of occupying settlers cleared it of its natural groundcover. Rose's quarter-acre section backed onto market gardens, first planted in the rich valley soils by the Chinese in the late nineteenth century and taken over by returned servicemen at the end of the Second World War. Then came an enveloping tide of houses, row upon row of square plain dwellings built by the state as rentals for low-income families. A wide river dominates the landscape; it eddies and swirls beneath willow trees, and it can flood the entire valley. A delta fans back from the river and flares towards the Wainuiomata hills, which burn brown beneath summer skies of cobalt heartache blue. In the years after Albert Black left Naenae, I came to know the place well. For thirty-five years Ian taught at the high school there. He had a little office at the periphery of the school buildings where he saw troubled kids each day. Most of them lived in those huddled post-war houses.

―――

In 1953 the Hutt Valley became the centre of a storm about teenage morals. Underage girls, the newspapers trumpeted, were said to be having sex on the banks of the Hutt River and 'petting' in the back seats of the local picture theatres. To make matters worse, they were meeting leather-jacketed boys who rode motorbikes around Elbe's, the local milk bar. The movie *Rebel Without a Cause*, starring James Dean, was still a couple of years away, but the influence of a different kind of culture, an American one, which people saw as having started with the 'Yanks' in wartime New Zealand, was becoming pervasive. It had to be stamped out.

> Bodgies and widgies, comic books and Mickey
> Spillane, suggestive American songs on the hit
> parades. The bodgies wore stovepipe trousers
> and thick-soled shoes, and hair greased with
> Brylcreem touching their collars. And coloured

socks. Lime green or red or pink, colour
manifesting itself after the drab years of the war.
The widgies wore their cardigans back to front
with the sleeves pushed up to their elbows, one
of the sure signs a girl was going off the rails.
Or, pedal-pushers, tight three-quarter-length
pants, another sign of degradation.

Prime Minister Sid Holland, who had swept into power in 1949
on promises to treat farmers well and break the power of the
unions, had used strong-armed tactics during the 1951 Waterfront
Dispute. His government had also restored the death penalty,
which had been suspended by the Labour government of the
previous fourteen years. Now he ordered a report on this dangerous delinquent behaviour.

Sex, he made clear (although he preferred the
term carnal knowledge), was not something polite
people talked about, and young people had no
right to get up to it. Young girls needed protecting
from themselves. (It wasn't so bad for boys.)
They would never get husbands if they got up
to tricks beforehand. If a girl fell pregnant, she
got sent away, out of sight [usually to work as a
domestic servant in a rural household or to a hard
labour 'home' for unmarried mothers], or hastily
married in her parents' front room if the father
could be captured. That is, and here the voices
lowered even further, if the girl knew for sure who
the father was. Or if she was even old enough to
get married.

The man chosen to head the inquiry into the morals of teenagers
all over the country was a high-profile and God-fearing lawyer
called Oswald Mazengarb, who had a flair for the dramatic in
court, and political ambition. He was also a close friend of Sid
Holland. The revelations from the inquiry shocked the older

generation and fulfilled their worst nightmares: teenagers were running amok. Mazengarb's report was made public and landed in the letterboxes of anxious parents, just before the 1954 election, which National would win again by a handsome margin.

There is no way of knowing for certain why Albert decided to abscond, as it were, from his bond. There is a recurring suggestion that he was homesick, that the Hutt no longer appealed to him and that, if he could make his way to Auckland, he could earn more money and return to Belfast, or perhaps work his passage home on a ship. Nothing I was told suggested that he was involved in the Hutt scandals and Peter Simpson certainly was not. In January 1955, Albert would become the temporary custodian of a boarding house at 105 Wellesley Street in Auckland.

This is the way I half imagined, half learned of his leaving:

> Paddy [Albert] arrived in Auckland after an
> overnight train journey through the central heart
> of the country late in January. He had slept little.
> The train stopped often at sidings and small towns
> lit by dim lanterns over station platforms, staying a
> few minutes, then seemingly picking itself up with
> a mournful blast of its whistle, hurtling further on
> into the night. Twice there were stops long enough
> for passengers to alight and join a crush of people at
> the counter where they bought food. He remembers
> buying a pie and a cup of tea in a thick white cup at
> one stop, a rock cake and more tea somewhere else.
> He sat upright in a second-class seat, and in the
> shadowy darkness of summer he glimpsed canyons
> of bush and, it seemed to him, desolation. His
> heart felt as if it would explode with grief. He had
> left behind the only people in the country who cared
> about him, the woman who had looked after him as

if she were his mother, his friend who had emigrated with him, children who had welcomed his presence, the wee cutie who had danced on his feet.

Peter had been awake when he left. He was lying under the covers of his bed, smoking a cigarette . . .

'Paddy, my old mucker, don't go,' Peter said, as Paddy stuffed his duds into his suitcase.

'I have to, mate. I've got to get home to Ireland.'

The tangle of wooden houses, with their verandahs and alley-ways between, have been replaced by high-rise buildings. There is nothing left to show what 105 Wellesley Street looked like in the 1950s. But it's still just a five-minute walk to the main thoroughfare of Queen Street, past the neo-Gothic St Matthew-in-the-City, the turn-off to Albert Street and on to Smith & Caughey's, the venerable department store. While there is no record of how Albert came to be in charge of the boarding house, we do know that the woman who owned the property was to be away for a few months. They had met within days of Albert's arrival in Auckland. In return for taking care of the property, he would have free lodgings. He was not to allow people to stay there.

This is where things came unstuck. Albert was still only nineteen. Down the road and around the corner, in Upper Queen Street, was a café known as Ye Olde Barn, where patrons could buy cheap steak and chips. It was also a meeting place for the very people he had left behind in the Hutt Valley, mostly Kiwi kids done up as bodgies and widgies. Teddy boys congregated there too, and often young seamen, whose clothes were stylishly Edwardian to distinguish themselves as English. Or they may have come from Britain as children. New Zealand was one of several Commonwealth countries that took orphaned or abandoned children after the Second World War. Often, on arrival, they were sent to unsuitable homes like farms, where they were required to do heavy manual work or domestic duties and received little education.

I see myself sitting on the school bus in the Far North. At the front, a girl sits alone. Her name is Margaret. She wears a white blouse and a pleated skirt. Her face is very pale, her long hair caught in a bow. I think you'd call her pretty, but aloof. Or that is how she seemed to us other children on the bus. I remember we were told to leave her alone because she was unhappy and wanted to be by herself. Her surname was that of a local family, but then we heard that wasn't her name at all. In fact, she wasn't related to this family. And then she disappeared. How long did she sit there solitary and withdrawn? I don't remember. Weeks, a few months at most.

At one of the farms where my husband lived as a child, he remembered another girl, whose name was 'Jane'. She was supposed to be his sister. Or his cousin. Or something. She married into one of the families in that neighbourhood, and never left. We saw her now and then in the decades that followed, a righteous woman who bore a certain air of contempt when she talked about the locals, particularly those of colour. You could see it behind the smile; she wore her anger like a shroud.

Jane never left the farming area where she had been sent. But when many of these children were old enough to walk free, they tended to drift towards the cities, which felt more like the environment they were used to. There they banded together and proclaimed their differences.

———

Not long after Albert moved in, the house in Wellesley Street became party central. His new friends at Ye Olde Barn Café flocked to visit him and soon he was agreeing to people staying. He began to drift, moving around various labouring jobs, not staying long in any of them. He was also meeting and sleeping with a number of girls. It seems likely that at Rose's house, where certain rules were observed, he had not had much opportunity to explore his sexuality. Now his options were wide open. He was undoubtedly handsome and he liked to sing and dance and to make love.

In the last month that he would live at the boarding house, six months into the Auckland sojourn, Albert turned twenty. Among the people lodging there was Alan Jacques.

Born in London, in January 1936, he was a year younger than Albert, although he passed himself off as twenty-four. He had been sent to New Zealand in January 1952 when he was almost seventeen, an age when he might have been considered old enough to refuse migration. He came as an unwilling companion to two younger sisters, under the auspices of the Child Welfare Department, who placed him with foster parents on a farm in Hawke's Bay. His sisters went to other parts of the country. His mother was then living in Essex; it remains unclear why she allowed her children to be sent so far away. Alan was a well-developed youth, five foot eleven, with broad shoulders. It was said that he had done his three months' compulsory military training immediately after being released from the farm. I was not able to confirm this but the theory makes sense and perhaps explains his undeniable fighting skills. (Albert appeared to have avoided service up until that point, possibly because he was indentured to the government.)

Alan Jacques modelled himself on Mickey Spillane's Johnny McBride, the central character in *The Long Wait*, and assumed his identity. That novel was one of the books I had guarded on the mezzanine floor of the library. I reread it recently. Its violence, accounts of beatings and constant degrading encounters with women appal me. Johnny McBride, the character, carried a gun; Johnny McBride, the boy in Auckland, was known to carry a knife. McBride, the character, frequently insulted his enemies as 'yellow bastards'. McBride, the boy, was known to use this epithet too.

From the outset, Albert and Jacques, under his McBride alias, rubbed each other up the wrong way. Survivors of that time say that Albert was terrified of McBride and his bullying ways.

Albert asked his lodger to leave 105 Wellesley Street. The landlady was due back and he needed to clear the house. Jacques, with nowhere to go, was angry and resentful.

Throughout much of July, Albert had been sick with a heavy cold. His twentieth birthday came and went. But as the time drew close for the landlady to return, his friends persuaded him to let them organise a party on Monday the 25th as a wrap for the occupation of the boarding house and, for Albert, a late birthday celebration.

The following day, the young men at Ye Olde Barn made plans to pick up beer and invite the girls. Albert asked one particular girl, although he had a steady girlfriend who had already been invited. I called her Bessie Marsh. The other girl was a sixteen-year-old I christened Rita Zilich. Rita went home after her work as a shorthand typist, ostensibly retired early and then climbed out of the window of her parents' house, in order to go to the party. I did the same when I was sixteen. That yearning for the unexplored life, the wild energy that catapults us into our futures.

It's not clear whether the invitation was directed to Rita as a potential partner for Albert, or whether she was invited because of the coterie of girls she would bring with her. As it happened, Alan Jacques, the uninvited guest, turned up at the party and, before long, Rita was making out with him in an alleyway beside the house. Albert appeared and ordered her inside. It has always been maintained that he was jealous of this interaction. Perhaps he was, or perhaps, recognising her age and some vulnerability, he wanted to protect her from Jacques. Bessie had left the party earlier in the evening.

In the violent clash that followed and spilled out onto the street, Jacques kicked Albert in the testicles, blackening his eyes and otherwise delivering bruising blows. Jacques left, pulled away by other partygoers, promising to finish Albert off the next day.

Rita stayed behind. Subsequently, there was some dispute over whether she had stayed willingly or wanted to go with Jacques. While Albert lay down to recover, she tidied up the living room, putting away a scout knife that Albert appears to have brought from Belfast that had been used for opening beer bottles. Albert talked in a generally maudlin way and they attempted to have sex, but he was too injured for this to happen. Rita appears to have been a willing partner. According to the evidence she later gave against him, as the night wore on, Albert muttered that he would kill Johnny McBride. He told Rita he expected to die young. She left around three in the morning, when Albert called a taxi for her.

The following day, the young men who had been at the party drank in a desultory way around Auckland's pubs. Albert got up late, finished cleaning the house and later in the day, carrying his knife, went to a pub where he drank until he vomited and was thrown out. He then retreated to Ye Olde Barn Café where his mates, if that's what they were, had assembled to eat. A group of Teddy-boys-turned-seamen also entered the café and sat down near the jukebox. One of them was another former child migrant from England named Richard Douglas, although he became Henry in the novel.

And it was at this point that the 'incident' occurred.

There are two versions of what happened. Albert would maintain that Jacques came in, told him to come outside and fight, called him 'a dirty yellow Irish bastard' and hit him in the face. Earlier that day, during Albert's absence, Jacques had gone back to 105 Wellesley Street and put his belongings in a suitcase. Albert would state that he believed he was about to be killed. In order to save himself, he pulled the knife he was carrying and stabbed Jacques in the shoulder, hoping to scare him.

That is one version.

At the trial, the young men sitting by the jukebox would say that they saw nothing, that there was no exchange between Albert and Jacques. As Jacques stood, choosing a song, Albert had got up, walked over and stabbed him.

That is the second version.

Whichever you choose to believe, Albert left the café, accompanied by another youth. They walked to the nearby police station, where Albert made a series of muddled statements, claiming self-defence.

Back in the café, some of the young men had rolled Jacques over onto his back. The knife had sliced through his neck and emerged from his nose. Blood sprayed in all directions and panic ensued. Jacques died within minutes. A pathologist's report would say that the initial stab wound was the cause of death – it had penetrated soft tissue and cut Jacques' spinal cord.

The youths were terrified out of their wits and, it later appeared, believed that they had caused the death. When the police arrived, they offered themselves as witnesses but were told there were enough already. They then left the premises as quickly as they could.

Richard Douglas is still alive. He has a clear and exact recollection of that evening. In his version, an altercation did take place in front of the jukebox, before Albert retreated to his seat. Albert, he says, tried to play the Bing Crosby version of 'Danny Boy'. His little brother back in Belfast was, of course, Daniel, or Danny. Jacques overrode this choice with, according to popular narrative, a song called 'Evil Angels'. It seems more likely that it was 'Earth Angel', recorded by the Penguins in 1954.

Richard was therefore one of a number of potential witnesses who were not called at the subsequent Supreme Court trial in Auckland the following October. But, from his different vantage point, he maintains that there was a disagreement between Albert and Jacques, and that the threat Albert complained of may have been made then. Although Richard doesn't recall a punch, his detailed memories of the ensuing minutes have been put to the test over a number of interviews and his story holds up. All these years later, we appear to have a truly credible witness.

Alan Jacques had immersed himself so deeply in the character of Johnny McBride that it was several days before his true identity was revealed, confirmed by the farmer for whom he had worked after his arrival in New Zealand. Jacques was carrying a clasp knife with a 4-inch blade.

———

A grand jury no longer features in the New Zealand justice system, but in the 1950s it was part of any serious prosecution in the Supreme Court. A collection of between twelve and twenty-three citizens had to decide and recommend that the case could go to trial before a twelve-person common jury. The same judge would preside over both juries, but the grand jury deliberated behind closed doors. Reporters were admitted but were not supposed to disclose the judge's comments until the trial was over. In this instance, however, they did make public what was said by the judge, a man called George Finlay:

> The offender is not one of ours, except by adoption
> and apparently comes from the type that we could
> well be spared in our country. He belongs to a
> peculiar sect, if you could call it that, or a peculiar
> association of individuals whose outlook on life
> differs from the normal. It is unfortunate that we
> got this undesirable from his homeland. It is a case
> of an apparently deliberate stabbing in a restaurant
> in Upper Queen Street, and there seems no opening
> of either provocation or self-defence, or any of the
> defences usually presented in a case of this kind.

These comments were reported in the *Auckland Star* and the *New Zealand Herald*. On the night before the trial began and on the morning it started, 18 October 1955, these newspapers were delivered to the rooms of the sworn-in members of the common jury, who were staying at the Station Hotel.

It seems impossible that a trial without prejudice could have taken place. Surely, one would think, it should have been aborted. Some contemporary legal experts agree that it should not have gone ahead. But it did.

My jury members are fictional. But I have been on juries and I know how they work and I know how prejudice can influence outcomes. I have seen it at work and it's ugly. If I have a regret about the book, it's that I reordered the events, placing the delivery of the newspapers at the end of the trial, rather than the beginning. Call it 'the writer's journey', so beloved of screenwriters. I would write that differently now. Nevertheless, it's damning, either way you look at it.

The testimony of the young men and women who gave evidence at the trial seems questionable. I think of Rita, turned Crown witness. From the transcripts of her evidence, it's clear that she was intelligent, quick-witted and, back then, perhaps too adventurous for her own good. She understood authority and parental boundaries but she was willing to break free of them, provided she didn't get caught. But she did. Her and Albert's accounts of what was said at 105 Wellesley Street the night before the incident in the café would vary.

Eye-witness accounts of the trial describe her as dressed in a fitting black suit and wearing a black beret on her tawny red hair. Her manner appears to have been defiant, perhaps as a mantle of protection. She was sixteen and one must assume that her truth was her own. But so much of this trial came down to one person's word against another, to things that occurred without witnesses. The Crown's case against Albert Black included the allegation that he had stabbed Jacques because he was jealous of the latter's relationship with Rita. That has never made sense to me. Rita stayed with Albert far into the night, towards the dawn, tidying his house, listening to him talk and climbing into his bed for sex. Hadn't Albert already won her?

What she told the jury, as a prosecution witness, was that Albert had threatened to kill Jacques. This was the crux of her evidence against him. Albert may well have said this. If so, it was unfortunate, but the heat of the moment is not always a rational time, especially for the young. What Rita failed to disclose was the extent of his injuries.

What would I have said, if I had been Rita, her life in tatters before her, as the truth of that night, and where she had been, and what she had done, emerged before her parents' eyes? This is something I cannot answer. It would have been just about the worst thing imaginable, the shame beyond the pale.

Rita and the girlfriends who had accompanied her to the party were granted name suppression. Not so the young men, though I have given them aliases. So what to make of them? We know from their testimonies that most of them had spent the day of Alan Jacques' death drinking at various hotels in central Auckland. They seem to have had collective amnesia about what they saw. For the most part, I invented their backgrounds. But where they had been and what they had been doing on the day is much as it really was, based on the transcripts of their evidence. Some of what happened in the hours, days and weeks that followed, I gleaned from subsequent newspaper accounts.

A night or two later, the youth who had gone to the police station with Albert had his car tampered with outside Ye Olde Barn. Another witness escaped to Rotorua and went into hiding. He had to be escorted back to Auckland in order to give evidence for the prosecution. Another youth called Claude Quintal, known as Pooch, had landed in borstal in Invercargill by the time of the trial, and was prevented from giving evidence. He would spend the rest of his life telling anyone who would listen that he had information that would have saved Albert Black from execution.

There is a theme here of witnesses who were absent but wanted to give evidence, and witnesses who were deeply unwilling to be there at all. Pooch apparently asserted that it was rolling Alan Jacques onto his back that killed him, not the stab wound. The pathologist disagreed with this, and presumably he knew better. But he did describe the wound as 'flukey'. What sets Pooch's evidence apart is that he was isolated from the other youths in the months after the incident.

In the fraught minutes that followed the stabbing, these young people did what they thought best, fearing, perhaps, that they might be implicated in the death. It's possible they then regretted it. There's an image that haunts me, of the café cook, a man called Laurie Corrington, running down Queen Street, screaming, his apron covered in blood. Later, he would speak to reporters of 'that poor kid who was killed and only had his suitcase and nowhere to go'. I find this poignant. I find this the story of two young men who had reached the end of their tether.

If Alan Jacques appears as the villain in this story so far, I think that's only partly the case. At worst, he was imitating a cardboard cult figure, too handy with his fists, an adolescent acting out his fantasies. Rather, I believe that this is a tale of poverty and unemployment, of abandonment and prejudice, of immigration gone wrong.

For me, Albert's claim that he was defending himself is credible. I like to think that if I had been on that jury, I would have found him guilty of the lesser charge of manslaughter. All the jurors were male, not unusual in the 1950s, although women had been eligible to serve on juries since 1942. It's hard not to imagine that a more gender-balanced group might have been more open to the circumstances of the case. In his lengthy summing up – longer than the time it took the jury to find Albert guilty – Judge Finlay said: 'If there was no assault in the café, there was nothing against which Black had to defend himself, and if there was no insult there was nothing to deprive him of his self-control.' It was immaterial whether the fatal blow was a fluke or not.

> Gentlemen, if I may seem to express any view of
> my own upon the facts, I want you to know that it
> is unwittingly that I do it . . . I thoroughly support
> Mr Davison's plea to you [for the defence] when he
> asked you to forget all you have read or heard about
> this case. It is difficult in a community like ours not
> to read the newspapers and not to know something
> about a case before it comes to adjudication. It is
> difficult for people not to discuss beforehand such
> cases as that.

So there it is: a trial that should not have gone ahead because prejudiced material was put before the jury, a judge excusing himself for his own remarks, witnesses whose evidence was variable, and those whose evidence was suppressed.

A friend of mine, who was a student teacher at the time, was present when the verdict was brought in. He had raced to the court with his mates when word travelled that the jury was deliberating. But their excitement would soon drain away. He still recalls the sense of chill in the air as the jury returned, the silence as the guilty verdict was delivered, the way the judge arranged the scrap of black material on his head that proclaimed the death penalty before the words were spoken. He remembers a pale girl who was led away weeping.

Prejudice was the basis of an application to the Court of Appeal in November, the month after the trial. The appeal was dismissed in an eleven-page summary.

Back in Belfast, Kathleen Black was desperately trying to gather support for a petition to save her son's life, which she planned to present to Clifton Webb, the High Commissioner for New Zealand, based in London. In the space of a week she collected twelve thousand signatures; this in a city where few people had telephones and word of mouth was the main form of communication. She wrote to the Queen, mother to mother, although Her Majesty may have been distracted when the letter arrived, as her sister, Princess Margaret, was that week renouncing Group Captain Peter Townsend, a divorced man, as her prospective husband.

Kathleen was also praying as well as pleading. She decided she would make the journey to New Zealand to put the case in person for clemency for Albert and, even if it failed, say goodbye to him.

None of it worked.

And this is where the New Zealand government's role and that of the Mazengarb Report come up for scrutiny. The attorney-general in Sid Holland's hanging government was a man named Jack Marshall, later prime minister and knighted. As it turned out, Clifton Webb was no friend of Kathleen. He wrote to Marshall saying that he hoped he had spared him the visit of another murderer's mother to New Zealand: he was referring to the case of Frederick Foster, who had been hanged earlier that year. Marshall concurred with this view, denying Kathleen entry to the country and turning down pleas for mercy. The Blacks did have an advocate in the form of health minister Ralph Hanan, who added his entreaties to spare Albert's life. But Marshall, supported by Holland, was unmoved. The process marched steadily towards its grim conclusion.

Based on newspaper reports, here is how I perceived scenes at Parliament on 30 November 1955 when the Executive Council, the highest formal authority of government, met to decide Albert's fate:

> It's a short meeting. The Prime Minister, Sid Holland,
> remarks again on the undesirability of men like Albert
> Black in New Zealand. If they can't be sent back to

where they came from, they have to be prevented from pursuing further crime in New Zealand. The reports on him suggest a highly immoral lifestyle, something that he and his friend Mr Mazengarb aim to stamp out. It will not just punish the crime that has been committed but serve as a short, sharp reminder to those who follow reprehensible modes of living and are sexually promiscuous.

Ralph Hanan says, 'So Black is to be made an example in respect of the Mazengarb Report?'

'None of them were up to any good. The youth who was killed had been reading banned books. He even modelled himself on one of Spillane's characters.'

'So two men die, thanks to Mr Mazengarb. Aren't we, as a government, succumbing to lynch law?'

The Attorney-General rolls his eyes, and the rest of the Council members sigh and look away.

The Prime Minister says that unless there are any further objections, it will be recommended to the Governor-General that Black's execution take place forthwith.

There is a time frame for the procedure. Once the Council has made its recommendation the penalty must be imposed within seven days. Hanan looks at his colleagues one at a time, until they look away from him and drop their eyes.

Hanan would become a major and successful advocate for the abolition of the death penalty. But that was of no help to Albert.

———

In the last weeks of his life, Albert converted to Roman Catholicism, presumably out of respect for Bessie Marsh, who was carrying his child. He was supported in this decision by Father

Leo Downey, well known for his good works among Auckland's prison population. During this time Albert also wrote numerous letters to friends he had made on the ship coming out to New Zealand. Peter Simpson kept his letters and later gave them to the family Albert had stayed with in Naenae. I have copies and parts of them appear in *This Mortal Boy*. They are the work of a thoughtful man who has grown into himself as he examines his conscience and accepts his fate. Peter, like many of his friends, would never stop mourning him. Albert died on 5 December 1955, just over a fortnight before Christmas.

There is a wind that evening, a noisy buffeting wind that lifts the canvas like a ship's sail in a storm. The scaffold is a high steel structure, with a platform reached by way of seventeen steps. Around the supports at the bottom of the gallows canvas has been lashed to conceal the space beneath. The whole scene is lit by a powerful electric light. The light shines on the white rope coiled beneath the gallows and on the noose hanging over the trap. The hangman stands waiting at the back of the platform, his back to the observers.

Albert appears, led by his guards. He doesn't walk along the polished corridors; rather, he shuffles because his body is harnessed by broad leather straps. The straps are crossed around his arms at the elbows, his crossed hands strapped in front of him, and his legs pinioned above the knee. In some ways, he resembles a log of wood, or a five foot eight tree stump. To further ensure that his body is as rigid as it can possibly be made, he wears a stiff canvas coat and a pair of heavy boots provided by the prison.

He ascends the stairs slowly, and the hangman turns to meet him. In the bright light Father Downey sees that the hangman is dressed in a felt hat pulled low over his brow, sunglasses hiding his eyes. His chin is sunk in the collar of a long topcoat buttoned all the way up the front.

Albert is facing Horace Haywood [the prison superintendent]. 'Have you anything to say, Black?' Haywood asks.

Albert turns and looks down on those assembled beneath him. In a grave voice, he answers, 'I wish you all a merry Christmas, gentlemen, and a prosperous New Year.'

Less than five months had elapsed since the incident at Ye Olde Barn Café. Three months after his death, his daughter, referred to as E. H. in the novel, was born. Albert has grandchildren too.

2

Newspapers were allowed only one reporter at an execution and they were under strict instructions to report nothing more than such details as time of death and how many people were present. Jack Young of *Truth* defied the rules and wrote exactly what he saw in language that moved his audience. A wave of revulsion for the death penalty followed.

It was this account, and public debate and protest, that strengthened Ralph Hanan's arm when abolition was put to the test in Parliament. By that time, he was the justice minister in the National government, elected in 1960, led by Keith Holyoake. Hanan was a man with a good instinct for public sympathies. In 1957, during the last months of the Holland administration, one more person had been hanged. His name was Walter Bolton, and even now, there are some doubts as to whether he did poison his wife. Between Albert's death, and abolition in 1961, there had been a second three-year Labour government, which again suspended the death penalty. Hanan saw an opportunity to reform the situation and remove this hit and miss political approach to executions once and for all. As justice minister, it was his responsibility to introduce the bill ratifying the penalty, but when he did so, he made his disagreement with it known. He convinced nine of his party colleagues, including Rob Muldoon, to cross the floor and vote with the Opposition, thus abolishing the death penalty.

If Hanan emerges as something of a hero in this saga, I am aware that other of his views were more conservative. Some contemporary historians see him as no great friend to Māori, believing that some of his legislation was detrimental to their welfare. It's hard to fathom how people balance out their priorities, or how, when in power, they determine the fate of others. Hanan remains an enigma to me. He died when he was sixty from complications of a lung condition contracted during his war service.

―――――――

Writing *This Mortal Boy* involved years of research. There is a moment of troubling realisation that comes in a writer's life, or it does for me anyway, when a book presents itself and you know, somehow, that you have to do it, you can't brush it off. In a way the research is a kind of procrastination, a delaying of the moment when the book must be started, the transformative act must begin. But I've always heeded the words of John Steinbeck who once said that it was best to get the research done first so that the process of writing would not be constantly paused while the hunting for background and 'facts' took place. I think he was right. For the act of researching takes you closer and closer to the characters, to the long months in which you must inhabit them. There were many days when I found myself inside the head of Kathleen Black and her desperate pleas for clemency for her son. I became that mother, a part of me living her anguish. And I didn't have to look far for Albert. I'd seen him for so many years of my life – the father who never went home, who mourned an Ireland from which he came but to which he never really belonged, as he didn't belong in New Zealand either.

I interviewed dozens of people, including Albert's friend Richard, whom I visited with my publisher and enduring friend, Harriet Allan. I have worked with Harriet for over thirty years. She is part of this story. Although we quizzed him about what he had witnessed at the milk bar, the police did not, deeming him and his companions unreliable.

Richard is in his eighties now, becoming frail but as clear headed as any youth. He lives alone in an immaculate Waikato apartment, home to his precise and detailed model ships.

I talked endlessly to the historian Redmer Yska, who had already written about Albert in his book, *All Shook Up*, and who provided me with transcripts of the trial and swathes of other material – not least Jack Young's account of the hanging.

I travelled to Belfast, where I'd talked my way into an invitation to the city's writers' festival, via my London publisher, and got put up in a historic high-end hotel for a week. I walked the streets where the Black family lived, stood in the cathedral where Kathleen and Albert senior were married, spent hours ensconced in the Linen Hall Library and was made welcome by the staff at births, deaths and marriages, who treated my search as if it were their own. A cousin of mine, an architect who had designed prisons, had access to the closed section of Mount Eden. I stood on the spot where Albert was pitched into space by the hangman, and I wept.

If this sounds vaguely like an acknowledgements section that should come at the end of a book (and did when I wrote the novel), it's actually about the lengths you go to, to find a way into a story. And to get it as right as you can.

The person I talked to the most was Ian. He knew Auckland in the 1940s and 1950s like the back of his hand. As a child during the Second World War, he had lived with his grandparents in a run-down building in Parnell called Paddy's Puzzle, the subject of another early novel. Young women who lived there entertained American servicemen, so Ian knew how the 'Yanks' or 'the American invasion', so called, had divided opinion and changed the face of youth culture. Ian often got to eat candy when there was too much of it for the recipients. He remembered the nylon stockings the Americans brought, their ice-cream sodas and their flowers, and the venereal diseases the girls in the building suffered. And during the 1950s, he had been a student in Auckland and seen it with different eyes again. How long would it take to walk from here to there? I would ask him over breakfast. Or tell me about the dance halls – what dances did you go to? He could recite the names of streets, ones I would often walk along during trips to Auckland, trying to soak up the feel of them, even though so many of the buildings that were there have gone.

As on some earlier books, Ian had become my collaborator. When I told him a day or two after I had written the end that I didn't feel the story was over, his eyes lit up. 'Another cause,' he said. He was glad, however, that I had 'come back'. He felt that I'd been away for a long time. I knew what he meant, though I didn't like to admit it then. I'd been consumed by that book and returning from it was hard.

———

I didn't find Albert's family when I was in Belfast. I had wanted to, especially for the sake of his daughter, whose birth was still an active secret. Since the book emerged, all the Belfast family that is left or known to exist have come forward. There is a cousin twice removed, and a very elderly aunt, but no sign of Daniel. I learned that Katheen and Albert's marriage did not survive Albert's death. I imagine their grief driving them apart, laying bare their differences, as so often happens when a young person has died a sudden or violent death. The family story of who did what, in order to save Albert, has varied over the years. Would I have written my book in any other way had I this access when I started? Perhaps in the detail, but not in the broad outline. Their fictional lives are still, for me, a passionate preoccupation, and a burden.

———

A postscript. One day not long ago I flew to Auckland and met Harriet. She was dressed in a quilted green jacket and sturdy boots, well prepared for walking.

We set off for Waikumete Cemetery, where Albert is buried. Armed with plot and row numbers in the Roman Catholic area of the huge cemetery, we thought it shouldn't be too difficult to find him. I had seen a photo of Pooch Quintal beside his grave, taken not long before his death. Pooch is bald and sad, wearing a fleecy-lined jacket and holding a black hat. In the accompanying article he is quoted as saying that he wanted to take Albert's remains home to Ireland to bury them beside his mother. Time, the item said, had washed away the name on the white cross that was shown.

The entrance to the cemetery was planted in fragrant purple stocks. The women at reception were dressed in black, though one had immaculate fingernails all painted white, except one that was bright red. They were kind and solicitous and interested in our search. In their burial records, Albert is shown as having been buried in Catholic E Row 8, Plot 70 on 6 December 1955, the day after his death. That doesn't match up with information that he was buried first in the courtyard; perhaps that was a holding point while a grave was prepared. Or perhaps the record is simply skewed and he really was taken straight to the cemetery. As we would discover, he is something of a mirage.

The sky was wide and pale grey above the natural basin in which the cemetery lies. The rows of graves are named like streets, and all the names are those of flowers or trees. We made our way along Amber Crescent, appropriately named on that wintry day, for a vast plane tree was shedding its foliage in soft drifts, bright scarlet on one side, turning gold on the other. Further on, we were showered by the pale lemon leaves of a gingko.

Soon we had left the bright trees behind, as we ploughed down a bank and found ourselves in a small gully squelching with swamp beneath our feet. None of the graves quite matched the numbers we had been given and there were many white crosses washed clean of any name. Harriet, who is a better map reader than I am, decided on one that lay beside the headstone for a small child. The graves are in order of date of death. In that row, according to the list of graves we had been given, lie two Williams, a Daniel and a John, all with unmarked graves. The one Harriet spotted had a cross sunken almost to its horizontal bar in the swamp, covered with rushes and a plant that could have been wild marsh iris but would be revealed only in spring. We made our way back to the office, where it was confirmed that we had identified the right place.

We went back and took photographs. I wished I had taken flowers; instead, I plucked a head of paspalum grass and dropped it among the rushes.

After that, we went in search of Alan Jacques, or Johnny McBride as he liked to be known. He was said to be in the Protestant Division A, Row 5, plot number 62. It was barely round the corner from Albert. On our way there, we came across a tidy headstone for Frederick Foster, the young Englishman who had shot his girlfriend in another café further along Queen Street, and was hanged a few months before Albert. Locating Alan Keith Jacques was harder. It took two trips to reception and another printout to find him – or where he might be.

A huge pine tree spreads its roots over Row 5. Alongside the remains of a tilting headstone for a man called Tom Strange, we believe, lies all that is left of Alan Jacques. Somewhere in the swamps and pine trees of Waikumete Cemetery these migrant youths have vanished.

――――――――

The story of Albert Black, of either of them, is not over. As Ian had predicted, Albert was another cause in the making. *This Mortal Boy* has been read by interested judges and lawyers who have, with careful restraint, volunteered their view that justice was not entirely served in this case. Even though Albert came from Northern Ireland, the Irish Embassy has expressed its concern, as have supporters at Otago University's Centre for Irish and Scottish Studies. At the time of writing, a group of lawyers is examining the case to see whether it might be brought back to the Court of Appeal, notwithstanding that any exoneration, or a downgrading of the case from murder to manslaughter, would be brought posthumously. Richard, the witness unheard until now, has made a sworn affidavit, detailing at length what he saw and heard on the night Albert stabbed Alan Jacques in Ye Olde Barn Café.

That is a story still in the making.

Alan Jacques is
buried beneath
the tree.

The cross marks
Albert Black's grave.

Frederick
Foster's grave.

Grave-hunting
at Waikumete
cemetery.
Photographs
taken by
Harriet Allan.

Pure Duras

Of late, I have seen women writers, it is always women, claiming Marguerite Duras as a favourite author. When I see their embrace of her, I am filled with outraged jealousy. You can't have her, I want to tell them, she belongs to me. They are writing about extremes of passion, about the realities of desire – that's if desire is ever real; it never really is until it's been consummated, and then it starts all over again until the next time. These women who want her for themselves, like a new discovery, are usually pretty good at what they do. They understand Duras, draw on her intensity, the recklessness of her mind. The rest see only her surfaces – the alcohol, the life lived with abandonment.

I became aware of her in the late 1950s when I read her first novel, *The Sea Wall* [*Un Barrage contre le Pacifique*], published in 1950. Then, in the very early 1960s, when I was newly married, I saw Alan Resnais's 1959 movie, *Hiroshima, Mon Amour*, which, as a screenwriter, Duras had scripted. It concerned two lovers, a Japanese man and a French woman, meeting in the aftermath of the August 1945 bombing of Hiroshima. The film portrayed the sensual beauty and desire of a relationship divided by war, in which each participant perceived the other as evil, and the way in which people of goodwill were torn apart by these differences.

The movie deeply disturbed me. I was twenty years old, or maybe twenty-one. Not long before, I had married cross-culturally, in the face of some opposition. I sat in the dim twilight of the old Regent cinema in Rotorua, where I was accustomed to watching romantic comedies or Elvis Presley movies, and knew I was seeing something different. Even though I was young, I recognised flashes of myself that had yet to be fully explored. Perhaps it was the image of shadowed slatted blinds across the man's naked back, an image that repeats itself in my work. I've described Duras elsewhere as having 'the spare and unsparing voice of human sexuality'. Or maybe it was the tension of war, the necessity to reach across boundaries in the face of adversity. I had already done that, one wet and stormy day in St Faith's Church by the lake, where, on certain days, sulphur and steam rose and fragmented the light. It was where I had married. These memories are inescapable.

I see myself as changed by that movie. I reread *The Sea Wall*. It's based on Duras growing up beside the Mekong River on a failing piece of land with her mother and brothers, her love affair with a Chinese man in Saigon when she was little more than a child, then her departure from the East for a life as a writer in Paris. (Perhaps my knowledge of her affair came later. To some extent, *The Sea Wall* obscures the facts of the relationship; they become clearer in *The Lover* [*L'Amant*], not published until 1984, but there are clues all over the earlier work.) My life did not mirror hers. She was an alcoholic who drifted into lengthy comas at the height of her addiction. She was married twice, once to the writer Robert Antelme, who barely survived the Second World War in Buchenwald concentration camp - like Duras, he worked for the French Resistance until he was deported - and later to Dionys Mascolo, the father of her only child. For a time, the three of them lived in a ménage à trois. She spent her last years in the company of Yann Andréa, a much younger gay man whom she loved and who loved her in return.

So no, I'm not like her at all, except that I'm a writer, and perhaps that is sufficient. There was enough of a reflection for me to be stirred in some mysterious way. I'm trying to explain the fascination for her that has followed me over the decades, how she has led me into danger, how I have defied the odds to find the essence of her. And perhaps, in the end, to let her go.

But in seeking to understand her influence on me, as a writer, I've returned often to an essay Duras wrote called 'The Black Block', about her writing process:

> It isn't the transition Aristotle speaks of, from
> potential to actual being. It isn't a translation. It's
> not a matter of passing from one state to another.
> It's a matter of deciphering something already
> there, something you've already done in the
> deep sleep of your life, in its organic rumination,
> unbeknown to you. It isn't something transferred –
> that's not it. It might be that instinct I referred to as
> the power of reading before it's written, something
> that's still illegible to everyone else. I could put it
> differently. I could say it's the ability to read your
> own writing, the first stage of your own writing,
> while it's still indecipherable to others.

As I read this, it suggests a sense of abandonment, a letting go when immersed in writing, with which I identify. Or, to put it another way, of bringing to the surface what has gone before, and finding in it what you want to say.

Duras was born in 1914 near Saigon, as Marguerite Donnedieu, the daughter of French schoolteachers. The family came and went from France. In 1921, during one of these trips, her father fell ill and died in Paris. Later, when Marguerite was establishing herself as a writer, she took the name Duras, which was the French birthplace of her father. She was often referred to simply as M.D. The remaining family returned to French Indochina – later to be known as Vietnam – where her mother worked for a time in a boarding house, believed to be near the Hoàn Kiếm Lake in Hanoi, before buying some isolated rice farmland in Prey Nob, near Sihanoukville. The family lived a desolate existence, eating what they could grow, while trying to repel the encroaching China Sea (not, as Duras calls it, the Pacific). Another failed property was at Vĩnh Long, beside the Mekong River, and it was from there, as nearly as I can pinpoint it, that Duras' relationship with the older Chinese man began.

Possibly it was these circumstances that led Duras to remark that mothers remain the strangest, craziest people we ever met. I adored my own mother, a plain-spoken, seemingly sensible woman, yet I understood all of this, I really did. After the war my father had bought land in the Far North that was not fit for purpose and we had been poor and eaten off the land; my mother had worked in a boarding house. Perhaps she had been crazy to keep following along, saying nothing, accepting, if not everything, then too much.

———

I'm trying to assemble the ghosts of things I've written before and I'm aware that I may be repeating myself, but there's no other way to recount it. In 1991, while on holiday in Thailand, I persuaded Ian to take a side trip to Vietnam because I wanted to follow the path of Duras, to go to Saigon, and from there take a boat trip along the Mekong to Vĩnh Long.

By then, Saigon had become Ho Chi Minh City, renamed for the country's leader. Sixteen years had passed since the fall to the north, and all of Vietnam was now under communist rule. Tân Sơn Nhất Airport was worn and almost derelict, but the boulevards appeared much as Duras had described them, fragrant with oleanders. We were the only Europeans at the Rex Hotel, accommodation for US military personnel before Saigon fell. On the opposite side of the road stood the turn-of-the-century Continental Hotel, the setting for Graham Greene's novel, *The Quiet American*.

While Ian went on an expedition of his own the following day, I walked alone through the streets, then stopped to sit on a park bench by a boulevard of towering trees. Behind me the twin towers of Notre Dame Cathedral stabbed the sky. It was Vietnam's National Day. Children passed me, blowing clouds and clouds of celebratory rose pink and blue soap bubbles, or shook rattles made from slit Coke cans. Young men were performing violent martial arts on a dais. Although the French had long gone, the bakery stalls still sold French pastries and French bread, alongside pots of steaming noodles and frog meat.

I remember a little girl sitting to pee in the dust alongside where I sat. When she was finished she stood up, rubbing her belly. She knew the word for hungry, repeating it with moans.

I hesitated, thinking that, as a European, I shouldn't be giving money to children. Her eyes were dark and angry.

My bag contained thousands of dongs, the Vietnamese currency. I opened it and gave her some; instantly a crowd of children rushed from the trees around us. As I made a hurried retreat I almost tripped over limbless beggars. Their sores bled from rubbing on the new tarseal. However it had looked on arrival, this was not Duras' Saigon.

I'd come no closer to Duras. After enquiring at the tourist office, I discovered that for $US100 we could have two guides for the day and the use of a flat-bottomed wooden launch to explore the Mekong Delta.

We started very early in the morning, the sky a dusky breaking blue. Fishing boats surrounded us as we drew away from the pier but then they fell behind and we were alone. The launch was more like a barge. There was a little canvas awning over the top and on the deck stood two folding deck chairs. As we churned through the brown swirling currents, I remember thinking at some point how foolhardy the whole endeavour was – not another boat in sight, sometimes catching glimpses of people on the shore, in their rice fields. It had been raining hard; there were signs of flooding and branches caught on the shoreline.

I'm still haunted by Duras' description of crossing the Mekong, on the ferry that plied between Vĩnh Long and Sadec. It's worth quoting again: 'Never in my whole life shall I ever again see rivers as big and wild and beautiful as these, the great regions of water soon to disappear into the caves of the ocean.'

We stopped often on this precarious journey, invited into houses for tea, exclaimed over with wonder. On an island called Tan Long we strolled through quiet orchards. Grapefruit as big as pumpkins hung above us. They smelled like breakfast. Marigolds grew as high as my chin and in the grass bright pink ten o'clock flowers opened to the sun. 'Does anyone remember a Madame Donnedieu and her family?' I asked, through our guide. There were blank looks, the shaking of heads. 'The daughter is a famous writer in France now,' I added, trying to sound helpful. The guide said, gravely, 'Until 1954, we had to bear the domination of the French. Until 1975, we had to bear the domination of the Americans. Now there is only us.'

I don't believe we reached Vĩnh Long, perhaps the outskirts. To be honest, I'm not even sure that we were going in the right direction. It didn't matter, I had seen the river she had travelled on and felt its power.

———

I might have given up on Duras, but I kept bumping into reminders of her and her life. She *was*, after all, still alive then. I came across her collection of essays, *Practicalities*, published in 1987. My concept of what an essay might be was turned on its head. These were more like conversations, reflections on her life, quite short, often terse, sometimes funny, but also domestic – the thoughts of a woman who ran a household. I loved that she provided a list of household products that she was never without:

table salt, pepper, wine, pasta, potatoes, rice, tinned tomatoes, yoghurt, eggs, washing powder.

I looked at my own list for last week, which begins: paper towels, blueberries, lettuce, wine, toothpaste. These are items that are always in my pantry (the blueberries are frozen ones in winter), or somewhere in the house. Batteries, butter, dishwashing liquid. And camembert. Plus a particular kind of lemon vinaigrette that is better than the one I make.

I stand at my kitchen bench and make these lists. My kitchen is a pale lemon shade. On the windowsill stand many blue glass objects the colour of the sea and sky; all down one wall hang old Royal Doulton plates, covered in painted pansies. My mother loved pansies, and these plates come from her life. On a shelf stands a row of creamy-coloured cups decorated with a shadowy pale green pattern of leaves, like tracings, part of a tea set given to my parents by our neighbours when they left the farm up north. Beyond the window above the bench lies a courtyard surrounded by native trees that Ian and I planted when we came to this house, and inside those a half-circle of white roses put in for a family wedding. Below me, on the other side, stands a grove of olive trees, just above the lip of the cliff that falls to the road far below. These were planted by my grandsons. I never do get to gather the olives, they are out of reach, but birds feast on them as they ripen. So many birds.

I add olives to the list.

I came across a book called *Writers' Houses*. The prologue was by Duras, and the opening pictures were of her house at Neauphle-le-Château, a market town between Paris and Chartres. The interior of the house wasn't glamorous. It was a bit shabby around the edges, with frayed cushions and tablecloths, but it was filled with light and jars of wildflowers and books. Not unlike a version of my own house, which is very light. I have a passion for light – windows that face the dawn, that let in the sun. Duras remarked that her house was a place of solitude, even though it looked onto a street and 'a very old pond'.

There was a picture of the pond and I was drawn to that, almost as much as to the house. It was round and edged by trees that swept its dark surface. I knew that I wanted to see this house and this pond. By this time, Duras had died (in 1996), but even if she had been alive, I was certain she wouldn't have liked intruders.

My yearning was satisfied in 2006, when I was in Paris as part of a New Zealand authors' tour of France. I had already spent much of that year in the city of Menton and, throughout my time there, the idea had been quietly fermenting that I must see the house in Neauphle-le-Château. As I have described in my second volume of memoir, with the help of my friend and fellow writer, Pierre Furlan, I found No. 1 Rue du Docteur Grellière, though it was empty and its exterior was sadly altered by neglect. But I was moved by the simple domesticity of what I saw through the windows: scuff marks on the skirting boards, dried flowers in a vase, expressing the reality of a life I had so often imagined. And the pond, its surface mirror still, was unchanged. Another example, I thought, of how Duras might see things, of how one might go into the depths of the pool and come up with something unexpected.

At the end of *Beside the Dark Pool*, there is a brief account of another journey, made some years later, to search for the boarding house by the lake in Hanoi, where Duras' mother worked when the author was a small child, and where she lost her innocence at the hands of a predatory boy.

Although Ian and I had been back to South Vietnam since the time we took the boat along the Mekong, we had never made it to Hanoi. Seventeen years later, I told him that we both had unfinished business in the north. I flew from Auckland and met him in Bangkok Airport where he had arrived hours earlier, after one of his aid trips to Cambodia. By the time we reached Hanoi, however, he had become seriously ill with a potentially fatal tropical virus. Although we were in Hanoi for two weeks, he spent the whole time in an intensive care unit. Alone in a hospital side-room, not permitted to see Ian, who I'd been told might not live through his first night there, I managed to contact our family in

New Zealand. My daughter had the presence of mind to ring the night desk at Foreign Affairs and, soon afterwards, a team from the New Zealand embassy in Hanoi appeared.

Through the days that followed, as my husband hovered between life and death, I found friends in this group. The ambassador was a man called James Kember. His wife, Alison, like Ian, had been a teacher in her other life - and, as it turned out, they knew each other, so she visited with me from time to time.

By day the Kembers took me into their diplomatic residence and gave me free run of the house and their well-laden bookshelves. In the weeks that followed there were many things I could have done in Hanoi, but I did very few of them. I lit incense in temples, read, visited the Temple of Literature, where white-robed monks moved in a stately silent fashion, and took a taxi across the city forty-one times to visit Ian. I think I saw Duras' lake, but there are many beautiful lakes in Hanoi. I sat by one that I believe was hers. I did think that Duras had brought all this about, although that was not entirely true. We had wanted to go there for all sorts of reasons, not least the simple curiosity that travellers have for the world.

The hotel where I was staying, in the Old Quarter, near the Hanoi Opera House, had a distinctly French atmosphere. If the perceived decadence of the French had been discarded in the south, in Hanoi the influence was still evident, encountered in buildings and food. Ian was, in fact, a patient at the Hanoi French Hospital. As the nightmare lifted and he began a slow recovery towards being well enough to travel home, Alison took me under her wing. In her company I entered a new friendship and felt that I was not alone. She also took me shopping, given that a refund on some lost side trips had been delivered in the form of American dollars.

What happened in Hanoi would later become the basis for a long story called 'Silks', which appears in my collection, *The Trouble with Fire*. It has become something of a signature piece for me but I cannot read aloud from it, though my daughter did, at Ian's funeral.

So we resorted to Pho Hàng Gai, Rue de la Soie, the
street lined with silk shops. I picked up handfuls of
different silk, holding them to my face, and in some
I thought I detected the scent of skin like warm
honey on the tongue, though it may have been that
of food cooking at the back of the shop or incense
burning . . . If I closed my eyes for a moment, I was
overcome with a young woman's ardour, could see
the golden sheen on the back of my husband, my
beloved, the play of light and dark, and I thought,
M.D., you haven't abandoned me. I was wrong to
doubt. I ordered jackets, and skirts and pants. I
went on doing this for several days, the sweet cool
fabrics slithering between my fingers, like the touch
of my lover, while hundred-dollar bills drifted away.

The reading ends, as does the story, with an account of leaving
Hanoi, an ambulance driving us to the airport and my husband
seeing the Red River for the first time. 'I took his hand, our two
skins crumpled together. Old silks.'

Some people expressed surprise at this reading; they may
even have been a little shocked. Sex isn't what you talk about at
funerals. But I knew it was right. I was very happy that she had
read it. It is, of course, in its origins, pure Duras. She had followed
us, my husband and me, from the beginning.

———

This should have been the end of it, the end of the affair, as I had
come to think of it. But things are harder to end than you expect.
Isn't it always the way? The year before Ian died, I had been to
Paris and stayed with Alison and James, who were on their last
posting before retirement. One morning we walked over from the
residence to Montparnasse Cemetery where Duras is buried. I go
there every time I stay in Paris. Her inscription is simple, just the
initials, M.D., cut into the stone. James took a handful of pencils

that morning. That is how you pay tribute to Duras, not with flowers to lay on the grave, but pencils. I had thought that I was saying goodbye to her then.

And, then again, at Ian's funeral.

That is not how it was.

A few months after the funeral, I went to Paris again. My publisher, Sabine Wespieser, had released my novel, *All Day at the Movies*, in translation and she was keen for me to go over and promote it. I thought Paris might help me to heal a little.

I was asked to go on Radio France's culture programme. The interview would go out live. I was met at the door by a young man dressed in a sharp black tunic over a forest green skinny rib and checked pants. The walls of the station were painted mauve and white, dotted with mauve and black cubes, one room leading from another over soft grey carpets, until we reached the mauve studio. The interviewer was a pretty, intense, clever-looking woman, wearing large dark spectacles. I was uncertain about how this would go, given language barriers, but, with a simultaneous translator working rapidly beside me, it seemed as if we had been talking together for years. After half an hour the interviewer indicated that they were going to extend into the next hour. Then she asked me about my interest in Duras.

I began to explain, or as nearly as I could. The interviewer asked me to listen to something she was about to play. It was an old recording of Duras. I had never heard her voice before, but there it was all around me, a deep gravelly roar.

I wept then, on Radio France.

Quardling around Glover

This essay is based on my 25 February 2021 review, on Newsroom, of *Letters of Denis Glover*, selected and edited by Sarah Shieff (Otago University Press, Dunedin, 2020).

I have only to close my eyes for a moment when someone says the name Denis Glover, to hear that unmistakeable concrete mixer voice, laced with English vowels, and to be back in his presence.

A while ago, I was invited to review a collection of Glover's letters, edited by Sarah Shieff. It was a vanity, perhaps, to begin with personal recollection, but it was also irresistible, given that a friendship of sorts spanned the last decade of the poet's life, and that those years included producing several voice recordings for radio that have survived as part of his legacy. If I qualify our friendship it is because I knew him during a time when, as Shieff puts it, he had become to many 'little more than a tiresome anachronism, a misogynistic old fart, a court jester, a drunken laughing stock - a *quardler*' (referencing his beloved poem, 'The Magpies').

Did he fit that description in my lexicon? Yes, and more. And yet I had also had the privilege of seeing the other man, that one who had been, and had not quite gone by the time I met him: legendary founder of the Caxton Press, brave and decorated naval officer, fine poet who identified with the land and its people, publisher and mentor to many writers, typographer par excellence. That man appeared when he sat down to record his poems and numerous interviews, the latter part of a series we called *Looking Back*, consisting of conversations with significant writers. The ones I produced, between Denis and broadcaster Elizabeth Alley, took place in the studios at Radio New Zealand. No matter that I had to get permission from the director-general of broadcasting to allow vodka in the studio in order to keep him talking, the other Denis came to the fore – thoughtful, reflective and in beautiful voice. But the conversations had to be recorded before lunch while he still had a semblance of sobriety.

It was up to Denis's wife Lyn, Pixie as he called her, to get him to the studio. Lyn was his second wife, a late marriage for both of them. She was older than him, a tiny bird-like woman who had wealth and an apparently relentless devotion to Denis. She managed his drinking by rationing it.

Lyn used to say that the whole point of her life was to look after her husband, which in a way seemed quite sad. She didn't appear to have much life of her own, although she had tried her hand at writing poetry, which Denis would promote. He did seem genuinely grateful to her, although occasionally she would voice a certain despair. But he somehow got people to do things for him, even when he was behaving badly.

Shieff's book contains some 500 letters, culled from around 3000, a wise and judicious selection, revealing the story of a life. That story had been told before by Gordon Ogilvie, in his biography, but this was different because the letters tell us what Denis himself thought of his life, and his friends and, God help them, his enemies. They reflect, too, a brilliant mind's descent into the shadowy darkness of alcoholism and the sense of loss he experienced as coherence began slipping away. The early letters reveal stylish prose that records Canterbury and other landscape, delighted accounts of occasions and interactions, a stunning eye for detail, all illuminated by genuine wit. The love letters to various women – and there are many, letters, that is, but also women – are tender and sensual. Those written to his first wife Mary, and the mother of his only child, are lyrical, philosophical, often profound. After that marriage ended, the wooing of women by mail continued, but his relationships never lasted, or not until he met Lyn. (It did become clear, nonetheless, that he was in his heart, if not his body, unfaithful to her from time to time.)

Writing to his erstwhile lover, Janet Paul, towards the end of his life, he said: 'Frenzied in not knowing what I wanted, I found it in you. I steered a bad course, but still navigate by your fixed star.' It was to Janet that Lyn, sometime after her marriage, blurted out during a chance encounter: 'I don't know what I did in my past life to deserve this.'

If Denis's love letters glimmered and shone, much of his later correspondence was riddled with almost childish banter, forced humour and invented names for people, as if real language were escaping him. Inevitably, I turned to the index in order to see whether I rated a mention, and what Denis had thought of me. Pride always comes before a fall. He wrote, in a letter to Allen and Jeny Curnow, 'Any minute now in this forenoon watch of the 10th, I expect Fiona Kidman, one of the few cowgirls, surely, who can milk by hand, as can Lyn and myself, so quaintly old-fashioned. She is doing poesy over at the Concert programme, where she works as some sort of editor. She got me to read some of my own stuff, and they were so pleased that I am now immured in the archives.' Not bad, but a couple of lines earlier he had written: 'Islands [the literary journal] stinks with academics, and when it breaks away we get the worst effluvia of young fellas and the ovary elegists who may perhaps have attained SC.' I flinched, knowing full well that the cross-referencing with me was no accident.

Perhaps this naked latter-day misogyny arose from the disappointment of the failed love affairs, but it could be unpleasant to be around. Shieff wrote, 'I have included quotations from inward letters from Glover's partners. Unconventional as this might be in a volume of this sort, I felt that the voices of these women should be heard . . . These intelligent, attractive women were clearly able to look past the grog-blossom complexion, terrible teeth and cauliflower ear.' I could not; I found him bordering on physically repulsive. No doubt he sensed this and so my status remained that of a literary handmaiden. Lauris Edmond, my great friend of those years, was closer to him. They had collaborated on her selection of A. R. D. Fairburn's *Letters*. In one letter to her, he describes her as 'jam to his wasp'. When she and I launched our first collections of poems at a joint event at the old University Club in 1975, Denis spoke for her book, *In Middle Air* (Sam Hunt launched mine, *Honey & Bitters*). In his speech, Denis rambled into a sour attack on 'the menstrual school of poets'. His friendship with Lauris did not entirely recover. And yet, this was the same man who had discovered, published and supported Janet Frame. In a letter to John Money, dated 16 May 1947, he said: 'I wrote to Miss Frame, and received a shy letter . . . I can't help making the Mansfield comparison all the time; and do you know, I think Miss Frame has her licked in lots of ways.'

While serving with the Royal Navy during the Second World War, he was based in Britain. At first, in his letters, he appeared to soon become culturally acclimatised, writing with delight about all he was seeing and learning. But his old feelings about the 'Mother Country', most famously expressed in his 1936 poem, 'Home Thoughts' – 'I do not dream of Sussex downs/or quaint old England's quaint old towns' – asserted themselves. In 1942 he told Curnow: 'Of England & the English I can't possibly write here and now. The place is what I thought it would be, only worse . . . They are simply appalling in many ways, but full of dogged virtues in others.'

That letter delivered me a sharp image of another evening spent with Denis. It was an occasion arranged with the British High Commission to mark the arrival of Michael Frayn on a visit to New Zealand, which I had helped organise.. I had also agreed to get Denis along for the evening as a mutual guest of honour. But Denis was paralytically drunk and began to tell our hosts what he thought of the British. They retreated, finally, to the far end of the room and turned on a transistor radio in order to listen to a cricket match. What else could they do? Frayn, urbane, watchful and charming, stayed with the New Zealand 'team'. As it all became unbearable, Denis turned to my husband and said, 'Deaaah boy, time to take me home.' That was Ian's permanent role in Denis's life, to take him home and carry him up the steps to his and Lyn's apartment in Strathmore Park. Frayn graciously offered to help. And so it was. Neither got a mention in Shieff's *Letters*, but perhaps they appear in the other 2500.

Glover would waver in his loyalties over the years. He continued to write fulsomely to Allen Curnow, although it was clear to many that the latter was moving on. Only now and then does the reader sense Glover's disappointment that Curnow's reputation had overtaken his.

But it was on full show at the national book awards ceremony in 1980, held in the old Alexander Turnbull Library in Bowen Street. Curnow had produced a book of poems called *An Incorrigible Music*; Pegasus Press had published Denis's collection, *Towards Banks Peninsula*, a work he had been creating over several years, about an old seaman called Mick Stimpson with whom he had had a close friendship. I recorded both poets reading from their books. Whatever the difficulties in recording Denis, they were small by comparison with Curnow, who insisted on keeping his distance and called me Mrs Kidman, a more circumspect reminder that I should properly be at home in the kitchen. The whole atmosphere suggested that he was doing me a favour, but I was aware that Denis had been in touch with him and presumably had persuaded him that an interview was a good idea. As I discovered in the *Letters*, he had told him that he should not do a phone interview but 'leave it to be de face en face with Elizabeth Alley; not only personable but knowing exactly what to ask. For this dream-series Fiona [Kidman] had to go as high as the Director-General himself. Do it when you are down, if at all.' It amused me to read that; it was the vodka, of course, not the *Looking Back* series that had required permission, but perhaps it was as well Denis never knew. And I had become Fiona by then.

Denis had made it quite clear to people in conversation that he believed he would, and should, win the poetry award, but it went to Curnow, and Denis was distraught. He sat in the doorway, as Lauris would later recall, a 'big, fat, whiskery creature'. The anguish in the room was palpable, as Denis called out 'impostor' and 'fraud'. He wasn't crying but near enough. I don't know whether he knew he was dying, or how fit he thought he was, but we all saw that he was failing and sick. Maybe, in writing *Towards Banks Peninsula*, he thought his life's work was done. That was almost the last time he was seen in the city. He continued writing to Curnow with no mention of the awards, his style chatty and newsy as ever, although in what proved to be his last letter, he addressed him as 'Noble My Stuffed Trout', a reference to a poem he had sent Curnow about exactly that, a stuffed trout. Still, it sat well with what I always perceived as Curnow's pomposity.

And, in a last letter to Olive Johnson, a librarian at Auckland University he had befriended years earlier, he wrote:

> What I have wrote I have writ. If out of print, in
> libraries for the curious to see. To fix MacBeth, 'I have
> supp'd full with honours.' Remotely I prefer to sit on
> Olympus, not garlanded nor placarded. Oh that I had
> stayed in the Royal Navy. But in between times there
> is too much ceremony and little chance of action.
>   A wildly squandered life, Olive dear – squandered
> but not altogether squalid. Those I love are many,
> those I hate are few.

On 9 August 1980, Denis died during a move to what was to have been a new house at Breaker Bay on Wellington's wild southern coast. I was phoned with the news around eight, just as I was leaving for work. I knew how the day would unfold. I wrote a script for a tribute to go to air that night. I called in Elizabeth to narrate the excerpts of poems and interviews I had chosen. We made the hour-long tribute with minutes to spare. There is no record of this, but I have a distant memory that we played Denis reading the opening to *Towards Banks Peninsula*, 'In Memoriam H. C. Stimpson [Mick] Port Levy':

You were these hills and the sea.
In calm, or the winter wave and snow.
Lie then peaceful among them,
The hills iron, the quiet tides below.

If we didn't we should have.

Over the years, I've been called on to speak of Denis often.
As I told Gordon Ogilvie,

> He was such an intelligent man and he was aware of
> his drinking problem, and he used to bluster to cover
> it up. But I think underneath there was a desperate
> person; he was aware of changes in the world, like
> the women's movement, which were leaving him
> behind . . . And he became more and more aggressive
> about those kinds of things . . . I think that some of
> Denis's grief at the end of his life was that he was
> willing to change his views but he didn't know how
> to – it was too late.

I still think that. And of course I recognise, with the long slant of
hindsight, that in spite of bad days and nights spent in his company, he did become a friend. Shieff's selection of Glover's letters
seemed like the record of a literary era of which I had accidentally
caught the tail wind. It told the real story of a significant life,
as gossipy as a neighbour's Christmas drinks party, in the end,
profoundly sad.

Some years ago, I was part of a group that supported the installation of concrete text sculptures, created by the designer Catherine
Griffiths, honouring local writers. It fell to me to choose the text
for Denis's. It's from his poem, 'The Harbour is a Laundry':

The harbour is an ironing board
Flat iron tugs dash smoothing toward
Any shirt of a ship, any pillow slip
Of a freighter they decree
Must be ironed flat as washing from the sea.

Some other girl: the case for Jean Batten

When I was young I worked in a library. It was situated in a long, light, airy room that adjoined a stuffy and neglected museum which we library assistants were required to dust once a week. There were a lot of insects captured in clear kauri gum, plus various bits of greenstone. Beyond the museum lay Rotorua's council chambers. One wall of the library opened through french doors onto a balcony that contained a garden, enclosed by a low concrete barrier. Tom, the gardener, had red rheumy eyes with sagging lower lids. Then he had an operation to correct the condition and this brought him great happiness. He was a bent and shrunken man but we cared for him deeply. He would cut flowers for us, and when one of us had a twenty-first or got married he would come bearing a gift, a carefully chosen china plate. Opposite what we called 'Tom's garden' stood the archway to Government Gardens, with steaming volcanic mud pools dotted here and there on the otherwise immaculate lawns. Sometimes a new geyser would bolt up through the earth and alter the symmetry.

I used to stand at the issuing desk in the library, wearing the latest fashions, balancing on stiletto heels. It was a library with a difference. The head librarian, who was beautiful and emancipated, expected 'her girls' to look their best for the public. Her hair was pale blue, like the head of a hydrangea, and she was having an affair with a married man, though later he became free to marry her. In my novel, *Songs from the Violet Café*, I modelled the character of restaurant owner, Violet Trench, on her. She was good to me, and for me. She gave me the incentive to broaden my horizons, to read widely, to take responsibility.

The library was a magnet for the locals, the social hub of the town, at least on weekdays and the evenings that we were open. There were several artists living in the area, then, Theo Schoon and Jan Nigro among them. Schoon called library assistants 'stupid' if they couldn't find the book he was looking for straight away. Nigro wore flowing colourful garments and it was said in hushed tones that she painted people in the buff, something we discovered to be true: her nude paintings are still sought after. The Little Theatre crowd came in too, full of 'dah-lings' and abhorrence for 'the ordinary'. We girls waited on them all, although I preferred the soft pouched faces of the elderly women who borrowed romance novels and offered us boiled lollies when they thought the head librarian wasn't looking. Forestry workers came in too, because the timber mills were just along the road. They offered dates at the weekend dances and we accepted some of those too.

All of these people, young and old, wanted information. It was assumed that, with all these books around us, we would know things, we would have knowledge at our fingertips. We were the digital warriors of the 1950s. We understood that knowledge was a kind of secret power and we did our best. But the idea that knowledge could come from anywhere but encyclopaedias never crossed our minds. It's just that we couldn't read them all. Nevertheless, questions were fired at us every hour of every day. And one of them that kept being repeated was 'Do you happen to know where Jean Batten is at present?' If we were to hesitate for even a moment, there might be flashes of impatience, as if we were ignorant or uncooperative, followed by a reminder that Jean was a famous aviator (although they usually said aviatrix back then) and she came from Rotorua. She had been born here, didn't we know, very famous indeed, a little odd perhaps, she seemed to have dropped out of sight.

———

I didn't know where Jean was. None of us knew, but I did learn that her birthplace was just two blocks away, in Amohia Street, No. 1200, though I didn't find that out until much later. Diagonally across the street from this house stood the rooms where her father practised as a dentist. It's where, it was said, he accepted favours in return for dental work on women who couldn't afford to get rid of their toothache any other way. But I didn't hear that until much later, either.

Jane (Jean) Gardner Batten, born in September 1909, was the third child of Frederick and Ellen Batten. Her two older brothers were Frederick Jnr, known as Harold, and John. Her mother was usually called Nellie. Jean would become one of the most well-known fliers in the world, dominating the air throughout most of the 1930s. Much of her flying was financed by public speaking tours for which she was widely acclaimed on trips back to New Zealand.

After daring but unsuccessful attempts to beat the women's record for a solo flight from London to Australia, she beat Amy Johnson's record by four days in 1934, in a time of fourteen days and twenty-two hours, flying a Gipsy Moth. She would go on to break record after record, later in a Percival Gull plane. In 1936, she became the first person, man or woman, to fly solo from Britain to New Zealand and then back. On her arrival in Auckland, on the last leg of her journey across the Tasman, thousands of people were gathered to greet her arrival. In a radio commentary I have listened to, the announcer cries out:

> The crowd surges forward, a large crowd of police,
> mounted police, foot police and traffic inspectors
> and they are having a great job to keep the crowd

back . . . Here she is coming down, she is down
about twenty feet now, about ten feet, she is nearly
on the ground, just very near the tops of those motor
cars and nearly touches them. A beautiful three-
point landing she is going to make . . . Here she
comes . . . I don't know whether you can hear me or
not . . . We can see a white . . . a white helmet . . .

She had that sort of charisma, that grip on the imagination.

During the course of her return journey, Jean's fiancé Beverley Shepherd, also a pilot, was killed in a plane crash in Australia.

What I did find in the library was her first book, a beautiful little memoir called *Solo Flight*, a young woman's exuberant account of her early flying adventures, punctuated with entries from her logbooks, which reflect the scope of her feats. There are sometimes forlorn reflections about loneliness in the vast stretches of the sky, when she was effectively suspended in the air by a contraption made of fabric and wire, with a compass to help her navigate and a torch to see her through the nights. Her private life remained largely a mystery. The engagement to Beverley was the nearest she came to marriage. Famed for her beauty as well as her exploits, she remained single, spending most of her time in Nellie's company. G-AARB, the registration number of her record-breaking plane, led to her being dubbed the Garbo of the Skies. At the beginning of the Second World War, her plane was requisitioned by the British government, meaning that Jean could no longer fly. By the end of the war, Jean and Nellie had disappeared from public view, rarely revealing their whereabouts. After Nellie's death in Tenerife, Jean reappeared in New Zealand sporadically, before dying alone in Majorca, in 1982. The Percival Gull was recovered and brought to New Zealand. It hangs in Auckland Airport alongside the international departure lounge. Outside the terminal building stands a statue of Jean.

If Fred was making a name for himself in Rotorua around the time of Jean's birth, so, too, was his wife. Nellie rode a white horse about town, wore a hat adorned with a bright feather and took acting roles in local drama productions. She had always lived this way, when she was growing up in the southern city of Invercargill. She had also developed an interest in pioneering flights. After Jean's birth, she pinned a newspaper picture of Louis Blériot, in his two-seater monoplane, above her daughter's cot. Just eight months before, the Frenchman had flown across the English Channel, the first person to achieve this feat, in a time of thirty-six minutes and thirty seconds.

The Batten marriage was falling apart. Several shadows were falling across their lives, not least the inconsistencies in their son Harold's behaviour. The family moved to Auckland, Fred went to war and, afterwards, he and Nellie separated. Charles Kingsford-Smith visited Auckland and when Jean heard him speak she decided to be a flier too, despite excelling as both a ballet dancer and a pianist. She and Nellie engineered a secret trip to Australia so that Jean could meet Kingsford-Smith, take a flight with him and get advice on how to pursue her dream. Before long, she and Nellie were on their way to London, on the pretext that Jean would study music there. Her father, on whom the pair relied for funding, was against the idea of her becoming a flier.

Jean's story now became a rags to riches one, as she began to take lessons at the elite London Aero Club at the Stag Lane flying field. It was the training ground of Amy Johnson herself, of dukes and duchesses, and the then Prince of Wales, briefly King Edward VIII.

So many people at Stag Lane were so famous, so self-confident. So rich and so well dressed. Nobody said the word 'colonial', but that was how she saw herself. When she opened her mouth, she didn't sound nearly as eloquent as she thought she had back in Auckland.

Of more importance than the glamorous line-up of would-be fliers, Stag Lane was the site of Geoffrey de Havilland's engineering school, and the creative industry that built the planes he had invented, the Gipsy Moth and later the Tiger Moth.

Jean learned engineering too, so she could service the planes she would fly.

———

Jean wrote more books about her life. None of them matched *Solo Flight* and none of them told the whole story. There are great gaps in her narratives, such as a missing seven years when she and Nellie ostensibly toured Europe in the 1960s. They had 'such fun', she would recount, staying at spas and travelling. A 1990 book called *Jean Batten: The Garbo of the Skies*, written by the late Ian Mackersey with his researcher wife Caroline Mackersey, did not account for the gaps either, or explore the deeper mysteries of her personality.

When I came across Mackersey's book several years ago, it puzzled me. I had been interested in the Batten story, without following it in depth. I'd met my husband in the Rotorua Public Library all those years before. Ian's love of planes was part of our lives from the outset. He had learned to fly in Tiger Moths when he was in the Royal New Zealand Air Force in the 1950s. Our choice of home in Wellington was determined by the proximity to and the view of the airport. The movement of planes was a preoccupation for decades. Batten's name came up from time to time. I would reflect on those enquiries people used to make about her whereabouts.

Mackersey's book did have an answer of sorts about where she and her mother lived while I was working in the Rotorua Public Library. They had been in Jamaica, not far from Goldeneye, home of the writer Ian Fleming, and closer still to Noel Coward's holiday house. But the two women portrayed in this book were decidedly unpleasant: Nellie a sour, domineering woman who ran her daughter's life, Jean a spoilt, vapid person who gave herself airs and graces and chased men to fund planes and her career, before dumping them.

The more I thought about it, the more odd I found this. There *was* a huge amount of previously unknown information in the book, not least the whereabouts of Jean's grave in Majorca, where she had lain unidentified and apparently lost to the world for five years before Caroline Mackersey discovered it. It was a brilliant piece of detective work. Jean had died alone in a hotel room, after being bitten by a dog; the authorities had assumed her name to be Gardner, her middle name, rather than Batten.

Caroline would be helpful to me when I set out on my own inquiries, but her husband remained unfriendly. Yet I kept asking myself if the witty Noel Coward would have had a flirtatious, albeit gay, friendship with a woman as off-putting as the one Ian Mackersey described. I had discovered that they danced and laughed and partied together. Winston Churchill was another admirer. And was Jean really a gold digger?

I read and reread Mackersey's introduction. What struck me was the account he gave of his first and, it seems, only, encounter with Jean. He was seven years old and travelling by train with his mother between Hamilton and Rotorua. As Jean boarded the train and entered their first-class carriage, Mackersey's mother greeted her, wanting to open a conversation, only to be rebuffed. Their fellow traveller sat hunched in her seat. This slight to his mother had rankled with the writer.

When I began to look more closely at this account, I realised that there was something interesting about when this journey took place. Jean had been touring New Zealand, giving speeches after her epic flight from London to Auckland, and was exhausted. She had just that day cancelled the tour, and was about to retreat to a hotel at Franz Josef for an extended recovery, funded by the New Zealand government. She was, in other words, having a nervous breakdown. Perhaps it was not so surprising that she didn't want to fall into conversation with strangers. It seemed increasingly clear that her enigmatic life had been explored from an unsympathetic point of view. I wondered why Ian Mackersey had bothered to write a biography of someone he so clearly disliked.

A number of things had drawn me towards Jean. There was the link with Rotorua, with some other girl who had lived in the town at a young age, as I had done. There was the similarity of the planes she and my husband flew. And there was another strange link – her brother Harold had farmed in Waipu. In fact, where we lived on North River, the road curled up the side of the hill beyond to Cave Road. Harold's farm jutted onto an area of caves, where glow worms gleamed in their dark tunnels. Jean would come there and stay. Our neighbours remembered how she would call to practise on their parents' pianos. Her visits were short. Harold's mind was in disarray. There had been a strange scandal, which had got into the newspapers, about a New Zealand youth in Sydney, arrested for forgery, but found to be hoarding gelignite and the makings of bombs. His name was Harold Batten. A case of mistaken identity, the family insisted, but nobody knew for sure. The real Harold had married an Australian woman and had children, but his past, even then, was clouded. Harold's life would end after years of illness in a psychiatric hospital. His wife, I learned, feared his visits home.

I began by asking myself whether the way Jean and her mother were portrayed really mattered. They were dead, after all. But what had been said had become the 'official' record. Wherever you looked – on every internet site and in documentaries, of which there have been more than one – the same stories appeared, as if they were the only truth.

As clues and trails emerged, I had to face a truth of my own. I knew in my bones that I was going to write about Jean, to try and find the other Jean, the girl I might have known had we been of an age, and who, I was certain, I would have understood, probably liked.

From the beginning, I knew that the book would be called *The Infinite Air*, from Gerard Manley Hopkins' poem 'The Wreck of the Deutschland': 'And so the sky keeps/For the infinite air is unkind.' It seemed to speak of the tragedies of the many pilots, contemporaries of Jean, who would die in their record-breaking attempts – and of the effect those losses would have on her.

Around that point, I began to experience a high level of anxiety. I knew the book would be unlike any I had written. For a start, when I write fact-based fiction, I travel to wherever the action has taken place, to see for myself the sights, hear the sounds, absorb the smells. This was clearly impossible. Jean had crash landed in Middle Eastern deserts, flown over Afghanistan, now a war-torn country. I lacked the resources to travel in her footsteps.

Yet there were surely other possibilities. I decided that if I could research the circumstances of every person Jean was known to have associated with, I might find some answers to the riddles. I would lay my hands on biographies of people she had known, interview every person who might have known the family. For on-the-ground research in the Royal Air Force Museum, where I'd had a hint there might be unseen letters, I hired a researcher who spent months uncovering the treasures there, and another researcher here to comb every 1930s newspaper in every little town where Jean had given talks. Jill Nicholas, who has lived in Rotorua on the edge of the lake for decades and has a passion for the town's history, offered to help with local knowledge. She's been a noted journalist all her life and a stalwart friend in the search for clues to the Batten mysteries.

I remember a moment in Oxford, north of Christchurch. I was giving a talk to a group of people about an earlier book. During question time, I was asked what I was working on now. When I replied that I was going to write a novel about Jean Batten, a man in the audience said, 'I hope you know a bit about flying. I'm an international airline pilot, and I know you need to get it right.' That was not all he had to say on the subject. He had met Jean Batten on her last visit to New Zealand. This was Jonathan Marrett, who has since become a firm friend. In retirement, he paints scenes from Jean's life.

But the conversation gave me a jolt. Ian knew a lot about flying and certainly about the planes Jean flew. All the same, I had to learn from scratch how these machines worked, to be able to think like a pilot at their controls. Added to my research were lessons in front of the computer with simulated cockpits and controls of Gipsy and Tiger Moths, where I 'practised' flying, with Ian as my instructor.

It was time, too, to start talking to the Batten family, Harold and John's children. John had been married briefly to Madeleine Murat, a novelist, who wrote also under the pseudonym of Dorothy

Quentin. John was an actor, starring in movies. The couple had had one daughter, who lived in England.

Except that these conversations with the Battens were not going to happen. With the exceptions of Harold's son, Jim, and Lesley, a great-niece who lives in Australia – I'm grateful to them both – the Batten family flatly refused to help. When I rang a great-nephew, he said he treated people like me in the same way he did stock agents selling manure. Others wrote and told me that 'Mr Mackersey had done such a wonderful job that there was nothing more to be said and there it must end'. I would learn from Caroline that one family member, at least, left money in their will to the Mackerseys. The source material had largely disappeared, given to Mackersey by her relatives, and the correspondence held by Barclay's Bank, where all her mail went, had also been destroyed.

In a strange way all this unpleasantness offered me freedom. They had had their chance. I wasn't beholden to them.

What was their problem? I think there were some terrible family secrets. Freedom is a two-way thing, of course: it demands respect. I was a fiction writer, but I was not going to invent their secrets. That would have been too easy. I spent months on a false trail with a woman, now dead, who believed she was Jean's daughter, and had been given up for adoption. Initially I thought the story was credible but after an exhaustive search of records, it became clear that Jean was in Europe at the time of the woman's birth. The one positive thing that came out of our conversations was a meeting I suggested between her and Jim Batten, and I believe gave her comfort.

Do I have a view about those Batten secrets? Yes, I do. I think they lay within the shadows of the family and siblings and stretched back to Rotorua. I believe that Nellie knew she must do something to protect her daughter, and that this was why she took her away from the family. Divorce, in the early twentieth century, was unthinkable for most women. Nellie appears to have had compelling reasons to leave and they seem to have centred on her daughter's safety. Protecting Jean became her lifelong mission.

Despite whatever was withheld from me, and whatever I

chose to leave out, a mountain of revealing material had begun to present itself. In the Royal Air Force Museum in London, a wonderfully funny document had appeared, an unpublished manuscript called 'Memories of Stag Lane', by Bernard Collacott, who had worked as an aircraft mechanic while Jean was there. He details the idiosyncrasies of the rich and famous, including the Prince of Wales' drunken exploits and how, one evening, his fellow pilots saved him from himself by rolling him up in a blanket in the back of a laundry van and dropping him off at the back door of Buckingham Palace. In a West Australian newspaper, I discovered a review of Madeleine Murat's first novel, *Sidestreet*, featuring movie sets and film directors and homosexual men having complicated relationships with women. This didn't seem too different from her own relationship with her husband, John Batten, the brother from whom Jean would become estranged for many years. And an interview Jean gave to a newspaper after an evening spent with King George VI and Queen Elizabeth was a splendid find. She provided intimate details of the informal supper she had been invited to at the end of her return flight to New Zealand, describing what everyone was wearing, what they ate and how Princess Elizabeth came running in to show off her new puppy. Revealing such details was a departure from protocol but nonetheless, Jean had some impressive medals bestowed on her by royalty.

I also began a patient re-examination of the negative accounts of her romantic life. Jean Batten was a gorgeous young woman, and conscious of her glamour. She usually dressed in white, except when she was working on the engines of her planes or flying, and would step off her flights with perfect make-up, wearing her white flying helmet, before retiring quickly to change into a white silk dress. There were often men in her life. An early romance was with a man I chose to call Frank Norton, one of the few aliases in *The Infinite Air*. I did this for the sake of his descendants and because, in a sense, his real name was not important. He was a New Zealand-born RAF pilot whom Jean met on a ship while returning home from England. She was twenty-one and he was eight years older, and already a hard drinker. He fell deeply in love with her and, on learning that she wanted to fly, offered to finance her lessons. It was clear that she accepted some assistance and that he also lent her money. Jean was not in love with him, although he would pursue her in New Zealand and follow her back to London, where he continued to court her. But she was already involved in a relationship with a man called Victor Dorée, who had learned to fly in Australia, while he was there selling silk and linen. Dorée came from a wealthy London family, who would offer to fund the purchase of Jean's first plane. They showered lavish hospitality on Jean and Nellie, who were barely getting by, often hungry and cold in their bedsit. They took this friendship seriously.

Young women make mistakes. Frank Norton was Jean's. Well, actually, so was Victor Dorée, but for different reasons.

Norton was ready to settle down and return permanently to New Zealand. He assumed Jean would follow him, but she turned him down. Perhaps she had made promises to him, or perhaps not. You could say that she was foolish to have accepted money that she then had no means to repay. You could say he was foolish to have given it to her. What men and women say to each other in the heat of the moment can be confusing in hindsight.

In the event, he left England bitter and angry. You could say his heart was broken, never mind his wallet. Over the years, when Jean visited New Zealand, he would be waiting at stage doors to intercept her, demanding the return of his money. He married and had children. At some point, Fred Batten persuaded Jean to give him a cheque for £250. Norton died in his late forties.

The relationship with Victor Dorée had flourished. A plane was acquired and registered jointly in Jean's and Dorée's names. It had belonged to the Prince of Wales and was in need of repairs. During the restoration, the couple quarrelled over the condition of the con rods, which had a record of being prone to metal fatigue. Jean wanted the engine dismantled but Dorée insisted that this wasn't necessary.

On 9 April 1933, she set off on her journey to Australia from Lympne Airport. It was supposed to have been a secret but at the last minute Dorée invited the press to see her off. There was high excitement. His family turned up, wearing furs and fancy clothes, and a filmmaker appeared. I found it interesting the way Ian Mackersey commented on this farewell. He wrote: 'One is impressed by the way in which all the activity revolves around Jean. She appears as a very diffident and innocent-looking young woman of below average height – she was 5 feet four inches tall – holding centre stage and accepting the VIP treatment. She is composed and unexpressive, possibly overawed by the warmth of the farewell party, and in none of these scenes does she radiate much joy.' The real sting in the tail is yet to come.

After a number of adventures, which included a landing in a desert, the plane crash landed near Karachi. A con rod had broken. Jean was unhurt but out of funds. The Dorée family turned their backs on her; overnight, it appears, their fortune had vanished. Jean was left to find her own way back to England. She did this thanks to Lord Wakefield of Castrol Oil, who would become her mentor for future flying attempts. It would be another year before she set her first record.

Mackersey wrote: 'In neither of her two books, nor in her unpublished manuscript, did Jean describe her departure from Stag Lane that spring afternoon on what was the start of a flying career that was to realise all her aspirations for fame and success. She was not prepared to acknowledge publicly, even over forty years later, her indebtedness to Victor and his family. She appears to have viewed their patronage simply as the due entitlement of a woman of destiny.' I see it differently. I think she might have minded quite a lot that she was abandoned by her sponsors in a foreign country.

More than fifty years later, as the Mackerseys were researching their documentary and book about Jean, they had what they saw as an amazing piece of luck. The widow of Frank Norton wanted to talk to them, but they would need to hurry because she was dying. On her deathbed, she told them how Jean had ruined her and Frank's lives because she had taken all his pension money and this meant they had to delay their marriage. I am puzzled by this. We can't know what happened – what her husband told her and whether it was true. He drank heavily. Was the real answer that he had lost his money before he met his wife? He did, after all, have the means to support Jean when he left England.

This was not the only widow the Mackerseys managed to track down. Shortly after Jean's crash in Karachi, a notice had appeared in the *Times* announcing the engagement of Victor Dorée and Mary Swan, an heiress. It was to Dorée's widow that they now turned. The widow assured them that Jean was a bad lot who had taken her husband for his money. This is at odds with Jean's own account, in an unpublished memoir, that she repaid her erstwhile fiancé back. And it is at odds with the circumstances of Mary's own engagement to Dorée.

Taken together, these stories don't add up. These men appear to have wanted the golden trophy of marriage to a world-record-breaking flier, and thought that money would buy her. In the case of Victor Dorée, her failure to perform seems to have triggered instant rejection.

There were other men, but Shepherd appears to have been Jean's one great love. Her relationship with Ian Fleming is almost impenetrable, although Jim Batten ventured to me that they had been close. What does one make of the fact that Jean and Nellie sold up and suddenly left Jamaica the same week as Fleming made a hurried marriage to Ann Charteris, Viscountess Rothermere? Fleming impregnated Ann not once but twice and the viscount had had enough, divorcing her quickly on the grounds of adultery. Fleming was her third husband; she was his only wife. (She later abandoned him in favour of the Labour politician Hugh Gaitskell.)

Jean Batten may not have fulfilled the image of the perfect hero, but there seems to be a dismaying trail of unreliable witnesses in the stories we have been told about her. She was a woman pursued by demons and trauma, and the deaths of many friends. There is much that is still not known about her. Someone, some day, may find where Nellie and Jean disappeared to in Europe for seven years before settling in Tenerife. The clue may lie in *Keep on Dancing*, a memoir by Sarah Churchill, the daughter of Winston. The Churchills' holiday home was at Cap d'Ail in the south of France. Sarah recorded the sense of sadness she perceived in Jean when she visited in the early 1960s. Her sister Diana, the same age as Jean, had committed suicide.

Perhaps Jean and Nellie travelled Europe, 'having fun' and 'laughing and laughing'. Or perhaps, between the good times, there were necessary bouts in spas and health clinics, to repair Jean's fragile mental health. This seems a possible explanation for the extreme secrecy with which they shrouded their lives during this period, directing all their mail through Barclay's Bank, so that their movements couldn't be traced. Jean persisted with this arrangement until the end of her life.

Not long ago I stood in Amohia Street in Rotorua with Jill Nicholas. We were outside No. 1200, looking across to the spot where Fred Batten's dental practice once stood. All traces of those houses have gone, replaced by square modern buildings. But the sturdy trees that have been a signature of the Rotorua skyline for as long as I have known the place, and the heavy smell of sulphur on a summer's day, were there still. I thought of Nellie pinning up the newspaper cutting about Louis Blériot and about how mothers could dream for their daughters' happy lives. At the height of her fame, in the 1930s, Jean had met Blériot and been invited to stay with the family in France. Like these two aviators, I have been honoured with the French Légion d'Honneur, something I am proud of and gives me a particular sense of connection with Jean Batten.

In my mind's eye, too, I saw Nellie riding her white horse through the town. And I saw a lost child, a girl who could make it only by flying as high as she could. 'Very lonely,' she would write in her logbook, 'no land in sight.'

Rotorua is like a foreign country to me now. Some other girls lived there. Me, the girls from the Violet Café, Jean Batten. The real and the imagined.

Flying places

Two black super-light suitcases stand in my bedroom. One is an overnight bag; the other, a little sturdier and larger, is for the long weekend. Going to literary festivals has become part of the professional life of writers and during the festival season I am poised for flight. That season gets longer every year as more and more towns host their own events. I have lists of items for the quick pack.

For the most part, writers have solitary lives, sitting alone in front of a computer. When we go to festivals, we are performing and selling our work and ourselves. The two merge into each other. We want to be liked. (Sometimes it is easier to be famous than it is to be loved.) For a short time, we enjoy the hospitality of people who, for the most part, are strangers. We are the outsiders looking in, just as we are when we sit down to create characters, people we know and can never entirely know, and will abandon when we start the next book. And yet we are changed by our experiences in the cities and towns we visit. We leave behind our books, our signatures, our dirty linen in hotel rooms. We take away with us fragments of shared lives, the enthusiasm of our readers, a renewed sense of belief in what we are doing. We are less alone when we leave.

Judging by the number of people who attend, audiences have an ongoing love affair with festivals. Writers usually speak as part of a panel or are 'in conversation', as the saying goes. A bookseller is on hand at the end and the audience, if they are sufficiently moved, rush to a signing table where the author or authors pen their names and a few thoughtful words on the title page. And so it goes. Behind the scenes there is usually a group of volunteers – particularly if it's a small-town event, though the 'internationals' will have paid staff – who have been toiling for months to bring the event together: booking the writers, arranging their contracts, their travel and accommodation, preparing their biographical notes for publicity, contacting media, hiring venues, sound systems and so on. I know all of this. I've organised a few events in my time; now I benefit from the generosity of others.

I go to lots of festivals. I love them. I love getting on aeroplanes and flying off to some other place where it will all be new all over again, a different hotel, fresh people to greet, old friends to reconnect with, and those who say, Remember me, we went to school together, and to marvel at each other, how the years have passed, and here we are and still alive. Nothing can beat the Auckland Writers' Festival on a bright day in May. And what author's vanity can resist the lure of an event that draws audiences of seventy thousand. But, with one or two exceptions, I prefer small festivals to those featuring international writers. I'm not keen when occasional visiting writers see themselves as stars, aloof figures who don't have time to greet readers, who turn up from afar, take one look at their hotel room and demand a penthouse suite. I like places where you can sit down and eat your lunch with your readers, who sometimes know more about your books than you do yourself. Often they remember characters you have forgotten, and it's good to have them brought to life again.

Things often happen when you go to festivals. Or they do to me. I met the late great Angela Carter at the Vancouver festival and we became friends until the end of her too short life. That was back in 1988. The friendship was swift, as is often the way at festivals. Frequently, they fall by the wayside within weeks or months of the festival's end, before you move on to another, but it was not like that with Angela. She and I got lost one night on Granville Island with Margaret Atwood, dumped by a taxi on a lonely strip beside some railway tracks, having to find our way back through the dark to the distant lights of the venue. Afterwards Angela invited me to have tea in her room at our hotel, where she proceeded to tell me the story of her life, and describe her favourite bedtime reading. Recipe books, she declared.

Not long before Angela died, she wrote me a long letter from her home in England. Somehow it got lost in the mail and, judging by its date, had taken six weeks to reach me. The editor of a local newspaper rang me the same day. Would I write Angela's obituary? That was the first I knew of her death. I remembered her love of good food, her size eleven shoes and the little son she had brought to visit me in New Zealand.

Ten years later, I was back in Vancouver for their festival. I had been on tour for the Women's Book Festival in New Zealand just the week before I left for Canada, visiting two or three venues a day in Waikato, driving from one place to another. During those days my aunt lay dying in a small cottage hospital in Te Aroha. I raced from one place to another and back to the hospital. Those two tours would form the basis of a long story called 'Silver Tongued', in which a character called Flo is dying; the narrative moves back and forth through her past. This fluidity of time in fiction fascinates me. I have always been interested in the way the past informs our lives in contemporary time. L. P. Hartley famously described the past as a foreign country, but I've never been sure of that. I'm familiar with the past, despite the complex messages it often sends me. If memory were a house, I would know its interiors, the locked and unlocked doors. I'd say it was just the furniture that got shifted around. The way our differing selves slip in and out of our histories often informs our futures as well. It's possible to see the exits before you reach them. Or those of others.

In 'Silver Tongued', the narrator recalls dashing from one town to another:

What followed for me was a kind of dreamtime, a
compulsion to keep going that I still can't explain.
Driving, speaking, coming back in the middle of the
night to be with my aunt. What did I say to people I
met? So you want to be a writer. Well, you must learn
to live with yourself, however difficult that might
be at times, because you're on your own in this job,
you need to make space in your life, settle on your
priorities. A writer's life is not spent in an ivory tower.
Learn to accept that real life is full of interruptions.
You have children? Yes, of course, many of us do.
Write for fifteen minutes a day - it's better than
nothing at all. No, I agree this is not about craft and
style, but it's about how to survive, which is the best
I can tell you right now. Can I guarantee this recipe
for success? No, no, of course not. Nothing is certain.
Forgive me, I have to leave now.

My aunt died on the second to last night of the tour. The next day
I gave the last talk. Because that is what you do: there are all those
people to whom you have promised yourself, and you cannot let
them down. Then we buried her, and the following day I went to
Vancouver.

On the first night, before I joined the festival, I stayed at the
Sylvia Hotel at English Bay.

[It] seemed the most perfect hotel in the world. It was
covered with ivy; the interiors had dark old beams
and rich stained-glass windows. I slept in a bed of
such deep comfort in a large airy room that, when I
woke up late in the afternoon, I was happy and felt
free. I walked to a shopping centre and bought a face
mask from a cosmetics supermarket, complete with
an open cool bin of products that looked as if they
should have been in a delicatessen. The face mask
was made from shiitake mushrooms and came in a
pottle, resting on ice inside another little container.

Elsewhere, I bought an umbrella and a Vancouver
newspaper. I went back to the Sylvia Hotel and
put the mask on my face. It seemed as if flesh was
being drawn to the surface. Afterwards, I felt totally
cleansed, as if I were making myself over into a new
person. I sat and watched the sea and ate chicken
breast stuffed with ginger and grapefruit.

It was on that tour, which extended to Winnipeg and back to
Calgary and Banff in the weeks that followed, that I met the
young man who could have been romantically interested in me
but turned out not to be. And what would I have done with him
if he had been? Nothing at all. On these tours I looked neither
to left nor right emotionally, guarding myself as a writer outside
scandal, the work at the forefront, until age simply overtook any
hints of gossip that might have emerged. Nevertheless, I was
flattered by the attention, and I was someone to whom he could
tell his troubles and his own dark little secrets.

———

The Toronto festival is called the International Festival of
Authors: Harbourfront, though it used to be known just as
Harbourfront. In its early days it was so exclusive you just about
had to dribble print to be invited. It was a pleasant surprise when
my turn finally came. I stayed in a glamorous hotel on the edge
of Lake Ontario, where I spent many hours watching light fall
on the water. At the first event I was rebuked from the chair for
briefly greeting the audience in te reo, and then a fire alarm
went off and we were evacuated for almost the remainder of the
session. I had dinner with Stephen King and found him the most
pleasant of men, a person who asked interested questions and
listened to the answers. He and his son were a big, gambolling
double act. I got told off for mispronouncing a Québécois writer's
French name and apologised, citing hearing loss, which is real,
and was forgiven. I wore the tiny red insignia of my French

Legion d'Honneur and was asked several times if it was for real.

I had a nice time but it took me a little while to learn the rules.

At the end of the festival, I met up with my friend Judith McCann, who had flown from Ottawa to spend time with me. She used to be the chief executive of Film New Zealand but had gone back to her home country to live. In her company, I began to see the city for what it was and loved it. We flew from there to Halifax, where I was able to catch up with the MacPhersons, friends I had made thirty years earlier when I was researching *The Book of Secrets*. John and Sherry, and John's mother Jean, from Port Morien to the north of Nova Scotia, all looked much the same to me as in that long-ago spring when I was ensconced in their households. The daughters gathered with the family to celebrate my return, and to eat a giant lobster feast, just as we had done on my first visit.

One evening, Judith and I travelled along the coast to Peggy's Cove to meet friends of hers. I remembered the wooden fishermen's houses that faced the Atlantic, the Wedgwood blue and white of the shallows. This is the original home territory of the poet Elizabeth Bishop, whose work I love. There is a famous lighthouse to which I had walked during my first visit. But since then Peggy's Cove had been caught up in a giant tragedy.

On 2 September 1998, Flight 111 was heading from John F. Kennedy International Airport in New York to Cointrin International Airport in Geneva, Switzerland, when it crashed in a bay near Peggy's Cove. The fishermen turned out in their boats to bring in whoever and whatever they could. But they brought back nothing and no one.

> . . . *it is another story*
> *to come here at evening when the white*
> *rocks are glimmering against the burning*
> *bush, the red stain of wild azalea leaves*
>
> *turning in autumn's last light*
> *before the Nova Scotian winter sets*
> *in, the shingled houses like abandoned*

> *grey ships on the shore. And even more*
> *different to stop and climb from the road*
> *to a memorial for the people of the air*
>
> *disaster Swissair Flight 111, 229 names*
> *set on a hillside . . .*

There was no ceilidh in the world that could give them their due, no song that could be sung. I stood for a long time looking at the hillside where the names are written on slabs, and shivered in the fall wind, thinking about the price people may pay for flying places.

And yet this is what writers do, over and over again, even in this time of Covid, as our horizons narrow to our own country. We get in planes and we fly.

Sometimes, as I set off, and despite the pleasures of the journey, I wonder why. Festivals are unpredictable. As you get more practised they are easier to navigate, the terror of fluffing the event less palpable. But still there can be mishaps. One of my first international festivals was in a large Australian city. I was excited when I saw that I was to have a whole hour to myself at the beginning, in a venue that looked enticing in the photos I'd seen.

There were three people in the audience that day.

The venue stretched, empty and bleak before me. A short way off, hundreds and hundreds of people crowded a theatre for the opening event of the festival, featuring seven of Australia's most prominent writers. This event ran simultaneously with mine. I learned that day that the three interested writers who chose to come to my event were as important as a thousand. We parted well. They said they had enjoyed the session.

And in Edinburgh, on a rainy early evening, five 'Australasian' writers - which meant writers from Australia and New Zealand - appeared in a tent in Charlotte Square, before an audience of seven. That included the husbands of the two New Zealand writers, of which I was one. Ian didn't usually travel to festivals with me, but we had been living in Menton that year, and it had seemed like a great opportunity for us to see a new city.

In the yurt the next day, Ian said, 'I know that chap over there. We do know him, don't we?' The man was surrounded by fans and security guards. He was dark and dapper, with black beetling eyebrows.

'Hush,' I murmured.

'But we do,' he insisted. 'I'm going over to check him out.'

I said, 'It's Sean Connery.' And I'm really not sure why I didn't just say to Ian, Go on, just go and say hello. I feel bad about that. Ian was, after all, the audience too.

It kept on raining all that week and it was too wet to go to the Edinburgh Tattoo, although we could hear it from our hotel. It was our forty-sixth wedding anniversary, and Ian fell ill.

There are some places you just need to go back to, in order to see them in the best light. But at least you have had the opportunity, and I am forever grateful for that.

There were seven in the audience at Belfast too. If that in any way sounds churlish, it's not meant to. For the most part, I had a wonderful time in Belfast. As mentioned, I had talked my way into that festival; I was then barely known in Northern Ireland. My English publishers had managed to get me a gig there because I was researching my next novel, *This Mortal Boy*. I was offered an hour in conversation with a wonderful chair called Cathy McNally who was associated with the Seamus Heaney Centre. I was able to roam Belfast's streets, talk to people, do my research.

As well, I was given a week's accommodation in the fabled Europa Hotel, which stands in Great Victoria Street, opposite the Crown Bar, a one-time gin palace and still a vibrant place to hang out. During the Northern Ireland conflict, The Troubles, most of the journalists covering those difficult years stayed at the Europa and drank at the Crown. The Europa was bombed so much that it earned the name 'the Hardboard Hotel', after the boards nailed over its windows. The Provisional IRA damaged the place so badly in 1993 that it had to be rebuilt. Perhaps people do it for a laugh, but there were bomb threats on three nights that I was there. I got used to huddling outside in my dressing gown and nightie while the place was cleared. It is a grand hotel, mighty comfortable, and bomb scares are a quick way to make new friends in the dead of the night. Who is to complain? Management said it was people smoking illegally in the rooms and setting off the fire alarms.

That was also the week of the stalker.

In the audience of seven who appeared at my session was a man I had met once some years earlier, at a talk I gave in New Zealand. Will (not his real name) was eager to chat, a bulky lonely man who had quite recently suffered the loss of someone close. Over the first cup of coffee, he cried. And over the second.

I was sorry, what else could I say?

I tried hard to escape the third cup, but he was always there.

On my last day in Belfast, he suggested we go for a walk in the Botanic Gardens that lie alongside the festival venue. It was a pleasant afternoon. I thought it perhaps a nice way to say goodbye and go on my way.

We walked on into the gardens. The afternoon seemed to have darkened.

'Sit down,' he said, inviting me alongside him on a seat in the rose gardens.

But I didn't want to sit with him. Something felt wrong. I said that I'd just remembered that I had to speak to the organiser about an urgent matter. I hadn't been paid for my appearance and I needed to collect the money. This wasn't true, but was all I could think of.

Will agreed we should return. But the organiser was busy and Will had ordered another cup of coffee. I needed to see the organiser on my own, explain my predicament. We sat in grim silence, and suddenly the organiser had disappeared. Nobody I asked knew where he had gone. Back home, maybe, someone said. Nothing had passed that seemed to justify calling for help. It was a crowded room. I was just having a cup of coffee with a friend, a fan.

'I need to get back to the hotel,' I said, more lies accumulating on my tongue.

'But what about your money?'

I explained then that I had had a strange lapse of memory. Now that I thought about it, the organiser had said he would drop the money round to the hotel.

'I'll walk you there,' Will said.

'I can't possibly walk that far. I'll catch a bus.'

I knew that he knew I was lying. And when I look back on it, I see how women are never really prepared for what's coming to them. Yet still I thought I could shake him off.

We stood at the bus stop and a light rain began to fall. No buses appeared. I said I could walk after all. He followed me down the street. He seemed calmer, and asked me to explain the way writers got paid, and asked what were the rates like - a general sort of conversation.

And then, there in the street, he flew into a strange rage. 'It's despicable,' he cried, 'a terrible thing that you haven't been paid.' He was going to sort it out. His face was contorted and he stamped his feet.

'No,' I said, 'no.' I walked away down the street, without looking back.

I arrived at the hotel. Will was behind me. I stepped into the lift, closed the doors, glided up to my room. Inside it, I leaned my head against a wall and sobbed quietly. It was over.

Around midnight, the phone rang. Another bomb scare, I thought, although there were no sirens in the background.

At the other end, Will sounded strangely disembodied. He had sorted out the organiser. 'I've told him about your money. I've told him what a bad person he is. You'll get your money, I've seen to it.'

I lay awake, shaking, in the Europa Hotel. This was no bomb scare.

At six o'clock in the morning I rose, showered, dressed myself and went out onto the streets of Belfast. A black taxi that takes people on tours of the 'trouble spots', the divide between Falls and Shankill roads, two communities still divided by 'peace walls' in the wake of The Troubles, was waiting below for the first curious tourist. In a bleak early morning light, we drove around the walls that stand between Catholics and Protestants, saw political murals etched on them, silent testimony to the conflict.

I left Belfast an hour or so later.

I supposed that Will had extracted some kind of revenge for not having received the attention he sought.

Weeks later, I sorted out the story with the organiser. He was pleased to hear from me, he wrote. It had cleared up a few things for him. He had thought that Will must be a very close friend of mine. He was sorry that this had happened to me.

The seat in the rose garden features in the last pages of *This Mortal Boy*. Kathleen Black sits there, after she has received the telegram telling her that her son Albert has been hanged in New Zealand. This is a fiction, but nothing should be wasted in the hunt for a good story.

And the sense of oppression happens to be true.

St Malo on the edge of France, in Brittany, there was that festival too, and such a good time. My publisher in Paris, Sabine Wespieser, organised for me to go to the vast annual book fair one year. To be published by Sabine is to be introduced to the pleasures of Paris style. Her publishing house, Sabine Wespieser Éditeur, is in the heart of the Latin Quarter, situated in a thirteenth-century building, the steps worn into grooves, the walls thick and heavy, the huge beams of wood above the winding stairs low and dark. The door opens on rooms full of filtered light and simple, elegant décor, just like Sabine herself, the quintessential Frenchwoman. The covers of her publications lining the walls are all cream. Only the blocks of colour behind the lettering for the title and the author's name differ for each title. She publishes twelve books a year, just that and no more. Each achieves maximum publicity. Her authors' list includes Edna O'Brien, Tariq Ali and Claire Keegan. I have been one of her authors for the past fifteen years.

She cultivates French bookshops assiduously, which I think is a big factor in her success. When I go to Paris for a launch there may be festivals, or fairs, always a round of media, and always the bookshops. There was a night when my novel, *All Day at the Movies* (*Comme au Cinema* in translation) had just appeared. We set off for L'Attrape-Cœurs, in Montmartre. Like so many French bookshops, it was tiny compared with New Zealand stores, but crammed with titles up to the ceiling, and on the night we visited, with people too. Shops like this are not situated in the high street, nor surrounded by other shops, but tucked away in quiet places, a destination for local communities. That night in Montmartre the crowd stretched into the street and clapped and cheered when we arrived, raising glasses of champagne in the air. The questions flowed for a long time, rapidly translated as we went. That session stretched for two hours, deep questions exploring every motivation of the characters, questions about their psyche, some of which I found hard to answer.

Afterwards, Sabine took me up to Sacré-Cœur Basilica to see the lights of the city beneath us. Can there be any other way to see Paris by night, except on that hilltop beside the towering church? On the way down we got lost and went the wrong way down a one-way street, the oncoming driver aggressive, forcing a fast reverse up a winding hill.

'I think it's time to go home, Sabine,' I said.

'But that is what I am trying to do, dear Fiona,' she said, and suddenly we were laughing until we cried all the way back into the relatively safe haven of St Germain.

Sabine loves to cook. There was a big dinner at her house the next night; the gatherings are always large. The five-course dinner began with an excellent cold zucchini soup and ended with clafoutis – it was cherry season. Sabine's authors are probably the best-fed writers in France.

The trip to Brittany for the St Malo Book Fair was a five-hour journey on a high-speed TVG that was entirely occupied by writers from all over the world. All of Sabine's contingent were in the same carriage: me, Belgian-born Diane Meurs, Duong Thu Huong from Vietnam, Takis Theodoropolous from Greece. Two other New Zealand writers with different publishers were further along, in other carriages.

St Malo is a walled stone city overlooking the Atlantic. My hotel had a slit window with a view across the sea. My friend, Nelly Gillet, a translator and lover of New Zealand literature, had travelled from Angoulême. When Sabine was off duty, we sat together in the sunshine at the front of the stall exhorting passersby from the throngs of thousands to call in, explore what was on offer, buy books. We thought we were impressive salespeople. In the evenings, Sabine sat us down at restaurants where we feasted on scallops - coquilles Saint-Jacques heavy with cream - Breton crêpes and galettes. On the return journey back to Paris Sabine provided patés and cheeses, salami and fresh fruit and several bottles of splendid wine. Before long, our carriage began to fill as hungry writers migrated to 'those people with all the food and drink'.

At Montparnasse, our final destination, Takis stood on the platform and sang 'My Darling Clementine' at the top of his voice, calling for the rest of us to join in. I have a happy memory of standing in the lights of the station roaring about Clementine's shoes that were number nines and herring boxes without topses, the only other writer who knew the words; of exchanging addresses, and somehow knowing that I was unlikely to see or hear from these people again.

Except Sabine.

So many festivals. They become a way of life. If I have written at length about those excursions overseas, there have been dozens up and down New Zealand. I feel so grateful to all the people who care enough about the work to invite us and make these events happen. One that will always stand out is an evening in the tiny library in the central North Island town of Taihape, near where my mother was born. There was a local ukulele band and we all sang along and I got to sit in the mayor's chair. The two booksellers who were on hand had travelled for an hour or more on a dark winter's night. I love library events, and those in pubs and bookshops, and theatres, and community centres. There are bad beds and good beds, 1970s motels and luxury suites and even a penthouse or two, there are bottles of fine wine and Presbyterian abstention.

Then there was a festival in Blenheim when *The Infinite Air* came out. Wearing a helmet and a long white trailing scarf, like Jean, I was flown in a two-seater plane like hers; we did loops over the sea. All these things and more.

I gave the keynote address at the wonderful Going West Festival that's held in Titirangi. When I was sent a copy of this recently, I saw what I had written about festivals twenty years ago:

> Not everyone understands the way a writer's life
> really is. It's not too bad, it's just different. Little
> wonder that we enjoy talking and socialising with
> people who understand what our day is like, who
> know that the phrase, 'Did you get much done
> today?', is meaningless. People for whom you don't
> have to fill in the picture of your life to make it sound
> like a real job, even if it doesn't look like one from the
> outside. People who understand that when you say
> you want to be alone, that's what you really mean,
> and no hard feelings. People, too, who understand
> that the condition of money is an erratic, fluctuating
> and constant anxiety, or it is for most of us. I suppose
> it's like any union or association of workers, with a
> simple common understanding of the unspoken, and
> a shared way of life.

Just sometimes, you can be blindsided by a festival and its outcome. It's possible, as I did, to get tangled up in your own history. A year or so ago, I was a guest at the Whanganui Literary Festival. My accommodation was at the Rutland Hotel, one of the town's old establishments, which had been rescued from ruin and restored in fine detail. As I walked to my room on the first landing beside a small sitting room, something made me stand stock still.

I have written often about the time when I lived with my grandparents on their Waikato farm, about the breakfasts taken with my grandfather at a long table, a ceiling-high carved dresser beside us. After my parents and I left to go and live up north, my grandparents died. Everyone drifted away from that household until there was little left except reflections of the past, the dresser and my Uncle Robert, who took an English wife when he was in middle age. Her name was Augusta but he renamed her Jane and built her a new brick house. This was designed to accommodate the dresser so that, when I visited the farm, as I would for more than fifty years, there it was still and I coveted it. My daughter would love it one day, as I had, and with it the stories of my childhood. I thought it would be mine but along the way I had a cousin, the child of another uncle, and this is who Robert decided was to receive the dresser. She was the only child of the eldest son; I was the only child of the youngest daughter. There was an order about how things were decided. I begrudge my cousin nothing, she is a generous-hearted woman and we are friends.

But she already owned two dressers from her mother's side of the family. She offered her new acquisition back to Jane, who was happy that the space on her wall would still be filled.

Years passed. Jane continued to live on the farm. But loneliness eats you up. She met a retired school inspector, when she was seventy-five. The next thing there was a wedding; Augusta, who had become Jane and was about to reclaim her real name, as well as that of the inspector, was the blushing and ecstatic bride.

The inspector had a son who had also been recently married. Bear with me, this story is going somewhere; it is following the dresser. The time came for Jane and her husband to leave the farm; the dresser moved to a new home in another town. And then there was a move to a rest home, and when the elderly couple dispensed with their belongings, the son's new wife was given the dresser.

Jane died.

The son died.

I didn't know where the dresser had gone. By this time, I had said goodbye to it anyway, the lost symbol of my childhood. I forgot about it, more or less.

But there in Whanganui, in the Rutland Hotel, stood my grandparents' dresser. No mistaking it. It had been nicely French polished and it gleamed in the afternoon light. I walked over, my heart pounding, my head exploding with disbelief. I knelt and fitted my fingers into its crooks and crevices.

There was an attendant, a tiny woman, full of stories. I asked her where the furniture had come from, even then doubting what I had seen and touched. Was it by any chance in the hotel when the restoration was started? No, she said, no, all the furniture had come from second-hand places. She and I took the dresser apart, pulling out the drawers and turning them upside down. I'm not sure what I was looking for, perhaps a name or something that would indicate the provenance of the piece. There was nothing – the interior had been carefully cleaned, no traces of the past. But I knew.

I went for a walk in the pretty town where hundreds of cherry trees were in wild and riotous bloom, past the Savage Club standing back from the street, a big red building where someone was playing tinkly old-time jazz, on down to the bank of the wide river. Then I walked back to the hotel and that night I slept in the Rutland Hotel in the room next door to my grandparents' dresser, and I was a child again.

People have asked if I was tempted to make an offer for it. If I did, it was a fleeting temptation. It looks very nice where it is.

On small planes

It's the same again this weekend, wild weather,
rain and delays, and a long way south, suspension
on a cloud, books take you everywhere.

My epitaph may be that she was a small woman
who spent her days in small airports flying
on very small aeroplanes to middle-sized towns.

Preparing for flight at the Marlborough Book
Festival, Blenheim, 2014.

The body's
sweet ache

On being massaged

1

I was lying naked on the massage table, staring down through the hole where you put your nose. It's called a face cradle. There was a lotus flower beneath me, artificial, but a nice touch. The towels were clean, although they had the roughened thin quality that suggested years of use. The person massaging me had moved silently into the darkened room, with a soft swish of a pretty dress I saw as I glanced sideways. The task was begun with quiet efficiency, using strong spiny fingers. I was asked whether the pressure was too hard, too soft, or just right? The voice was surprisingly deep.

There was a time when I would not have imagined myself in this twilight world of body and stranger, nor the vulnerability that demands acceptance and a degree of fortitude. What of the earthquakes that threaten us here in this shaky city where I live? How long might I have to stand wrapped in a towel on the street outside in the company of this unknown person? That's extreme, I suppose, but it's the level of exposure that begins as you strip off your clothes and slide under the towel on the high spindly-legged bed, not knowing how things will turn out.

You never know, you just don't.

On this particular day, it was mid-morning and I had elected not to eat breakfast beforehand. There is the problem of wind when you are being borne down upon. Flatulence, burping, call it what you like - I was being considerate. But I am a breakfast eater by habit; it goes back to the farming days of my youth, when beginning the day without food was considered to be courting disaster in the hours that lay ahead. That morning, minus the regular blueberries and muesli and yoghurt, my stomach took on a life of its own, gurgling and cackling away with an increasing clamour. My therapist began to laugh. Note that word therapist. I understand it is discourteous to refer to a person who performs health massage as a masseur or a masseuse; there is a subtle difference in the duties they perform. Or so I am told. People like me, looking for health benefits, go to massage therapists.

At any rate, my therapist's laughter turned into a different sound, and it is one I knew very well.

'A duck,' I said, 'that's a duck.'

'Many ducks: *clack clack clack . . .*'

We had flocks of ducks on the farm. My parents raised them for Christmas fare. My father's job was to chop off their heads, my mother's to gut the creatures, and mine to pluck their feathers, before their carcasses were handed over to the buyer at the farm gate.

My therapist let out a low yodelling sound.

'How do you know ducks?' I asked.

'My mother, in Thailand. She had many ducks. In the morning she called.'

And so the chuckling and quacking and calling continued and gradually my stomach subsided.

I've been back to this person. And, more than once, I have been transported to the steamy depths of a Bangkok hotel.

Bangkok, 1990. We had been through a bad patch, the way people do. We had had an extension built onto our house that took months longer than it should have, meaning no kitchen and a dog that had become irascible in the face of strangers. Earlier in the year, I had turned fifty and done nothing special to celebrate the event. Then I had an unexpected windfall. There were all sorts of ways we should have spent that money but I said to Ian, 'Let's have an adventure. Let's go to Asia.'

Of course, people go to Thailand all the time these days; at least, when there is not a virus sweeping the world. But to us, thirty years ago, Bangkok was a destination, a place of mysterious possibility. We landed at midnight. As we were driven through the empty streets, our surroundings seemed as foreign as a moonscape. I remember drawing close to Ian as the smell of durian fruit filtered through the car's air conditioning, thinking that it was the stench of open sewers. I had yet to learn that it was the fruit of the dying, so enjoyed in life that it was often pleaded for before death.

We were delivered to a riverside hotel called the Menam, on the banks of the Chao Phraya. The entranceway was tiled with marble, the corridors dimly lit, carpeted in green. I remember that there were large boxes of sand for smokers to stub out their cigarettes, and that the smooth surface was stamped with patterns of flowers. In the morning, we opened the curtains of our room, and below us lay the river and its bustling ceaseless traffic – ships, dredges, ferries with high piping whistles that signalled when they were pulling in to pick up passengers, traditional long-tailed boats. The Chao Phraya flows for nearly 400 kilometres through low-lying silty plains until it reaches the city and spreads into waterways and canals; these canals have been modified and reconstructed over hundreds of years. The name of the hotel, Menam or Mae Nam, is the Thai word for river. On old European maps, the city of Bangkok is shown as Menam. The Chao Phraya is also known as the river of kings. Upstream from Menam sits the vast glittering Grand Palace, for centuries home to the kings of Siam, or Thailand as it became.

I don't believe a tourist can ever become part of Bangkok; the city has its own mysterious interior life. A brilliant façade of colour and movement invites the traveller to believe their experience is unique, but it shouldn't be taken at face value. You can, though, allow yourself to be changed by it, as we were. On the river it's possible to set yourself apart, out of the traffic snarls of the inner city and away from the tuk tuks waiting to whisk you away to distant warehouses. We became instant fans of the longboats and the River Express ferries that carried us from one riverside station to another. In the process, we fell in love with the river itself, the water swarming with hundreds of varieties of fish, dragonflies hovering above its slow eddying tide. There were houseboats that looked poor to our Western eyes, yet they glowed with garlands of orchids and bright rugs put out to air. Orchids, there were orchids everywhere.

A raised terrace ran in front of the hotel, intended as a viewing platform for the river and the spires of the magic city beyond. Often, we would be the only people there late at night, when lightning tore across the sky. It seemed close and thrilling.

We had begun an affair with that hotel and that river which lasted for decades, when age and indisposition put a stop to our ramblings in Asia. It became our base, our place, each visit like a homecoming.

Ian had been closely involved with the lives of young people who came to New Zealand to study and later in his career he became an international student director. We had friends in the city, so at night we would set off from the pier by the hotel and land at the River City Pier, en route to Sukhumvit, the main street of Bangkok, to meet people, visit the night markets, and eat sometimes from the street, other times in restaurants. One of the students had tried to disembowel himself when exams came round and Ian saved him; his family would take us to places we might never have found for ourselves, their hospitality endless in thanks for their son being returned to them. Or, in the old Oriental Hotel on the riverbank, we would take tea in the Authors' Lounge, once visited by people like John Steinbeck and Joseph Conrad. Its walls were screened with bamboo, its white rattan chairs scattered with green linen cushions decorated with cream elephants; the terrace overlooking the river was flanked by orchids. We bought a print at the hotel gallery that we both loved at first sight; it faded in the bright sunlight of our house after it had been on the wall for a few years. Ian wanted to hang onto it until it was nothing more than a smudge. I insisted that it should go. Perhaps he was right; perhaps there are some things you should never let go. But then, as I've learned, there are some things you can't hold on to, however hard you try. Sometimes the dark side of the city would confront us: a hotel lobby would not be that at all, but padded red walls covered with photos of girls seeking work.

And it was in Bangkok, in a small basement room of the Menam Hotel, that I had my first experience of being massaged. I saw it offered on the hotel information sheet and because our whole lives seemed suddenly different and daring, I knew I needed to try it.

I descended a flight of marble stairs and made my way through a labyrinth of passages, into the bowels of the hotel. I came to a reception desk, with an older woman behind it, who sized me up as she greeted me with a wai, that placing together of the hands, the slight bow, the smile that could hide anything and everything. I practised my greeting and was waved on. I entered then a damp room musky with something I would come to think of as the smell of wet soil. I was aware that I was beneath the river, and thought that this must be the smell of water pressing against the walls. Only a wide-eyed girl, who looked as if she might be about twelve, and spoke no English, was in the room. We greeted each other, her bow deeper than that of the receptionist, her smile more tentative.

> *. . . a skinny*
> *girl who should perhaps*
> *have been in school, huge*
> *eyes and fragile limbs*
> *and fingers of steel . . .*

I hadn't understood the finer points of the language of massage when I wrote that poem. The girl is no less for how I have described her.

I pointed to one garment after another. Should I take it off?

Yes, yes, she nodded, until I came to my knickers. She nodded, her face becoming still and grave. She had guessed it was something I hadn't done before.

She gestured, her fingers like threads in that damp river-smelling room, turned away hastily and disappeared. I thought about leaving. Instead I climbed onto the bed and waited for what happened next.

I will never forget that young woman, the delicate pressure of her hands, her knees on the back of mine, the swish of her hair as she leaned over me, her musky fragrance. To enter into this personal contract, this sensual pleasure, yet at the same time to respect the distance of the other, is something you must learn. It doesn't matter the sex of the other person, they are not your lover, they are your therapist. Remember. But I was so overcome with languor and delight that evening in Bangkok, that it was like an addiction. I went back to the girl in the basement every night that I was there. On the last occasion, I offered extra money, just thinking it would make her life easier. She shook her head. I saw that this might offend. I asked at the desk. Could I leave more money? I asked, offering a handful of American dollars. They were quickly taken, more wai exchanged between me and the receptionist. Would the girl have got any of the dollars? I have no idea.

Friends unfamiliar with massage ask me what actually happens. What do you do? What is the procedure?

It's simple really. There is the bed with a towel or blanket lying folded on one end. Your therapist will discreetly disappear while you undress and, once you are lying face down on the cradle, you draw the folded towel up over your body.

Do you take all your clothes off, or do you leave your knickers on? It depends; it pays to ask. In Thailand, you are expected to be completely naked but here you may be asked to keep them on.

In a few moments the therapist will reappear and the towel

will be lifted back and the massage begins, usually with a few smart taps on the back, oils and lotions applied. And while all this stroking and kneading is taking place you will lie very still, until the time comes to roll over. While that is happening, towels will be held up to shield your nakedness, and dropped back over you, so that you maintain the illusion that your private parts are guarded.

There are a number of massage techniques. Most therapists will specialise in one kind or another. Expect to be kneaded, tapped and sometimes pummelled, depending on the kind of massage you choose. My body knots up as I sit over my computer day after day. Deep tissue massage relieves the pain in my muscles. Swedish massage will relieve stress and anxiety. Expect Thai massage to be firm. I once asked for traditional massage in northern Thailand, in a place near Chiang Rai, not knowing that traditional in those parts meant exactly that, and different from what passes for Thai, as administered to Westerners. It involved being thrown in the air, suspended by the therapist's hands and upstretched feet. She was angry when I collapsed on her. I fled.

For the most part, you will be at peace with yourself as the body's sweet ache is relieved. When it's over and you wish that it had never ended, your therapist will say quietly, 'All done now, take your time getting dressed', and withdraw from the room. Then you just have to put your clothes back on. And pay on your way out. And be in harmony with yourself for the rest of the day. It's that easy.

Only there was nobody to tell me this, that first night in Bangkok. I experienced a kind of rapture, a removal of the self from the body, a kind of surrender.

———

I came home to Wellington, my body longing for that calming touch that had so beguiled me in Thailand. I needed to learn more about massage, its values and what to expect. I have suffered high blood pressure for more than half my life; massage offered relief from the physical effects of stress. And my life was stressful. I had become a full-time carer for my mother, who had come to live with us in our newly extended house. It was what I wanted to do; I had chosen this course as increasing frailty and the pain of rheumatoid arthritis overtook her. She and I got along so well – and we did for the remaining years of her life, seven of them spent with us. But it was often back-breaking work, and constant. The journeying that had begun as Ian and I discovered Asia was possible only when we could find suitable live-in carers, or my mother had respite care in a rest home. Before long Ian was travelling alone as he took up voluntary work with landmine victims in the region. I accompanied him when I could. But often it was just the two of us, my mother and me, and her need for care was constant.

I found a woman who was beautiful, with pale skin and long dark hair. She worked near a pool; the air was thick with the smell of chlorine. She had a foreign name although she had been born in New Zealand. Her touch was deep and sure. We talked little, which I prefer. I shy away from therapists who want to tell me their own problems: their chatter distracts from the flow of meditation that goes on during the procedure.

I felt that we had a connection that I couldn't have described. Some kind of electricity was transmitted as she worked. And then, one afternoon, this feeling became transcendent. I was moved in my mind to some other place, somewhere exultant and free. Did anything physical take place between us that was different from the run of a massage? No, and I doubt that I would be telling this if it were so. And yet, I knew that there was some indefinable magnetism between us, and when it was over I was crying. So was she.

Thank you, I said, and then she thanked me and we never spoke of it again; nor did the experience repeat itself.

I continued to see her for some months after that. Before she left, she did tell me she had been a prostitute earlier in her life. She told me in a matter-of-fact way as I lay on the table and it neither surprised nor shocked me. She was happier working as she did now, she said. She liked sex but her boyfriend had got tired of her sleeping with other men commercially and, when she stopped, she discovered that she was tired of it too.

What I took from her was not just the memory of that day but also a sense of her generosity. Like all of the best therapists I have been to, this giving of the self is something that shines through over and again.

After she had gone, another woman took over and I stayed with her for several years until she gave up to start a family. She was a down-to-earth, highly trained woman who helped me to stay grounded throughout the time my mother lived with us. The massages were never highly charged, but she was a steady, calm influence in my life. I remember her telling me once about how the widowed would come to her, and how, at her touch, their emotions would be released, remembering the sensation of the lost other body. That was something I would come to understand.

Later, I stayed faithful to another woman for a good many years. She was from China and practised Qigong, a form of ancient Chinese healing. Meditation and controlled breathing are involved in Qigong practice, which is sometimes described as mastering one's energy. On my first visit, she put on a tape of repetitive Chinese music and, as the years passed, she continued to play it, until I knew every thrumming beat, and where there were pauses as if the tape had been spliced. Above the massage bed there was a railing on the low ceiling. She held onto this as she walked up my legs and then along my spine; she was tiny then. It took an act of faith on my part to stay still and allow this to happen.

In the beginning, we had little to say to each other. But I discovered, in brief conversations before and after the sessions, that she returned to her 'master' in China once a year and that the meditation would involve living in a cave underground. She helped me to write one of my novels that featured a Chinese character and I learned about Chinese food and culture from her. We drifted apart. Perhaps in the end there was nothing more to say, or we had tired of each other in some way. When, after some time, I looked for her again, her rooms had been closed and there was no way of finding out where she had gone. Perhaps the spirit of adventure had deserted us; she had got heavier and it was no longer safe for her to walk all over me.

Over the years there would be others. There was a man once, whom I hadn't expected when I made the booking. He was abrasive and rude, and rough - the only time I have felt afraid. There were many cups of herbal teas along the way, served after the massages. There was a woman whose large dog shared the room as she worked and occasionally it growled. There have been tired young women who hadn't been trained well or have taken up massage because they could get no other work. You know them soon after they have started: they talk too much, or they slap you up and down without rhythm, they sigh heavily. It's not always perfect but you have committed your body to this process and once on the table, short of assault, you have to see it through.

For the most part, though, this laying on of hands, as it were, is a powerful tool for being well.

I'm not a person given to talking much about healing, and people's spirits are their own business. Massage is, in the end, a personal meditation on your own body, a way of offering it ease, a way of honouring the self.

2

One of my grandsons, a medical practitioner, told me that the best answer to wakeful nights was to sleep naked. There is much to be said for it. The body, unfettered by the binding of clothes, lies between the sheets as if they were a skin. It's the fifth sensation, that of touch, which in the absence of *another* carries its own sensual message.

It was years before I reflected on the body, as such. It's not all about beauty, something I understand as I get older. I cannot entirely buy into the idea of the body as temple; if so, there are a few crumbling ruins to consider. Angkor Wat and the ruined palaces of the Greeks come to mind. Yet these are the places where we go sightseeing. Just to look at a fold of skin on a beloved person can still fill me with awe and a certain delight.

The first unclothed body I saw was that of my father. This was one of the primal scenes of my early life. I can describe it no other way. It happened when my parents and I were living in the cottage in the Far North. A curtained window linked the kitchen and the bathing area, in the lean-to. This is from my story, 'All the

Way to Summer', in which the narrator thinks of Oliver Reed in the movie version of D. H. Lawrence's *Women in Love*: 'I raised the curtain and he was rubbing himself dry in the dark room, lit only by a single bulb and the reflections of the flames from the copper fire . . . that same pale English flesh, the colour of potato flesh. He was long and spindly, his chest slightly concave, and yet in the flickering light I found him mysterious and oddly beautiful.'

Bodies were more private when I was a child than they are now. I didn't see my mother's body until she was an old woman, but then I think she covered up a lot of things that were hard for her to acknowledge. Her hair was as dark as a blackbird's wing when she was young, her eyes a gleaming brown that my father said were black when he first knew her, her skin never tanned even though she often worked outdoors. She was a tiny woman who worked like a dervish, as hard as any man, and in the end her body became a damaged shell full of pain, the spine a bent 'c' shape. I wished that I had seen it when it was young.

I don't recall whether I was curious about my own body in childhood. I know I was hungry all the time, rather plump, with straight brown hair that suddenly curled in adolescence. I know I told outrageous stories about bodily functions to other, usually older, kids, gleaned from my imperfect reading of adult books. In my fevered imagination, none of it applied to me. I knew my body was different from the one I had seen through the window, that my father's had an unexpected attachment. But the body was a secret taboo subject, and children had to be covered up. Girls were taught to keep their dresses over their knees, to reveal nothing. A part of me understands that. To love children well, the gaze of adults must remain chaste. This means not just one's own children, but everyone's. There are many who cannot be trusted. If the sight of impoverished children in the back streets of Asia pained me, so too did the sight of men, wearing gold chains at the throat of their open-necked floral shirts, eyeing them. It's a pain that doesn't leave me.

Yet it was in Asia that I discovered how bodies fascinate children. In the streets of Saigon, children would come up to me, pinch my flesh and run away laughing. They would come back and do this again. How old? they would ask. They would want to press their arms against mine to compare the colours, to trace the lines on my hands.

I was sixteen, turning seventeen, before I became truly aware of my own body and its power. I was necking with an older boy and he ran his hands over me. 'You have a beautiful body,' he said. 'Do you understand that?'

Later that year, I was invited to be a beauty queen. It was suggested that I parade in a bathing suit at the local summer carnival in Rotorua. How it all unravelled forms the basis of a story called 'At the Lake So Blue'.

I had been hanging out with a summer crowd and we girls were oiling one another's skins to improve our tans, as we lay in the grass beside a lake. The young men with us were part of a water-skiing group. In a desultory kind of way, they eyed us up, contemplating who would be a good candidate to represent the group as beauty queen of the year. The other two girls had already had a turn, so they looked to me. I had felt like the plainest girl there, but all of a sudden, they were telling me what a great figure I had, and asking me my measurements. And I found myself looking at what I had to offer and knowing it was good.

In the end, I turned them down, in the face of disapproval from family and the woman I worked for. It wouldn't do to show off my body like this. It cost me the friendship of the group but I don't recall any regrets. I found myself agreeing with my elders. When I revealed myself, the audience would be of my choosing. But I had learned some things about myself.

The power of the body.

Soon my body would be busy with other things besides being admired.

It hasn't been a particularly clever body. It was only a moderately good dancer, it wasn't the body of a gymnast, it learned to stand on its hands once, and only once, it missed balls when they were thrown. But it has served me well enough.

I remember these things sometimes when I'm stretched out on that table, experiencing the body's burn of skin on skin.

The way one looks after it, comforts it as it ages, in moments of
bliss gives oneself over to it.

> Outside I hear voices of people
> walking past in the street,
> which is reassuring when the rough
> stuff begins, although it turns
> out bearable enough. When it is done,
> I accept the cup of chrysanthemum
> tea, the assurances that my liver
> is sound, that I am indeed
> a healthy person, if a little tender.
> I eye the reservations book.

Playing with fire

The year 2018 marked 125 years of women's suffrage in Aotearoa New Zealand. Twelve women were invited to write essays about objects in Te Papa Museum that reflected women's experience. I was allocated Anolvar 21, the first contraceptive pill to be widely available in this country. After several false starts, I decided that the only way to address such a tiny yet powerful object was through personal reflection and experience. At the time of writing, the New Zealand Abortion Legislation Act 2020 had not been passed, something I have addressed in this account, slightly adapted from that original essay.

One day when I was a child my mother suggested I tidy the top of her dressing table. It was a plain piece of deal furniture crammed into the corner of the partitioned-off area of an old army hut that my parents called their bedroom. There wasn't much on it: a lipstick, a box of Coty face powder, some hair clips, a few bills. I soon got bored so I opened the top drawer. Inside was a little rectangular box, and inside that were some capsules that looked like brown jelly. I can't remember whether some were wrapped up, but certainly some were exposed. I took them to my mother and asked her if they were lollies. She snatched them from my hand and told me that I must never, *never* touch these again. It occurred to me later that, every now and then, a packet of about the same size would arrive in the mail and that the package wouldn't be opened in my presence.

They were, of course, contraceptive pessaries, something I would later, briefly, use to control my own fertility. Indeed, my mother slid me a packet on the eve of my wedding. I found them disgusting. They may have been Rendell's pessaries, although I think the packaging was the wrong colour. These definitely came in a black box.

All of this is by way of saying that my first encounters with reproductive control were tinged with the belief that something illicit was going on, something not talked about, and certainly not a topic for unmarried women. A prudishness was evolving in the late 1940s that burst into full bloom in the 1950s. It's well documented that women developed new freedoms during the Second World War, as they managed independent lives, worked and brought up children alone while their husbands served in the forces. But when the men returned, the women once again put on their aprons. The kinder side of me thinks that this reversal was not so much authoritarianism, or not all of it, as a primal urge to regenerate the species. All the same, as we wartime children arrived in our teen years, it made for lives that were hidden from our parents, hypocritical double standards and, worse, a reiteration of them when we married. The status quo had to be maintained. Yet we teenagers, particularly those of us who frequented dance halls and the rock'n'roll scene, had glimpsed freedom.

When I was seventeen, I fell in love with a man with whom I had frequent pleasurable sex. We fell into bed whenever we could, usually without precautions. I remember the day he said to me, 'We're playing with fire, aren't we?' He meant, of course, that I might get pregnant. It was fine by him because he was planning to marry me anyway. He had already proposed.

Not long after, I fell out of love with him, and in love with someone else. But by that time, I was cautious. I had had a narrow escape and the consequences of such abandon had been brought home to me. Friends got married in a hurry, or in their parents' front rooms with the minimum of witnesses. Young women disappeared for months at a time and when they returned they were instinctively shunned. Older couples, if a girl was lucky, appeared to have an impossibly late baby who grew up as her sibling. At least the child stayed in the family, but most did not. Not only was the unmarried mother avoided, but she wore a look of profound shock, as if she were in mourning. A close Catholic friend told me that she had sinned with the boy she really loved, and that they had broken up because the temptation to sin again was so great.

And then, of course, there was abortion. I didn't know much about that or how women went about having one. They were illegal. The images described in an underground way suggested some sort of charnel house awash with blood, overseen by a manic baby murderer. Later, I came to understand that a doctor of my acquaintance, a gentle, civil man, had 'helped out' some girls in our town in the orderly surroundings of his general practice. But he was the exception rather than the rule, and perhaps his reputation suffered a little as a result. I knew about a girl who had died after visiting another abortionist. And a friend had a botched abortion that rendered her sterile for the rest of her life.

Terror, that's what it was. We lived in terror. Our bodies were ready for sex, whether or not we had yet found the right mate but, back in the 1950s, the results could deliver shame and grief in equal measure, possible rejection by our parents, giving birth alone in cruel and unfeeling surroundings, the loss of children, bitterness and shame. Such outcomes have followed generations of women, not to mention those in search of their birth parents, and for many it's still an unresolved issue.

My own out-of-wedlock pregnancy scare was, in the end, just that, but it hastened the date of my marriage, one that would endure for the next fifty-seven years. I got lucky. But we didn't have two beans to rub together, as the saying goes, and we weren't ready for a baby. The doctor frowned on hearing this. It would be best, he thought, if I were to get on with things. After all, I was twenty and healthy. He reluctantly fitted me for a diaphragm. It probably wouldn't have made much difference; after I gave birth a couple of years later, I never conceived a lasting pregnancy again. Something had gone wrong, but I wasn't to know it then. I was still seeking birth control when someone mentioned at a coffee morning that there was a pill to stop you from getting pregnant. 'Coffee mornings' were a euphemism for local mothers to get together while their children were at kindergarten or school and tell each other all about their lives.

We dressed up for these occasions in twinsets and pearl necklaces. Ideally, most of us wanted two children, although three would be fine if they were spaced enough for us to catch our breaths between pregnancies. It was the mid-1960s. We stayed home and looked after children, there was disapproval of women who worked outside the home (though I managed to break the mould somewhat by working inside the home), we admired the whiteness of one another's napkins on the line, we preserved jam, and some slept with other women's husbands. Fear still lurked beneath the surface of ordinary domestic lives.

Anyway, somebody in our group had read about the pill being distributed to women of means, in America. There was talk that it would soon be available in New Zealand. The end of the messy undignified birth control methods we used, or of our dependence on our partners to use condoms or practise the rhythm method, or withdrawal, was in sight. Every drop of sperm counted, as couples discovered too often to their dismay. If this seems unduly intimate, for the majority of women, the reproductive period of our lives, how we had our children, or not, is one of our central and most enduring narratives, the stories we tell and retell, whether it be to others or our secret selves.

I encountered the pill somewhere in the late 1960s, and Anovlar 21 is almost certainly what was prescribed for me. By then, in one manner or another, including adoption, I had become the mother of two children, and briefly of three. I had also suffered some devastating miscarriages and further attempts at pregnancy became unthinkable. I asked my doctor about the pill and it was prescribed. So what do I know about it now? I have found out that it was manufactured in Germany by Schering AG and there were twenty-one tablets in a blister pack, which came encased in foil, within a box. You took one every day for three weeks, and then there was a week without them, during which there would be some light bleeding (an added bonus for women with heavy periods). Later contraceptive pill packs offered twenty-eight-day packs, with seven-day placebos, so that women would take their pills on a regular basis and not forget to restart them.

The little green pill seemed like a miracle at first. It contained 4 milligrams of norethisterone acetate and 0.05 milligrams of ethinyl oestradiol. Well, that's what I know now, though it wouldn't have occurred to me to examine the details then. I believe it was a pretty heavy dose of hormones. Unfortunately, it didn't agree with me. I felt nauseous all the time, with headaches, blurred vision and painfully swollen breasts. My reproductive life ended with a tubal ligation when I was in my early thirties. Yet for millions of women all over the world, life changed for the better. Women could plan their lives, think about occupations outside the home without fear of unplanned pregnancies, giving point and meaning to studying for professions; space their children in a manageable way; and, perhaps most of all, enjoy sex in a new and less inhibited way.

With an old woman's eyes, I'm still slightly taken aback when I read regular columns about how to have the best sex, how often one might hope to have it, how the best orgasm can be achieved and so on. It's not that I disapprove, it's simply that the focus of sexual activity has moved from childbearing to pleasure and the conversation about it has altered. In the 1970s, when the women's movement changed all our lives, and the pill offered greater sexual freedom to choose alternative partners, orgasm was the buzz, the anticipated outcome.

There was opposition to the pill's availability, of course, and it was considered unethical to prescribe it - or any form of contraception - to unmarried women, the very people for whom unplanned pregnancies usually had the most devastating effects.

Far right conservatives and fundamental church groups around the globe resisted it strongly. It's interesting to look at the lyrics of songs about birth control pills: they are almost all in opposition, and penned by extremists. There was one song, however, that was recorded in 1972 by the American country and western singer Loretta Lynn. It was called 'The Pill'. Lynn had had four children in her teen years, followed by another two. She hailed the pill, singing about her overused incubator, and the blessing the medication offered it. The song was a huge hit.

Although my own childbearing years were over, I hadn't forgotten the ones who still conceived in difficult circumstances. There were many couples for whom unprotected sex led to abortion, and there are still many today. Of course there are. Desire doesn't always wait for a chemist's shop to manifest itself. I knew that very well. When I left the provincial town where our children's lives began, I was swept up in movements to demand access to abortion. There are heroes in the history of contraception in New Zealand. Among them was Ettie Rout, who campaigned fearlessly during the First World War for measures to prevent venereal disease among the Anzac troops. Sexually healthy men meant sexually healthy partners after they returned home. Subsequently, Rout wrote *Safe Marriage,* a contraceptive and prophylactic manual for women that was banned in New Zealand in 1923, but published in Britain and Australia. She also, in 1925, wrote *Sex and Exercise,* specifically for women. Some in New Zealand hailed her as a hero but she was widely reviled for her efforts. The age of hypocrisy was alive and well. Rout's life has been eloquently documented by Jane Tolerton in *Ettie Rout: New Zealand's safer sex pioneer* (2015).

My contemporary hero is Dr Dame Margaret Sparrow, who has devoted most of her life to women's sexual and reproductive health. A feisty battler throughout her long medical career, she prescribed the pill for unmarried women long before it was acceptable. She was President of the Abortion Law Reform Association of New Zealand (ALRANZ) for more than thirty years. In the early 1970s, desperate young women would come to her seeking abortions, which she could not legally offer. But abortion had been legalised in Australia and so Sparrow devised a plan whereby women requiring abortions could be assisted to cross the Tasman. It was called SOS, which stood for Sisters Overseas Service. Tickets were booked for the women to go to Sydney in the early morning, have an abortion in a safe clinic and return the same night. It meant funding had to be found and accommodation for country women provided so that they could catch that early plane.

Our place was one of these 'safe houses' where women came to stay. These were harrowing times. They were not all young; there were middle-aged women, too, who already had large families and were experiencing financial hardship. Deciding to stay in a stranger's home and travel alone for a medical procedure must have been an unspeakable ordeal. Contrary to some studies, which concluded that Māori women did not avail themselves of this service, I know that some did. More than one stayed with us.

I was in Parliament, as was Margaret Sparrow, when the Contraception, Sterilisation and Abortion Act was passed in 1977, confirming abortion as a crime and sanctioning it only if two consultants agreed it was necessary for the mother's mental or physical health. A group of us hung out that evening in the office of Marilyn Waring, the young National MP who had vigorously campaigned to legalise abortion and tried to persuade the government of which she was a member to support her. I have never forgotten the abuse that was hurled into the room where we sat. A clearly very drunk and red-faced MP stood at the door and shouted that we were a bunch of whores. Other swaying men appeared and berated us.

Sparrow has been quoted as saying that it was 'one of the most despairing moments of her career'. She was so disappointed, she said. How could rational beings come to such a conclusion? My own memory of that night is that the conclusion was reached not by rational human beings, but rather by drunk, belligerent men who saw the proposed changes to the legislation as a threat to their domination over women.

However, the act that was passed, disagreeable as it was, opened a chink in their armour. An abortion through legal channels could be negotiated, although it demanded guile and good performances of mental impairment. Many terminations were performed by doctors of conscience, within the act's pre-scription. Yet, forty years later, the legislation had not changed. People, mostly men, were still arguing about the moral right of the foetus to survive until a full-term birth, regardless of the welfare of the woman.

Pregnancy is the biggest alteration that can be made to a human body, and the consequences for a woman are far reaching. Yet in order to terminate the pregnancy, she had to endure a battery of tests that no other medical procedure required. New Zealand was out of step with much of the developed world. Restrictive abortion laws violate women's human rights not only as enshrined in the Universal Declaration of Human Rights (1948) but also based on agreements made at the United Nations International Conference on Population and Development in Cairo in 1994, and the Fourth World Conference on Women in Beijing in 1995. High on the agenda at those conferences was the issue of protection for women from unsafe abortion services.

It was ironic that here in New Zealand people could legally have elective surgery to various parts of their bodies, including operations that altered their appearance or their body shape, physically change their sex and decline medical interventions to save their lives (except in the case of children whose parents may have refused it on religious grounds), yet women and their doctors risked being criminalised if a woman chose to end an unplanned pregnancy.

I held fast to the belief that things would change, must change. New Zealand led the world in several areas of women's emancipation, notably the 1893 change to the Electoral Act that gave all women the right to vote. I knew that women had not stopped fighting for justice and personal freedom.

When the Republic of Ireland reformed its abortion laws in

2018, I felt in my bones that the change would happen very soon. We had long heard of the repressive measures taken against unmarried mothers in Ireland, and how religion had dominated the discourse. But the people of Ireland had voted for change in a referendum and it was happening. Surely we, in enlightened New Zealand, would follow suit.

We had to wait until 2020 and a referendum of our own before it happened. Under a Labour government, the New Zealand Abortion Legislation Act was enacted in March of that year, decriminalising abortion and making abortion services available without restrictions to any woman who was not more than twenty weeks pregnant. Royal assent was given on 23 March and the following day the new law was in practice.

The face of the government had changed: it was younger, more diverse, more tolerant, more female. The rise of the left, with its inclusive mix of young men and women, convinces me that the old ideologies of the past are being left behind. I have hope in the young. They are as capable of making mistakes as we all were, but I think there are more with courage and conviction. I wrote a poem in praise of the young activist Malala Yousafzai, who was prepared to die for young women's right to be educated.

> *The route we women*
> *took when we were young*
> *was always harder than we knew:*
> *your difference is that you did . . .*
> *we weren't ready to die.*
> *You were. Knowing the risks*
> *you took bullets and lived.*

She speaks for her generation. In the same way, I hope, women's right to control their fertility will be understood not just as a personal freedom, although that matters too, but as a measure of social justice and equality, and improved relationships between the sexes.

In the time of Covid

1

Self-isolation made perfect sense to me when news of the pandemic and its reach into New Zealand first appeared. My mother lived on her family's sheep station near Ōpōtiki during the 1918 influenza outbreak. She and her siblings stayed comfortably in the grand old homestead, untouched by the epidemic. Night after night they heard karanga and lamenting from tangi across the valley, as word spread of deaths accumulating at the nearby Māori pā. One world separated from another by a dip in the landscape, and much else besides. On the other hand, I knew about the famous Dr George Smith who helped to save Hokianga from even worse suffering than it endured, through armed roadblocks into the district. His daughter Janet was my good friend. I visit her grave at Rawene as often as my journeys take me north, remembering her stories of that time.

So when my son paid a lightning visit from Australia in early March 2020, and hurriedly returned as their border closed the following day, I decided straight away that I must isolate myself. It didn't seem hard. I have a large house, a garden, a view across

Cook Strait. What was there to be brave about? This would soon pass. By the first day of the official lockdown my chin had started to quiver. It was, in fact, my eightieth birthday. There was to have been a family gathering, people arriving from around the world – London, Australia and from the north. I ate fried rice on my own that night. But lest I make it sound too bleak, there had been calls all day, including neighbours ringing to say they would be leaving small gifts at the gate; my daughter coming to wave from a distance; a house full of flowers delivered in the previous days. Somehow, by the time I went to bed that night, it felt like a birthday. My challenge was to be a brave woman, reminding myself of my privileges, and that it takes courage to be old. I read that somewhere, and in that time of reflection, I could see that it must be true.

Neighbours kept dropping by with baking, leaving it at my door. I thought I should be doing the baking, that's what I would have done once, but now I had become, involuntarily, an old person who needed to be minded and cosseted and, for the time being, I was grateful. I walked regularly and the way we distanced ourselves in those early days of lockdown interested me: going down the middle of empty roads to keep apart from oncoming walkers, jumping on and off the pavements, like a new dancing ritual, laughing and waving to one another all the same.

In this brief span of time there seemed to be a reordering of the natural world, one we would look back on and say that this was the way it should be, without cars, without planes. Some days were harder than others. I love the bird life that teems all around me here. Not just the humble sparrow, but tūī and pīwakawaka. For three days a long-tailed cuckoo took up residence outside my kitchen window, eating ripening olives. It is a migratory bird and rare. I worried that it should be leaving for its journey. I tried to imagine where that was.

Small amounts of work came my way but, contrary to what was expected of me, I wrote very little. Other writers have said the same. A great quietness had halted the impetus to write, as if communication with the world beyond were no longer important. The focus was getting myself through each day, making lists for my daughter when she shopped for me, making sure I ate well. I did keep in touch with family and friends, but that was enough writing for the moment.

Once the immediate crisis began to move away, I found it harder than I anticipated to return to what passed for ordinary life. The solitary existence had become the way it was. At nights I had looked out to where the airport lies. I couldn't remember, in fifty years of living above it, a night when it didn't glow with the green lights that illuminate the runways. During the lockdown, they were extinguished; it was as if an arm of the sea had extended out into a new tributary, linking Cook Strait with Evans Bay, a dark river of nothing. One night, for the first time in several weeks, I caught a glimpse of a passing Interislander ferry, like a stately lit castle above a sea of night. A return to the world seemed just possible.

That return brought challenges. I looked at myself in the mirror, seeing my wild, long hair, my unadorned face. There was a need to dress well again, to accept invitations, to shop for myself. I hadn't entered lockdown thinking of myself as old, but now there had been this apparent transition. It was one which, as I discovered, I was ready to accept. I had not, as I had assumed, given myself permission to be like that. A part of me wanted to return to my former way of life and this would mean fighting for myself against the view that others now clearly had of me. It takes humility to learn the art of acceptance. Perhaps I'm lacking in that. I may have accepted that the face I saw reflected that morning was past its best, but the spirit that has always sustained me hadn't been quenched. There's a difference, I think, between acknowledgement and acceptance.

The world beyond has darkened as the virus has spread. It occurs to me that I may not travel far ever again. That saddens me. In London, one of my grandsons fell ill with Covid-19 and was very sick. Since then, he has been to visit me, after a time in quarantine at the border. He said when he was here that in this country, where the illness is held at bay, we didn't understand that we were living in a different universe. It's true, in a sense; we've been practising an almost wild sociability, living while we can, but with an underlying element of fear. Enough old people died during lockdown for we who are said to be old to feel afraid. It could happen again. It could come for us. We yearned for our vaccination, the jab that would give us safe passage through more days, and we were not disappointed. But the virus is not done with us, as it rears its ugly head in various mutations.

This is, I suppose, a meditation of sorts on a process that comes to everyone sooner or later. Covid has hastened it. But the fight is not over, or not for me. I have discovered that it is still possible to be happy. Friends come to my door, bringing flowers and conversation. We talk through days and nights. There are travels within the countryside here. There is a fine rapture about the embrace of the lives we still have.

After a time, I was taken by a familiar urgency, the stirring of words. As a writer, there is still the will to work. Always that.

The new beginnings, another book.

Going south

At Pike River

1

The drive from Greymouth to the Pike River picket line is as wild and beautiful as any tourist could hope to see. You pass through stands of native bush - towering rimu and nīkau palms - and cross bridges over surging rivers. You come then to open farmland and, on the side of the road, there is a space, a corner that a farmer has set aside and on which have been placed twenty-nine rocks, brought up from the river below. Each carries the name of a worker who died in the explosion at the Pike River Mine on 19 November 2010. Most of the rocks have a little headstone bearing messages and tributes. It's like a tiny cemetery - except, of course, that it's not a cemetery, because there are no bodies. The area is known as Atarau, and this is the Atarau Memorial.

Ian and I set out for the picket line on a Friday morning, 2 December 2016 because, after six long years, the families of the miners who died were no closer to retrieving the remains of their loved ones - their fathers, sons and grandsons, brothers, husbands, lovers - than they were at the beginning of the nightmare. At the time of the disaster, then prime minister, John

Key, had said: 'The first thing I'm here to give you is absolute reassurance: we're committed to getting the boys out and nothing's going to change that.'

But something did change.

We believed these grieving families needed our support. Ian had a history with the West Coast, stemming from the days when he was a young teacher working at the Blackball school, not far from Greymouth and Pike River.

The stories that had emerged from a royal commission of inquiry, conducted in 2012, revealed a worksite that had been set up in haste and was under-resourced from the beginning. Coal has been the dark living heart of the West Coast for more than a century, its production essential to the livelihoods of thousands of people above and below ground. It's dirty work, hard work performed in subterranean tunnels, away from the light, with the danger of explosive methane gas ever present. There had been deaths before: the Brunner Mine in 1896, sixty-five dead; the Strongman Mine at Runanga in 1967, nineteen dead. In both explosions, all but two of the bodies had been recovered. Not one body at Pike River had been brought out. For there was a second explosion, five days after the first. The families were told that rescue was impossible and that all the men would have been consumed by fire.

As fossil fuels were replaced by natural power sources like wind and solar systems, coal production on the Coast had slowed and the region had become poorer. This new mine was to have been a saviour, a revitalising shot in the arm for Greymouth, the town at the edge of the sea, where most of the men lived. But machinery and other equipment in the mine were inadequate. Chaos, we were told, often ruled, and the workers themselves had begun to question health and safety precautions. The owners, an Australian Consortium called Pike River Mine, were desperate for a return on their investment, but little coal was being produced.

The picket line Ian and I joined had been set up because Solid Energy, the state-owned enterprise that bought the mine following the accident, was about to seal it off with 30-metre walls of solid concrete, so that it could never be entered again.

In fact, nobody had gone into the mine since the day of the first explosion, which meant that nobody was quite certain what had happened, and what they would find if they went in. That was the problem. Some experts on the Solid Energy side said it was not possible to enter safely. But the people of Greymouth had been offered expert opinions that suggested it was possible to enter, if not the mine proper, the area known as the drift, where it was believed that many of the men lay. These locals, who had often spent their lives in mines, were willing to go in and find out.

If they couldn't prevent the seal-off, the families would never know what Solid Energy, and by implication, the government, needed to hide. Because no one had ever been held accountable for the manifold failures that we now knew had occurred in that mine. In her first-rate book, *Tragedy at Pike River Mine: How and why 29 men died*, investigative journalist Rebecca Macfie had outlined a dreadful string of mistakes, from consent being given for a mine of unsuitable design and the lack of proper monitoring equipment, to the pressure from management to ignore safety requirements and the provision, effectively, of only a single exit. Was there more? We didn't know. But as far as the families of the Pike River men were concerned, the mine was now a crime scene.

The Solid Energy trucks carrying workers preparing for the seal-off drove along the road around seven every morning. A locked gate barred entry to everyone else. This was where the family members stood in the picket line, hoping to stop the trucks. It was a last stand, a brave cry of defiance. It interested me, however, that some local contractors and electrical companies were standing with the families, refusing to go to the mine, even though work was hard to come by on the Coast and times were lean.

So lean that getting to Greymouth was almost a deterrent in itself. There were no flights from any cities. It was possible to get flights to Hokitika to the south, or to Westport, a couple of hours' drive north. From there it was a case of finding ground transport to the town. All the same, Ian and I decided to go. We thought of the thousands who had gathered for memorial services in the first years after the disaster. But when we watched images of the picket line on television, there was just a handful of people, perhaps about twenty. And out there in that wide space, they looked so lonely. I remember turning to Ian and saying, 'Shouldn't we be there with them?' Ian was going on eighty-five. He looked at me and said, 'Let's go.'

We made contact with Bernie Monk, who had lost his son, Michael, in the mine and is a leader among the families, to make sure that we would be welcome. The answer came back, 'Please come.'

And so there we were on the eighteenth day of the protest, sitting on the road, the police line behind us. The sun was breaking through the clouds, the nearby mountain wreathed with mist, as we waited for the trucks to arrive. Across the gate the protesters had placed messages to the government, which alone could now prevent Solid Energy from continuing with its nefarious task. The messages were aimed squarely at John Key. 'NATIONAL CARES ABOUT WORKERS' SAFETY – YEAH RIGHT', or 'THE KEY TO THE MINE IS JOHN KEY', and others, more bitter and personal. What struck me most, though, were the photographs on a board of the dead men. Some of them were the ages of our grandsons. If we had had moments of wondering why we had made this journey, the reason was here in front of us. It was impossible not to be moved to tears before the faces of the lost.

The muster when we arrived was larger than the day before. Cars blocked the roads, a steady stream of protesters arriving by the minute. People who saw each other most days of the week nonetheless embraced. I met Dean Dunbar, whose seventeen-year-old son had died on his first day in the mine; Rick 'Rowdy' Durbridge, father of a missing son; Sonya Rockhouse, who lost a son too (his brother was one of only two people to escape the fatal first blast). Her friend Anna Osborne, whose husband had died, was ill that day and couldn't come; she and Sonya were forces in the movement. On the back of a truck, breakfast was being prepared: sausages sizzling on a portable barbecue, home-made chocolate muffins, strong hot coffee. Flowers and wreaths were placed in front of the men's pictures: a handful of roses, yellow chrysanthemums with two fabric monarch butterflies hovering over them. Weka emerged from the side of the road and tried to carry off these bright trophies. I shooed some away as I talked on my cell phone to various media outlets, while the people stood gathered behind me. When I went out live on *Morning Report*, the broadcast was being relayed on a speaker; hearing my own voice gave me the strength to say some of the things I believed about this situation. I said that I had some messages for Mr Key. I said that governments rise on promises, but fall if they break them. When the interviewer suggested that the prime minister had only committed to trying to get the men out, I said that there was still time to try harder, and that I hoped that he would.

There were hugs all round after that. The trucks arrived, the police moved in. This had been at all times a peaceful protest led by responsible people. There was no violence on this picket line, just determination on the faces of people in despair of being heard. Eventually the trucks were allowed through, although there were raised fists as they passed. We stood there for a little longer. Some announcements were made and then over the speakers a song boomed out. It was 'Brothers 29', written by local journalist Paul McBride, who was there that day too. He had composed it and sung it for the first memorial service; it had become an anthem for the Pike River families.

Some of the protesters considered staying on to stop the trucks leaving, so the drivers could see what it was like to be locked on the other side. Not that they would leave them there for the weekend. That was not their style. As Dean told me, 'They should be able to go home at the end of their day's work. Our men couldn't.' Joseph, his son, just a kid, had dreamed of going into that mine.

On the drive back to Greymouth, Bernie Monk stopped at the side of the road so that we could walk quietly among the tributes on the farmer's land. As we did so, Bernie told us about some of the men who had died. His own boy, Michael, had worked with a building contractor; he was not a regular mine employee. The fresh face and wide smile in his photo, the broad shoulders, suggested his father's build. Bernie is a rugged Coaster, with a shock of white hair and a barrel chest. He's the owner of the hotel at Paroa on the outskirts of Greymouth, where we had stayed the night before. It's a family business, has been for generations: another son, Al, works there, and a daughter, Olivia, was working in the kitchen at the time (she now owns a café in Greymouth). Kath is the quiet matriarch, a Coaster to the bone from further down south, a big Catholic family. The pub, with its low-ceilinged, timber-lined bar and restaurant, stands at the edge of the grey and green rolling Tasman.

Ian and I tramped along the white stony beach in the afternoon before catching a ride back to the airport, wondering if we had made any difference. As we walked back to the hotel, I glimpsed Bernie, wearing an apron and standing behind his pub counter, an energetic man stilled for the moment. From the beginning of the nightmare at Pike River, he had been the stalwart, fronting the media over and again, speaking in his earthy growl, supporting family members even when his own and the family's grief threatened to overwhelm them all. Earlier that year he had been made a member of the New Zealand Order of Merit for his service in this time of crisis. I remember his face that day, caught in repose – set, stoic, a look that said we will never give up.

Someone got in touch with me after we had travelled to the barricade to say, in justification for sealing the mine, 'that the men were lying in a beautiful place'. They are not: they are entombed in a mountain in the wreckage of a mining disaster. In a country that has a tradition of respect for its dead, whether here or in war graves on the other side of the world, that attitude seems peculiar to me. This is something I return to often when I think of Pike River.

In the week that followed, support surged from many quarters. In Auckland, Alexandra Dumitrescu, a writing colleague of mine, began an online petition asking the government to stop the sealing of the mine from going ahead. It quickly gathered several hundred signatures. Damien O'Connor, the West Coast Labour MP, advised us to get the petition into Parliament the following week, before the Christmas recess. It was essentially Alexandra's petition but she volunteered to put my name to it, given that I had made the public stand. The credit was hers.

While that was unfolding, there was a shock announcement on 5 December, three days after our trip south: John Key had resigned. Nobody seems quite sure why he did this. I believe it was coincidence. But a shiver ran through me when he was asked by a journalist if he had any regrets. He shrugged, as he was wont to do, brushing it off with his apparently affable, yet steely-eyed smile. 'Oh, I'd like to have got Pike River done,' he said.

I was racing against the clock, preparing the petition that now had more than five hundred signatures. Bernie suggested I contact the PR people who had been helping to put the case before the public.

It wasn't a very satisfying meeting, as I was repeatedly asked to explain myself and my intentions. I sensed, in the uneasy atmosphere, a desire for ownership of the situation. But then, I thought, it would be easy for someone new to undo or undermine the work that had been done, to make mistakes.

Ian and I rushed through the corridors of Parliament House on the day of the deadline, urged on by MP friends from the left. The petition was presented with fifteen minutes to spare before the recess began. Afterwards, a flash mob of supporters gathered on the edge of Parliament grounds. Bernie had come up from the Coast, along with other members from the family group. Someone got me a soapbox and we took turns addressing the crowd that had gathered in the street.

Six days later it was announced that a select committee, comprising politicians from both sides of the House, would meet in February to hear and consider the petition.

The royal commission of inquiry report in 2012 had found that Pike River Coal failed in its management, and that its health and safety systems were inadequate. Mines were overseen by the

Department of Labour, as it then was; the Minister for Labour in the National government, Kate Wilkinson, had immediately resigned her portfolio when the report appeared. In the wake of the inquiry, Key had offered an apology to the families. While the royal commission made it clear that the fault lay with Pike River Coal and, by implication, its executive director, a man called Peter Whittall, Key also agreed with the findings that the regulatory environment in the mine had not been effective for a long time. This should have been the responsibility of the Department of Labour, now known as WorkSafe.

In its report, under the heading, 'The Families of the Men', the commission had stated that the recovery of the remains from Pike River now lay within the control of Solid Energy and other parties to a July 2012 recovery deed. This had defined the new owner's obligations in relation to body recovery and contained mechanisms that enabled the government to exercise some oversight.

But here it was, six years after the disaster, and no attempt had been made to recover the men's remains. Solid Energy had said that the re-entry was too dangerous and that any attempt would further endanger lives. Had this been true, it would have been fair comment, but plans for a safe re-entry had been put forward. The mine was being sealed up at the behest of the government, thousands of litres of concrete poured daily.

Throughout that summer of 2017, I toiled over the statement to be made in support of the petition. Ian ran the household while I dealt with piles of information. The PR people and I came to an understanding of sorts as they fed information into the document. Most of it I wrote. It was a relief to know that technical issues would be addressed by Tony Forster, who had been Her Majesty's principal inspector of mines in Britain for twenty-five years before being recruited by the New Zealand government to be the chief inspector of mines here. Following the Pike River explosion, he had stayed in the role for three years before returning to England. He was also a board member of the International Mines Rescue Body. He would be sitting alongside me when we headed into the select committee hearing. Tony was also the brains behind the re-entry document. On his other side would be Bernie, there as spokesperson for the families.

In the background, another scenario was playing out. Earlier, Anna Osborne and Sonya Rockhouse had taken a case against WorkSafe for accepting a payout to the families from Peter Whittall's insurance company, in exchange for dropping negligence and criminal nuisance charges against him and Pike River Coal. The two women argued that this was unlawful and that nobody had been brought to account for failures in the mine's management. The courts were not showing a lot of sympathy, but Anna and Sonya were preparing to battle the case all the way to the Supreme Court. They had been supported in their struggle by Helen Kelly, President of the New Zealand Council of Trade Unions, the young warrior woman who had fought many battles on behalf of workers. Helen had died two months before Ian and I entered the fray.

———

The night before the hearing our team met at the headquarters of the Public Service Association to rehearse our opening speeches. Earlier in the day, Key's replacement as prime minister, Bill English, had made a concession, perhaps seeing the way things might go. Work on sealing the mine would stop. However, he said that under his watch nobody would ever enter the mine. The media was already heralding this as a victory for the Pike families, but we all knew it was a concession, not a victory in terms of what was really needed: a thorough examination of the site.

The next morning, we gathered again at a hotel room on The Terrace, up the road from Parliament. We stood around nibbling takeaway breakfasts and drank a lot of very strong coffee. At eight we made our way en masse down The Terrace, the yellow ribbons signifying our link with Pike River pinned to our lapels. The committee room was packed with family members and the press gallery was seething too. Seated down the left side of the room were four members of the National government; on the right, three members of the Labour Opposition, Damien O'Connor for the West Coast, Andrew Little, the Opposition spokesperson for mines, and Clayton Cosgrove, plus Winston Peters from his right of centre New Zealand First Party.

I spoke at length. Pike River Mine, I said, was situated in a remote rural area, difficult for most New Zealanders to access. Greymouth, the nearest settlement, was 46 kilometres away, and itself a small town, far from he main centres, on the margins of the land. Although most New Zealanders remained moved and saddened by the disaster and its aftermath, it was difficult for them to offer much practical support. As time passed, I told the committee, the families had become increasingly isolated from mainstream concerns. The petition I had presented sought to raise awareness of the difficulties they faced in getting their alternative evidence heard, in the hope that there would be more support for a proper intervention.

Tony spoke after me, with eloquence and a wealth of detail about how a re-entry could be made. Then he said something very personal. 'My family love me a great deal,' he said, 'and I love them. They're constantly terrified of the work I do. But I can tell you unequivocally that I would go into a mine when the necessary work had to be done to make it safe. It would be a measured risk.' He finished by saying he would have no hesitation about entering Pike River Mine. Then Bernie spoke for the families.

I rounded off our submission by pointing out that Solid Energy had sold its assets to three different companies six weeks earlier and that the sealing of the mine had begun just days later, suggesting commercial expediency rather than issues of safety. When I was asked what the motivation of the Solid Energy directors was, I said that I couldn't read minds, but I thought it might be convenient if Pike River disappeared from the books and the problem went away.

The chairman of Solid Energy, a man called Andy Coupe, who is a professional director, had the opportunity to respond. He was on record in the *Westport News* as saying that he was fed up with criticism from the West Coast: 'I'm a little tired of the pick, pick, picking away.' He thought the region should be applauding the board and 'frankly, the senior management, for what we've achieved and I'm never hearing a word about that. All we're getting is negative, negative, negative.'

Now he turned his wrath on me. I have never been so flattered by abuse. I was, he said, 'a woman with a total lack of comprehension of the complexities of the issues'. Ah, women, I thought, that's the problem. I was, he added, 'derogatory and offensive' in suggesting a cover-up. It was an interesting turn of phrase. What I had actually said was that the crime scene, if indeed it was, should not be covered up, meaning, of course, that the mine should not be sealed from view. Finally, it was done. We felt a sense of quiet jubilation as we made our way out, pursued by cameras. It had gone better than we hoped and there was definitely a sense that we had Solid Energy and their supporters on the run. The government members had looked crushed and disorganised. The Labour team had been vigorous in their support.

We carried on to the Old Bailey, a pub on Lambton Quay in the heart of downtown Wellington. Bernie bought lunch and drinks all round. Bernie and his wife Kath, Ian and me, Tony, Anna and Sonya – there's a photo of us all with our arms around one other, Tony a head taller than the rest of us. Dean and, as I remember it, Rowdy, wearing his trademark wide-brimmed hat, turned up. There was a sense of solidarity and togetherness. We would 'Stand by Pike', the motto that had emerged from the families and their supporters. There were hopeful tears, laughter, stories relived. It seemed as if we would be in it as a team forever.

October 2017 rolled around. After a bruising election campaign, Winston Peters had had the opportunity, for the second time in the country's history, to anoint a government, after the result was too close to call. He had chosen to go into a coalition with Labour and the Greens, led by Jacinda Ardern. During the campaign Labour and New Zealand First had promised to do all that was humanly possible to retrieve the miners from Pike River Mine.

Ardern's swearing in was due to take place towards the end of the month. On Labour Day, the 23rd, Bernie invited us to hear an afternoon concert in the Michael Fowler Centre, a 'Cantata Memoria' composed by Sir Karl Jenkins in memory of the children who died in the 1966 Aberfan mining disaster; it was also dedicated to the Pike twenty-nine. Three hundred performers, including an eighty-voice children's choir, took part in the concert, which was conducted by acclaimed New York conductor, Jonathan Griffith. The music soared around us, moving from darkness to light, ending with the 'Lux Aeterna', part of a Requiem Mass, a movement that develops with growing optimism, as the word 'light' is sung in various languages.

Three days later, Jacinda Ardern was sworn in as prime minister. Ian, a lifelong Labour supporter, was euphoric. We both felt so full of hope.

On the following Sunday, Ian fell. He died the next day.

Bernie was in town for his funeral. I didn't see him for a long time after that.

Over the next year or so, I was distracted. That's about the best I can say. I lost track of what was happening at Pike River Mine. I was aware that, in the month following the election, Anna and Sonya won a famous victory in the Supreme Court when the payment made on behalf of Peter Whittall was finally declared to have been illegal. With the initial support of Helen Kelly, who had died the previous year, they had made a powerful and principled stand, an achievement I respect. It was, they were quoted as saying, 'the end to cheque book justice'.

In that same week, Cabinet would approve the establishment of the Pike River Recovery Agency, set up to investigate what happened in the 2010 disaster and look into the possibility of manned re-entry of the drift. A government-appointed group, to be called the Family Reference Group (FRG), was also established to represent the families in relation to the Pike River Recovery Agency and the government. This was to be headed by Anna, a move I understood, in light of her newfound presence in the political arena. Sonya, Rowdy and Bernie were also appointed, as well as the PR people (one of whom is a documentary filmmaker). Nearly all of them had strong links to the union movement, as did Andrew Little, who had been national secretary for the Engineers Printing and Manufacturers Union (responsible for miners) at the time of the explosion. Little was appointed Minister Responsible for Pike River Re-entry.

Two families had consistently requested that there be no recovery because they did not want their relatives' remains disturbed, and one other had dropped out of contact. They were the only ones who were not signatories to the recovery agency's founding statement, in which they set out the following requirement:

> Stand With Pike Family Reference Group (FRG)
> has full and sole delegated authority from the
> overwhelming majority of the Pike River families
> (28 out of the 31 families) to represent them in all
> matters relating to and arising from the re-entry
> and recovery of the drift. The Agency will not
> initiate any contact with a Pike River family about
> the re-entry or recovery of the drift, except through
> the FRG. If a Pike River family contacts the Agency
> about a matter concerning the re-entry or recovery
> of the drift, the Agency will inform the FRG of
> the contact and the matters discussed, unless
> the family has requested the matter be treated
> confidentially, which will be pro-actively offered
> by the Agency.

The families, it appeared, were required to remain silent unless they spoke through the FRG. Anna headed the group. She, Sonya and Rowdy formed a nucleus, plus two of the PR consultants. At the outset, Bernie Monk was part of this group. This cloak of silence would later lead to insurmountable tensions within the group. Some would say that it turned inward and that government agencies were being protected. But at that point, I thought all was well.

On 14 November 2018, came the welcome news that the government had agreed to re-enter the drift, the 2.3-kilometre tunnel
connecting the outside world to the mine. At the beginning
and end of each shift a drift runner had been used to transport
the miners to and fro along the tunnel. Because the explosion had
occurred around the time of a shift change, there was a possibility
that some of the miners' remains might be found in the vehicle. As
well, the electrical components that powered a ventilator fan, and
other vital working parts, were housed at the far end of the drift. The
police had been asked to lay criminal charges of negligence against
the directors of the mine, but they maintained that until evidence
could be presented, they had no case. The government's decision
and the commitment of funds represented a huge breakthrough.

In late April 2019, Anna Osborne wrote and invited me to go
down and join the Pike River families for the mine re-entry at
the beginning of May. There would be a gathering in Greymouth
the night beforehand, where Prime Minister Ardern and Andrew
Little would be in attendance. The following day, we would all
travel by chartered buses to the mine entrance. I knew this was
something Ian would have wanted me to do. Both my children
were keen that I go and insisted on sending contributions for my
airfare to Hokitika. I rang Bernie and Kath and asked if I could
stay with them; they volunteered to pick me up at the airport. I let
Anna know that this transport had been arranged.

A curious thing happened when I was in transit at Christchurch
airport. Sonya phoned me to say the opening had been delayed.
Perhaps I would prefer to turn around and go back home?
Nonplussed, I asked if all the events were postponed too. After
a short silence, she said that they would go ahead as planned.
I continued on my way to Hokitika.

That evening, with the Monks, I attended the gathering in
Greymouth, which took place at a hotel in the town centre, in a
long room decorated with twinkling fairy lights. I sensed something was amiss. I looked for Anna and Sonya and saw them
among a throng of people. It was as close as I got. I sat at one
end with a small group. The prime minister went around the
room glad handing. She stopped at the table where I was sitting,

chatted about make-up and jewellery with a group of delighted women and then moved on. Other government ministers circled carefully. I spoke to Andrew Little. We had met, I reminded him, at the select committee hearing, two years earlier. Yes, he said, yes, thank you, of course. I approached Damien O'Connor. I'm talking to this lady, he said, bending towards an elderly woman dressed in red.

I was puzzled. Since those heady days at Parliament, something had changed. On the way back to Paroa, I mentioned to the Monks that I had found it strange that I hadn't caught up with Anna and Sonya. They were quiet and I let it go.

In the morning we assembled at the Moonlight Hall on the outskirts of town, surrounded by a big empty paddock, hundreds of us waiting to catch our designated buses. We had all received police clearances in the week or so beforehand. Everyone was given a lanyard with their name, showing which bus they were to board. The first bus would carry the zone one visitors right to the portal (the entrance to the mine); the zone two bus was for the next lot of invited guests, who would be set down a short walk away, at the White Knight Bridge. Everyone else would come in the following buses and make their way along the road from where they were parked. I have the lanyard still. 'Zone two' had been crossed out and 'bus two' had been replaced by 'bus four'.

So we travelled to the foot of that great mountain where the portal stood. Mist swirled around the black beech forest. When everyone was assembled, a loader was to have removed the seal that had been placed there by Solid Energy but, owing to the delay, that didn't happen. Members of the newly established Pike River Recovery Agency were to have entered the drift at this point. We did get to walk up to the portal face and touch it. There were blessings and speeches, and some songs.

Late that afternoon, back at Moonlight Hall, I caught up with the Monks again, and met Rebecca Macfie, chronicler of the disaster. As we stood in the paddock, I caught glimmerings of what had happened during my absence.

Because of the tight rein the government had put on the FRG, there was now a widespread perception that decisions were not being relayed beyond the nucleus of the group. When it came to information, you were either in or you were out. A year later, Bernie had chosen to be out.

Over dinner that night, I was told that some families later felt they were being excluded from information. Bernie had been asked to sign a confidentiality agreement, which meant that he couldn't be as open and transparent as he wished. His door had been open twenty-four hours a day and that was the way he wanted to keep it. Initially, he had signed the document, but when some of the families expressed their concerns, he had decided that what he was doing didn't sit with his beliefs. He was now a spokesperson for twenty-two of the families; this group is the Pike River Families Committee.

Bernie shook his head. 'Anna and I should be on the same page,' he said.

But they weren't any more.

I hadn't known any of this on my return to Pike River. It seemed that I was out too.

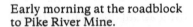

Early morning at the roadblock
to Pike River Mine.

3

I walked along the shingly rough beach again. It was a surly morning, cold, short, green waves curling and collapsing at my feet. I thought I might not come back, but then again, that a part of me might never leave. I knew about the margins of the world and about desolation. I knew something about coal. I understood that it was no longer as necessary in people's lives as it had once been. Were coal miners easy for the world beyond to forget? There are times when your life feels as if it is falling apart, when you think you're the only person in the world who is experiencing grief. I knew about accidents. Accidents happen. The moment is so sudden, so unpredictable.

But hadn't the miners who shovelled coal in the Pike River Mine understood that things were not right? Wasn't this accident one that could have been prevented?

'Things fall apart, the centre cannot hold' – that line from Yeats' poem may be well worn but it's still true. Grief is an irrational force, so overwhelming, so particular to the individual, that once it's entered there's no predicting how it will take and turn you.

What is one person's good decision is another's hell.

Bernie and Kath, Anna, Sonya, Rowdy - broken hearts, all of them, just like mine. But now the team was divided, torn apart by their sorrow.

Ian walked beside me on the beach that morning. I had a plane to catch, back to Wellington and another ordered world, one where I could plunge once more into the daily round of life, the place where I kept myself intact *after the fall*. I could have let the mine go then, the way I was trying to let go of the past and not having much luck.

But some things you can't quit. There were still no answers to what happened that day in the mine. The voices of the twenty-nine were still to be heard.

With Ian at the picket line.

4

The Legislative Council Chamber at Parliament is approached through a Grand Hall, covered with a ceiling of stained-glass domes. The chamber itself is an ornate room surrounded on its upper floor by galleries. A canopy of puriri supports Italian marble pillars and the panelled walls are made of heart rimu. The carpet is a deep shade of red. This lush room has been obsolete for seventy years when it comes to parliamentary procedure. It's used for formal occasions, like the state opening of Parliament by the Queen if she happens to be in New Zealand, or by the governor-general if she's not. It hosts other big gatherings that are important to the government, such as this commemorative service to mark the tenth anniversary of the first explosion at Pike River Mine. I'd been invited. The crowd was very well groomed.

By then the re-entry of the mine had been in progress for more than two years. It seemed to be going well, a skilful operation. Nobody had been hurt.

The room filled with hundreds of people. I introduced myself to the man sitting beside me, Steve Hurring, Helen Kelly's husband.

During the tributes, a clip of Helen speaking would be played.

As speeches were made – by the prime minister, by Rowdy and Sonya – we were reminded of the explosion that had happened at 3.44 p.m. on a Friday afternoon. And at exactly 3.44 p.m. on this day, we kept a minute's silence. We remembered the twenty-nine men who had died and also paid tribute to Daniel Rockhouse and Russell Smith, the two who had made it to the surface, barely conscious and smelling of methane. When the power failed, the ventilation fan stopped. And yet for the next five days the families were told that the men might still be alive in the refuge chamber, where there would be fresh air, first aid and drinking water. This was the refuge chamber that Daniel and Russell had attempted to use during their escape, but realised had been decommissioned months earlier.

Anna Osborne had written a powerful reflection for the order of service, remembering her husband. She reminded readers that Milton, or Milt, as she called him, had been a town councillor and a volunteer firefighter, who had spent his life helping people. She had to keep going for him. Anna has been unwell for most of the years since the explosion; she now uses a crutch. The toll of the fight has been heavy.

Drinks and refreshments followed in the Grand Hall. I didn't know anybody. I did spot the PR people, but they were busy. They usually were.

Down at Aratau, other mining families had gathered at the memorial rock garden.

5

It's 15 July 2021. Another six months have slid by. The other day a call came from Bernie Monk. The Pike River Recovery Agency had reached the end of the drift a couple of months ago, where they had recovered various debris, but neither human remains, nor the drift runner. About 30 metres between the end of the drift and the mine entrance there is a blockage, what they call a rockfall.

It's not a rockfall, Bernie tells me, it's coal - not hard for miners to shift. Tony Forster has formulated a workable plan to move the debris, to get to the electrical equipment and the vital evidence they're looking for. But the government has said, Enough is enough, we are not going any further. Too costly, too dangerous. They plan to seal the mine in a week or so.

So here we are, back where we started years ago.

I've been talking to friends about this over the past days. Some of them have told me to stop. Stop going on and on, it was all a long time ago. But of course it's a long time ago; that's what inert governments want people to think; they wear down opinion, just by dragging things out. My friends think I should stop beating myself up, it's not my responsibility. Neither is finding justice for Albert Black or seeking understanding for Jean Batten. But justice, understanding, truth – they are surely the responsibility of us all.

And with those thoughts in my head, I find myself on a Wellington street corner waiting for Pike River family members and their new lawyer, Paddy, who went to high school with Michael Monk. He has taken up the fight for an old mate.

I'm waiting with Tom and Jack, members of the World Socialist Organisation. Tom interviewed me a week or so beforehand. Friends have taken to calling me Pinko. I wonder to myself what my aunts and uncles would have said, and smile inwardly. They knew I was trouble. It's cold out here on the street. We were to have met at the café next door to the High Court but it's closed. The plane from Hokitika is late; it's graduation day in the city and the streets are teeming with students in their gowns; a major road into the city is closed for repairs and the taxis bearing Bernie and Kath and Paddy have trouble getting through the traffic chaos. Outside the High Court a bevy of media people shiver in the wind. We don't look at them; the moment hasn't come. We are joined by Chloe and Kilani, mother and twelve-year-old son, the boy an extraordinary young speaker, fatherless since his infancy; he will address the cameras repeatedly before the day is out. Carol and Steve arrive, their only child one of the twenty-nine. Carol had met one of her boy's mates in the airport. She hadn't seen him for a long time, and her first thought was, Goodness, he's got old. Then she remembered that her son would have grown older too.

Eventually, we are all together and it's time to go. We enter the High Court, through security that is tighter than at airports. While most of us wait in reception, Bernie and Paddy go through to the court's registry office and serve an injunction on the government, calling on them to stop. Stop sealing the mine. Stop.

This is how our press release begins:

> Twenty-two of the 29 Pike River families are
> supporting an application for a Judicial Review

filed today challenging the decision made by
Minister Andrew Little which rejects a plan to
continue a short distance into the Pike River mine
and instead begins a process to permanently seal
it before the Police underground investigation has
been completed. The Government has rejected a
proposal by the Pike River Independent Technical
Advisory Group on behalf of the families to
continue into the mine as far as the main fan,
which has been established as the likely source of
the explosion and the most critical forensic site
within the mine. The Technical Advisory Group is
made up of the very same advisors that wrote the
drift re-entry plan which was implemented by the
Pike River Recovery Agency.

The numbers had shifted. Twenty-two families in one group,
three in the other. And the PR people. Four now missing.

Things fall apart.

Divide and conquer.

So it goes. We are outside again, blinking in the deepening
day, the cold biting now. The reporters press in.

I don't know how this will go. I can't tell you what will happen.

I do know that the royal commission of inquiry's findings were
archived back in 2012, with instructions that they not be opened
for a hundred years.

So really, nobody alive will ever know the full story. Not the
families and their children. Not grandchildren born since the
explosion.

All we can know, on a cold day in the capital, is that the fight
for Pike River goes on. We will never stop fighting, Bernie says.
Never. I try to imagine what it would be like if 29 people were
buried in rubble under Wellington.

6

There are things I don't understand about the aftermath of the Pike River Mine tragedy, and I don't expect I ever will. Some will say it was about money, others that it was about individuals, others that it was simply a government which lost interest or had its own back to cover and that government agencies were being protected. I can't speak to those. Elsewhere, I have written about outsiders. I have felt like one myself – when I was a child, again when I was a young mother starting my life as a writer in suburbia and, later again, when I stood outside the mainstream of mid-twentieth century writing in this country. I cannot claim to be an outsider now. But I recognise it when I see it in others.

At Pike River, I saw a group of proudly independent people, battlers not victims, working at the margins of the land, who perceived themselves as outsiders, caught up in terrible events, struggling to make their voices heard. It had fallen to them to learn the language of power, the trappings and guile behind successive governments, to accept the indifference of people beyond the community who wanted them to 'move on', to hold on to what they each saw as the truth of their loss.

But truth is slippery and one person's truth is not necessarily another's. Perhaps that's what it comes down to, people seeing things differently. After a while, perceptions blur and what once seemed clear cut is not so any more. At least I understand that.

In March 2021, Andrew Little had told Cabinet he would not seek further funding to explore the mine workings. Apparently, he had told the Family Reference Group about this, but not the twenty-two families who no longer saw themselves as fully represented. In July 2021, the sealing of the mine began: 30 metres of concrete now blocks the access tunnel. In September, Little and Bernie Monk released a joint statement as part of an agreement with the families' lawyers to end the legal action begun earlier in the year. It says: 'Towards the tail-end of 2019 the Minister had foreshadowed to the Family Reference Group that going beyond the drift was unlikely. The Minister now accepts that the families who were not represented by the FRG were not advised and were not included in this communication.' Further on he says he 'accepts that his decision not to explore the feasibility of re-entering the mine workings should have been communicated to all Pike River Family members before it was presented to Cabinet' and that this 'caused hurt to several family members as a result'.

Post script. Subsequent to the High Court action which had to be abandoned, Pike River Mine was sealed in mid-2021. A process of drilling bore holes into the mine from the surface was then begun by police, and cameras dropped down them.

On 17 November 2021, almost eleven years to the day after the disaster, intact human remains were discovered. It appears that they cannot be recovered now; so far there is no evidence of a fire in the area where these men were found. We do not know how long they survived the first blast. This is one of those stories that can never end, will never be told in its entirety, a legacy of pain that can never be healed.

99 Albany Street

The journey to 99 Albany Street begins at Broad Bay, on the Otago Peninsula near the city of Dunedin. A huddle of houses sits beside a wide sweep of coastline, a broad scoop indeed of a peaceful sea. Its name, in the time of first settlement by Kāi Tahu, Kāti Māmoe and Waitaha, was Whakaohorahi, a place where food, including kaimoana and tī kōuka or cabbage tree, was gathered. Many hapū lived near the harbour and its estuaries, enjoying a hunting and gathering lifestyle. The peninsula's early name, and of the surrounding area, was Muaūpoko, and the main village was Ōtākou. In the 1830s, whalers and sealers from Australia arrived on its shores and, it is said, began referring to the area as Otago. This name was adopted by European farmers when they arrived in the 1850s. Meanwhile, historic Ōtākou Marae, near the harbour mouth, was one of the places where the Treaty of Waitangi was signed in 1840. Those who signed were descended from ancestors of all three tribes.

The main settlers had come from Scotland, buying into Wakefield's New Zealand Company scheme. The name of

Dunedin is from the Scottish Gaelic name for Edinburgh: Dùn Èideann. The bay became a shipping destination too. William Larnach used it to land materials required for building his famous castle further along the peninsula.

And for a while, in the Edwardian era, Broad Bay became known as a seaside resort. Seasonal regattas were held, newly wealthy town dwellers built pretty villas on the hill above, more informal cottages called 'cribs' were set up as holiday homes.

I stayed in a seaside cottage in the spring of 2021. It's called the Caselberg Cottage, after the previous owners, John and Anna, a writer and artist. They had wanted their home to become a retreat for artists like themselves, and it was acquired by a group of people who wanted to turn that dream into a reality. Before the Caselbergs, it had been owned by Charles Brasch, the founding editor of the literary periodical *Landfall*. I am one of a long line of writers who have inhabited this space, surely among the quietest places on earth. The garden overlooks a shaft of the sea, revealed between sentinel trees. I figure the trees have been there a long time. One of the oak trees has epiphytes growing on its branches, air plants sustained by its host, like Tāne Mahuta, the giant kauri tree in the north. Below lies the beach, steps cut in the bank to the rocky shore. In the evenings, I sat at a small table in the garden, drank a glass of wine, watched the bird life on the water, listened to the sound of my own breathing, counted the rhythms of my heart.

Each morning, I climbed a hill, and set off for the bus stop by the boatsheds. I passed other cottages transformed into chic houses, surrounded by vegetable-rich gardens; a place that looked like a latter-day hippie commune; a courtyard furnished by a table circled by eight large empty black chairs, as if a meeting were about to take place; the turn-off to a cemetery on a headland of bare earth dried by sun and sea winds, graveyard to Scots and Irish settlers. I boarded a bus that wound around the long coastline until I came to the city and made my way to a small red-brick building at 99 Albany Street.

99 Albany Street is home to the Centre for Irish and Scottish Studies (CISS) at Otago University. Earlier in the year, I was invited by Professor Sonja Tiernan and the department to be the inaugural Irish Studies Writing Fellow, and my tenure was to have lasted some months. In this season of Covid-19, and now of its rapidly moving Delta mutation, this was a truncated attempt to capture what might have been.

The room that I occupied was number 103, up two flights of stairs. The interior of the building is very blue – dark-blue carpet on the treads of the stairwell, doors painted ink-blue with black frames – though the door handles are brass. Some rooms are tucked into hidden spaces, with tongue-and-groove match lining. My room is one of the larger ones, my name on a plaque beneath that of the crime writer Professor Val McDermid, who was the Scottish Writing Fellow earlier on. The plan is to alternate the fellowships year by year. With me, you have two for the price of one, I joked, drawing on my dual heritage: the Sottish mother, the Irish father.

In order to be offered the fellowship one must have some Irish connection. True, I had written a novel about Albert Black, the Irish boy in *This Mortal Boy*, but that's not enough to cut it. It's because of my father that I arrived in this room. That mysterious figure I keep circling back to. If anyone has followed these narratives, they will have seen his uneasy presence throughout them.

I came to my father late, but then many women do. That is, I came to the point where I wanted to understand him better. It's strange the way fathers become kinder people with the long lens of hindsight. Mine was the one who dreamed seemingly impossible dreams, or, if he achieved them, let them go, like mercury in a bottle. Like the long-dreamed-of farm that he abandoned so quickly once it had been acquired. He had roamed the world for a long time before I was born. In San Francisco, he had sung in light opera and been engaged to a girl called Sybella; in Vancouver, he had jumped ship, and been saved from prison by his Irish uncles, who had emigrated to Canada and become Mounties; in Perth, he had waited on the railway station for my mother to cross the Nullarbor Plain and marry him. He had worn a Donegal tweed jacket and a tie, in spite of the heat, my mother told me. He would wash up with her in New Zealand, a country he never particularly liked, and never left after my birth. By the time that we lived permanently under the same roof, nearly six years and a world war later, he had become the delicate, sad person I never really understood, nor I believe did he me.

I have wondered from time to time what his original accent really sounded like. Although he had been born in Middlesbrough, and spent much of his childhood in Bandon, County Cork, he spoke what I recognised later as BBC received English, a cultivated voice with taut vowels. It was his wish that I learned to speak with his accent, to know 'the King's English'. To speak 'properly'. He sent up the way children I went to school with spoke, imitating them with exaggerated nasal noises. His mission was to transform my voice into that of a well-educated British schoolgirl and, when I spoke, he would often stop me in order to correct my pronunciation. Sometimes I would say, But did you hear *what* I said, not *how* I said it? Or did I say this under my breath? Or perhaps in my head, for I can't remember ever getting a response to this question.

He did other things, too. Like deciding to go off and wash his jerseys when my mother's brothers and sisters paid a Sunday afternoon visit.

Or refusing to have a car, even though we lived miles from anywhere.

Or, when I was a teenager, not allowing us to have a telephone in the house.

Most of all, not to have a Kiwi accent within earshot at the dinner table.

But, without him, I wouldn't have made it to Room 103.

Without his Irish DNA.

What did I do in Room 103? People asked me what my project was. Well, nobody ever asked me to have a project when I became the Irish Studies Fellow, and for this I give great thanks. Writers, and artists of most callings, have to account for themselves these days before they get any support at all. Tell us what you will write, the people holding the purse strings say. Allow us to decide how worthwhile this project of yours will be, let us monitor you, measure your creativity, and then we will think about whether you get these funds that we will proceed to audit with care. Never mind the desperation that has driven one to write an application based on any wild scheme that may be impossible to fulfil, once faced with computer and the blank space beyond. No. The Irish Studies people said just come along, and *be* a little with us. I love them for it. Which is not to say that I had nothing in mind.

I had had earlier close encounters with the department. The Scottish co-chair and professor, Liam McIlvanney, is a crime writer, and his brain-child was the Celtic Noir Festival, to which he had invited me two years earlier. It was there I'd first met Val McDermid, and Liz Nugent from Dublin, and Vanda Symon, the Dunedin crime writer. I'd been ushered into the dark halls of crime writing via *This Mortal Boy* after it won a prize for being the best crime novel of the year it came out. That still surprises me. I hadn't thought much about the crime when I wrote it, more about a young man's bad timing and misfortune. The book was never a whodunnit. It tells you what the crime is alleged to be from the first page, and what is going to happen to the perpetrator is writ loud. Yet, secretly, I was proud, because lurking in my short stories there is quite a lot of crime and problems to be solved. People have a habit of disappearing in mysterious circumstances, often near rivers. Crimes are hidden for generations in my stories and, in the end, nobody gets called to account, which I think is often how life is.

Anyway, I'd also met the writer Emer Lyons, who works in the department, and our first encounter had its own surprises. She is quintessential Irish, wide green eyes, red-blonde hair, a manner as lively as a dancer. Where is your home town? I asked her, to which she replied Bandon, County Cork.

And when I said, well, that is where my granny came from too, she asked the next question of me. Where in Bandon?

St Patrick's Quay.

That is where I grew up, she told me then.

So, there was already a feeling of homecoming when I arrived at Room 103, some innate sense of belonging. In association with the Embassy of Ireland, Sonja had conducted a survey the year before, mapping the Irish community and people of Irish heritage in Aotearoa New Zealand. There is an estimate, based on this research, that suggests some six-hundred-thousand people fit this description. I had never been alone, I just hadn't seen it. Nor, I guess, had my dad, but then this Irishness was not borne with distinction when he came here. Neither had it been a badge of honour when Albert Black arrived. There has been a steady influx of skilled Irish workers arriving in the country since 2000. The face of the diaspora has changed.

The Embassy of Ireland was established in Wellington in 2017 by Ambassador Peter Ryan. One of the things that I have noticed at gatherings he and his wife Theresa host is the diverse range of people they ask along: people from every walk of life, there is little sense of a formal diplomatic function. And the ambassador associates closely with Māori culture. In his company, New Zealanders are acknowledged as a mixture of people, and the embassy provides a natural meeting ground.

I thought about this a great deal during my time in Dunedin. It was never my project, but what I spent a fair bit of time doing in Room 103 was re-reading a play by the Irish playwright Brian Friel, called *Translations*. Peter Ryan had given me a copy of it. I wondered at first why he had given it to me, but as soon as I began to read I was struck by parallels between the colonisation of Ireland by the British and of Aotearoa, the way language had robbed the land, in each case, of its true meaning and identity. At almost exactly the same time as the sealers and whalers were arriving on the Ōtākou peninsula, in Ireland, the British were replacing Irish law and language.

I knew my Synge and Behan and Beckett and some other of the twentieth century Irish playwrights. But, somehow, I was not aware of Friel, who has been described — I've heard since — as the 'Irish Chekhov'. *Translations* is simply one of the best plays

I've come across in a long time. I need to explain here why that is: the play is set in 1833 in County Donegal in a hedge school, one of the small illegal schools set up to teach children from faiths that didn't conform with the governing Anglicans (in other words, Catholics or Presbyterians). A young teacher is coaxing a girl with speech difficulties to speak; straight away we recognise the constraints of language, the necessity to have a voice if we are to survive in the world. Manus, the teacher, is the son of Hugh, the master (Hugh, by the way, was my father's name). The audience is given to understand that the language spoken is Irish Gaelic, though the play is primarily written in English. Few of those assembled speak English, although Greek and Latin are taught and some of the cast are fluent speakers of these languages, too.

Manus is poor, like everyone there, but he dreams of marrying Máire. Close by, a detachment of the Royal Engineers has camped. Their job in Ireland is to make an Ordnance Survey, in other words to map the country for the benefit of the English government. In order to do this, they need the Gaelic place names to be recorded in an English version. Their surprise translator is Hugh's older son and Manus's brother, Owen, who has been absent a fair while and is now fluent in both languages. He comes upon the gathering of students and masters.

Manus asks his brother if he has enlisted, to which Owen replies: 'Me a soldier? I'm employed as a part time, underpaid, civilian interpreter. My job is to translate the quaint archaic tongue you people persist in speaking into the King's good English.'

And you can see how things will go downhill from there. The man in charge of the military detachment is starchy and self-opinionated Captain Lancey. He arrives accompanied by a lieutenant called Yolland. Yolland's job will be to enter the new names of every hill, stream, rock, every piece of ground in a Name Book. Owen's function is to pronounce each name in Irish and then provide the English translation. Lancey sets out to explain what is going to happen - a 'general triangulation which will embrace detailed hydrographic and topographic information which will be executed on a scale of six inches to the English mile'. He looks to Owen to interpret.

Owen says easily, 'A new map is being made of the whole country.'

Later, Manus will say to his brother, but you didn't translate everything.

So the days roll on, and Croc Ban, which means Fair Hill, becomes Knockban, and Bun na hAbhann, which literally means the mouth of the river, somehow becomes Burnfoot, and a ridge called Druim Dubh becomes mixed up with the name of the place they named the day before.

But even as the landscape takes on new meanings, Yolland is being drawn in and tempted by an Ireland that appears more appealing than his life in England. His eyes have turned with yearning towards Máire, and he wants to learn Irish. He says longingly, 'Even if I did speak Irish I'd always be an outsider here, wouldn't I. I may learn the password but the language of the tribe will always elude me, won't it? The private core will always be . . . hermetic, won't it?'

It's Hugh, the father, who tells the lieutenant that Irish is a rich language, full of mythologies of fantasy and hope and self-deception — a syntax opulent with tomorrows.

But the warning is not enough. Yolland will pay for his fantasies with his life, and in return Lancey will see that the village pays with their homes and their livelihoods.

And so, I see that some histories are universal. Wars happen, people are pulled apart from one another, land is lost because of words and the way they can be misinterpreted. I see how a people can be colonised by language. Inevitably, I look to the way that Aotearoa New Zealand's history was rewritten from the time that settlers renamed it. I may be from settler stock on one frontier, but I see what language does to strip people of their identity; it's similar to the way people of different cultures change their names in order to blend with what they perceive as the common voice, usually through anglicisation. I live in a village suburb known as Hataitai in the city of Wellington. But once I might have said that I lived in Whātaitai, named after one of the taniwha that is said to have created the harbour of Te Whanganui-a-Tara, otherwise The Great Harbour of Tara, and all of these old words are beautiful to say. The W has been dropped from Hataitai, and even if it were still spelled in its original version, the area referred to then is situated some kilometres away from here. As for Wellington, named by the New Zealand Company, it reflects the Duke of Wellington, the victor at the Battle of Waterloo in 1815. This seems utterly irrelevant in terms of our harbour.

As for the stretch of water that I overlook, it's called Cook Strait, after the English explorer Captain Cook, but Māori know it as Te Moana-o-Raukawa. Many places were named by Captain Cook; perhaps you can't blame him for this, he didn't know what to call places he saw for the first time and, like the Royal Engineers who couldn't get their tongues around the Gaelic words, te reo Māori might have been just too difficult. Some of Cook's names have a sting — he called Te Kauwae-a-Māui Cape Kidnappers, following an altercation with a local tribe member. Who knows what part language may have had to play?

For that matter, my father hero-worshipped Cook and, stripped away of its romanticism, his own cloudy past reveals some uncomfortable truths, including his family's association with the Royal Irish Constabulary, set up to police hedge schools. His accent and insistence on the King's English mark him out as descending from a position of authority, although that was not apparent in the life that he led in this country. It was not until I read Friel's play that I made this connection between the RIC and hedge schools. But perhaps I should acknowledge that in the English that I speak, I may have inadvertently inherited some of that long-ago privilege.

What we need when we learn a language are also the words that heal. We cannot undo the past, but in confronting it we have the opportunity to do better; in particular, to listen with respect to the languages that others speak. If learning correct English was painful for me as a child, I better understand how difficult it must be for those new to Aotearoa, speaking a different language, who must start from the beginning.

I do not speak te reo, although its vocabulary cross-references into my everyday conversations. But I have listened to the language for almost as long as I can remember, its rhythms and cadences familiar. Ian, my husband, spoke it as a young child when he lived with his grandparents in the King Country, but then lost it when he started school, where Māori was not allowed to be spoken. He felt this loss, and yet it was never really gone, lying dormant in hidden parts of his memory, suddenly appearing when neither he nor his listeners expected it. I remember his shy startled look when it crept up on him like that. While I lay no claim to the language, I believe that restoring it to its rightful place is essential to our collective understanding of who we are. In *Translations*, Hugh the father says, towards the end of the play, that 'it is not the literal past, the "facts" of history that shape us, but images of the past embodied in language . . . We must never cease renewing those images, because once we do, we fossilise.'

Which brings me back with sorrow and some regret to Hugh, my own father. I wish we had understood each other better. I wanted his physical presence and his affection in a way that was hard for him to show, and I think now I may have hardened towards him. He had lost the power of speech on his deathbed. It was a late move, but I told him I loved him and gave him the little notebook and pencil he was using to communicate. He wrote in shadowy lettering 'Nothing to say'. Perhaps he could have added the word 'more'— *nothing more to say*. If I thought at the time that language had failed us both, I think now that I was wrong. In some ways, my father had little, but what he had, he wanted to give me, his gift the power to speak with eloquence when it was demanded of me. To understand and articulate the language I was given. It has taken me further than either of us imagined. This was the best he could do and, in turning to look back over my shoulder, I see that he gave me a richness in my being.

But sometimes when I listen to Gaelic-speaking friends, I will hear a sudden familiar note, a timbre, and find myself wondering what else my father knew.

These are some of the things I thought about in Room 103. I didn't do much else.

The door to Room 103
at 99 Albany Street,
Dunedin, 2021.

This new condition

Truffles

This is not really about truffles, although they come into it. It's about a man called Luc Lanlo. Ian and I met him in Menton in 2006, that magical year when we lived in the south of France, purring away our days in a Provençal apartment overlooking the Mediterranean. The dream time. The place I wake up some mornings and still see: the blond sand on the seashore; the wild dahlia-red skies of evening; the town pink and gold in the afternoon light.

I was in Menton because New Zealand still honours Katherine Mansfield and sends a writer there every year to live in the south of France, as she did. We had been there just a few days when the deputy mayor held a reception for us. This was Luc, a vivid dark man, born in Madagascar. A man who loved this town and loved literature, and somehow, astonishingly, seemed to love us. The love affair between all of us began the moment we set eyes on one other. When I say all of us, there were Luc and his husband, art historian Michel Imbert, and Michel's mother Berthe, and Ian and me. Neither Luc nor Berthe spoke English, and Ian spoke no French. My French is halting; Michel and I bridged as many gaps as possible. I think back to the 'conversations' we had with Luc when Michel was absent with a kind of wonder. All I can say is that they worked.

That first meeting took place beneath a canopy of Jean Cocteau artwork, the ceiling of La Salle des Mariages, city hall's official wedding room. There was a small function held to hand over the keys to the Katherine Mansfield room in Villa Isola Bella, near the edge of the Italian border. Then Luc, in a sudden gleeful moment, decided that Ian and I needed a second marriage ceremony and so we were united again, before I could say a word. What followed, during that sojourn on the Côte d'Azur, were concerts with our new friends, beachside dinners, trips to the mountains, conversations in the town square, and surprises sprung upon us in a spirit of merriment.

Luc and Michel and Berthe owned a winter house on the edge of the sea in Menton and a summer house in the medieval village of Gorbio, which nestles among hills, bougainvillea lacing its walls. The people who live there are called Gorbarins. Beneath Gorbio lies Monaco, in one direction, and Italy in the other. Some days we would go to Gorbio on the bus and sit under the shade of a three-hundred-year-old elm tree that spread across the square, or some nights by car with Gordon, a friend from New Zealand.

On the last night ever that the two of us were in Menton, Berthe walked into Italy and gathered truffles. From a market, I supposed. I couldn't see her digging round the roots of oak trees, surely someone must have done that for her, but the truffles were fresh. I have always been fascinated by truffles, their mysterious underground existence, a fungus latched onto its host. I first saw them at a research station near Invercargill, where a scientist was experimenting to see whether they could be successfully grown in New Zealand. They were nuggety little things in a basin, emitting an odd cloying scent. I couldn't match them in my mind's eye with Colette's famous remark that if she couldn't 'have too many truffles' she would 'do without truffles'. But they fired something in my imagination. Years later, I wrote a whole novel dedicated to the search for truffles closer to home. *Songs from the Violet Café* is set in a nameless town, although it's so clearly Rotorua that I've never tried to deny it. There is a lake, an island, purple evenings. The imaginary café stands at the same address where Ian and I lived in the first years of our marriage, a place now occupied by a high-rise motel.

In Gorbio, we feasted on Berthe's ravioli flecked with white *truffe*, and it was different from any truffle I have eaten before or since. We ate saffron prawns too, and blancmange, and drank a dark chardonnay. The table was laid with heavy silver cutlery on a crimson cloth; the walls of the dining room were bone-white stone, decorated with dark red paintings by an Indian artist called Raza. And all the while the lights of two countries glimmered beneath us.

When we came to leave, the family showered us with gifts: a small mirror etched with a Cocteau sketch tucked into a red velvet pouch for me; for Ian, whose birthday it was the next day, a white bone-china plate decorated with a Cocteau drawing. It shows a young man with a flaring nose, a curled lip and a fish for an eye. It hangs in my house still. We all wept then, promising that some day we would meet again. We would come back. Or Luc would come to New Zealand. Somehow the magic would go on.

Luc was at the railway station the next morning to say goodbye again. He helped us load our cases aboard the bullet-nosed TVG bound for Paris. He stood on the platform, his arm raised as the train drew away, gathered speed, took us beyond Menton.

I would see him three more times. Ian never did.

A few months later, I returned to France for a writers' tour. There was a reception at the New Zealand embassy in Paris, hosted by the ambassador, Sarah Dennis. She told me she had a surprise for me – Luc and Michel and Berthe, who had made a special trip to see me. There they were, all lined up, shouting 'Voilà', laughing boisterously at my delight.

Years passed. Luc had relinquished his mayoral duties in the year following our departure. At New Year, he and Michel would phone up at midnight, shouting unintelligible greetings down the line. Then, in 2016, I made a trip south while on a visit to Paris, to see a friend in Marseilles. She and her husband were going to a conference close to Menton and volunteered to drop me off for the day. The town was crammed with people. The family were at their winter place and I had trouble finding my way back there, along the seafront.

It was almost like the old days, only Ian was back home in New Zealand, and the household in Menton had expanded to include Majod, whom Luc and Michel had adopted. I can't remember what we ate that day, but I remember the excitement, the exchange of gifts. One of Majod's roles in the house was to give massages. When I said lightly that was just what I felt like, I was ushered into their specially set-up massage room, facing the sea. I lay down on the table and was ministered to by Majod. It felt as if I had been re-admitted to the family. The new expanded family. We rang Ian and had a conversation that was sleepy at his end. It hit me then, just how much he had been part of the whole Menton venture.

Now Luc said we must walk through the town together. As we made our way through the crowded streets, I remembered other walks. The daily stroll to get an English-language newspaper at the news stand; the way we would often time this for lunchtime, to eat under a tree in the square. Things were the same but not the same. I bought a tablecloth at my favourite linen shop. Luc bought me a huge bottle of limoncello. Just along the street we came to the flight of stone steps that leads up to the local cemetery, where Ian had spent days admiring the ornate designs of the headstones and mausoleums. Our son-in-law had visited us in 2006 and taken a picture of Ian ascending those steps, wearing his little pack, a slight stoop in his back, heading away from us.

I hadn't realised that Menton had a new attraction on the seafront, the magnificent Jean Cocteau Museum, housing hundreds of works bequeathed by Séverin Wunderman, a watch manufacturer and philanthropic art collector. It is a white building that sweeps and swoons around the bay, harbouring what must be the largest collection of Cocteau's works in the world, floor after floor of them. Luc was immensely proud of the building, wanting to show me every inch of it. I had the impression that, while he was still deputy mayor, he had been instrumental in securing funding from a wealthy benefactor. But perhaps I misunderstood:

it was a point where language failed us.

I said goodbye to him after the tour. Somewhere in my heart, I was thinking that I would not go back to Menton, that one cannot recreate some of the best days of one's life when parts of it are missing.

But I did go back.

————

This last visit was unplanned. It was 2018. I had gone to Europe in haste, trying to shake off some demons. Ian had died a few months earlier. At his funeral, we had had the slideshow that everyone includes these days, and it had ended with that photo of his ascending back, as he trudged up the steps towards the cemetery.

All the same, I hadn't planned to go to Menton. I had stayed with a grandson and his partner in the village of Bargemon, in the French Alps above St Tropez, where we had hung out at the markets and eaten some fine meals. The partner's mother owns a splendid house on the perimeter of the village that is said to have been built, at Napoleon's request, for his doctor. My plan was to head for Nice and catch the train into Italy. But when I reached Nice, there was an Italian train strike, and I was stranded for a day or so. It was not so bad. I booked into a hotel. I had friends in Nice, and we arranged to meet for dinner. There was just the day to fill.

I knew where I must go.

So I caught the 100 route bus that took me past Villefranche and Saint-Jean-Cap-Ferrat, past Roquebrune-Cap-Martin, once the home of a distant cousin, the Empress Eugenie (through our common Scottish ancestors, the Kirkpatricks of Dumfries). Past the shining waters and the stone buildings, the unimaginable wealth of Monaco. And in an hour or so I was in Menton, walking the familiar boulevards, until I reached the square and sat beneath the tree that sheltered the lunch table. I phoned Luc and said I was there. I wept uncontrollably while I waited for him. The waiters were bemused. I explained as best I could – 'Mon mari est mort, mort.' I rocked back and forth. They brought me wine and small things to eat. They were kind and solicitous as if they understood this crazed woman from the other side of the world.

Luc came and put his arms around me, held my hands, murmured in French. It wasn't all right, but it was as all right as it could be. Soon Michel arrived too.

It was the best thing I could have done for myself. It was also the hardest. The grief had broken at last.

Now it is the time of Covid.

Luc has died, the first of my friends to be felled by this virus.

Luc est mort.

Adieu, mon ami. Thanks for the memory. Thank you for the laughter.

The blue room

The blue room looked as if it hadn't been slept in for months. In the dull light hanging from the blue ceiling, the windowless room, with its blue painted walls, blue bed cover and blue carpet, seemed shrouded in gloom. It was one o'clock in the morning in Paris. We had travelled, my husband and I, by train from Rome. The man at the desk at the little hotel in Montmartre had no record of our booking. But I did, and so we found ourselves in the emergency room below stairs.

What will we do for a fortnight in Paris? my husband asked. I had been to Paris before but he had not. Right then I had no answer. We would move in the morning, somewhere, anywhere but here, I promised. In the morning we woke to bells chiming. We staggered to the breakfast room. A manager appeared, offering apologies. We would immediately be transferred to the red room upstairs. The red room was as red as the blue room had been blue. We looked now directly into the source of the chiming bells, the exquisite Art Nouveau church of Saint-Jean de Montmartre.

My husband's spirits were lifting. We went outside. On a wall next door to the little hotel the words 'I love you' were painted in one hundred and thirty-two different languages. 'I love you,' my husband said. 'Je t'aime,' I said. 'Te amo,' he said, going all Spanish on me. The words, they were in te reo too. By the metro station at the end of Rue des Abbesses, a man was playing an accordion. My husband went and sat beside him. They smiled at each other.

We decided we would stay on at the little hotel. The next day we were promoted again, to the yellow room at the top. Now we looked directly into the bell tower of the church, and the room glowed as yellow as Monet's kitchen table, as yellow as sunflowers. We declared that we never wanted to leave. Each day we read more and more of the phrases aloud to each other, and each day the accordionist played as if we were the only people in the street.

We came home to New Zealand. Over the years we went back and forth to the little hotel. The last time I was alone and visited without staying. The phrases on the wall had gone. But there was the accordionist, grey, bent over. He played something familiar, as if he remembered. I entered Saint-Jean. I lit a candle. For memory. For hope. Light in dark times.

On widowhood

It was early summer in London: the trees were pale green clouds, the lilacs were out. Because the Chelsea Flower Show was in progress, the arches and doorways of hundreds of shops were decorated in floral splendour. I had an Art Nouveau-style apartment in Lower Sloane Street. In the mornings, fifty horses, perhaps more, were ridden past by uniformed men from the Royal Stables.

During those weeks, I met people, talked, gave readings, laughed feverishly. I did interviews at the BBC. I was also in the first season of widowhood.

———

When someone close to you dies, an undertaker may send you books about grief. The one who organised my husband's funeral did. The little booklets, written by two women who had been widowed, were called *The Colour of Grief*. At first, I was angry when they arrived, as if nobody could access my state of mind, as if my grief was different from that of everyone else who had been through a similar experience. I threw a couple of them away. When I think about that now, I see I was wrong; there was a lot of sensible advice in those booklets. I still have the last one, about the approach of the first anniversary of the death, and recognise how much common sense it contains.

One of the things I like is that the writers acknowledge that people who are grief-stricken can be angry. They might not have liked that I threw their books away but I think they would have understood. Some bereaved people have told me that anger was the last thing on their mind. Others, like me, have felt a sense of rage.

I think it has something to do with powerlessness. Death is not interested in what you want; it gets on with its business and you can't stop it from happening when it's ready. My husband died from an accident at home and it seems, from everyone I've talked to, that sudden death is a likely trigger for what looks from the outside like an unseemly response. That, and medical misadventure.

Men often appear to deal with bereavement differently from women. They either fall apart in an inconsolable way and die. Or they get married again very soon. They are sought after. They get asked out to dinners. People don't refer to them often as widowers. People say, Oh, his wife died, poor chap. Of course, there are exceptions and I hear myself being accused of generalisations straight away. In his memoir, *The Only Story*, the writer Julian Barnes describes the grief of his wife's death in a very intense way. He allowed it to show. But a lot of men don't.

Because I understand widowhood from a female perspective, through the simple fact of being a widow, I chose to talk to other women in the same situation. There are a lot of us around. Even the Queen is one now. Not that widow is a term I care for. It puts a stamp on you. Not in service. Use-by date passed. Or, in a worst-case scenario, huntress on the prowl.

Around about a year after my husband died, I was attending a gathering. A man I knew slightly sat down beside me. 'Found yourself a husband yet?' he said. I nearly fell off my chair. He was an educated man, in a good government job. I think he was sober but you can't always be sure.

'I'm not looking for one,' I said, and it was true.

'Oh, that's what they all say,' he responded, turning away. 'You'll find one.'

I felt a sense of outrage then, of violation, not just of my husband's memory, but of me. I had no interest in finding a husband, and nor have I in the years since. There are pleasures in solitude and the freedom of the single life. They are not exclusive of the company of men, but marriage for the sake of it has not been for me.

What I might have said, that confused evening, was that I had already had some overtures from men who were hardly an advertisement for their kind. One of them clearly wanted a roof over his head. It hadn't occurred to me that I had such financial cachet.

On the make. On your bike, I had said in effect.

Then the question of sex arose, a certainty from others about what I *needed*, and I was undone by this too. I took astonished, diffident trips to the mirror. It was years since I had considered my appearance in this way. Wasn't I already old? I thought of myself as interesting rather than sexy, when it came to men. An interesting friend. It wasn't that I was averse to the notion of sex for older people, but at that moment I had no wish to be touched.

There is a contrariness here, I suppose. What I have missed since my newly single state arrived is touch. Age might have contained desire, but there is a terrible longing for the simple acknowledgement that the two of you exist as living bodies – the hand held, the touch on the back when you are out together, knowing there is someone there when you reach out at night. In the beginning, the loss of touch is a near-inconsolable grief, an ache that dulls with time but doesn't go away. All the same, I knew that whoever might touch me in any way at all had to be of my choosing. In that first bewildering year I felt vulnerable and afraid.

Finding a husband? Not likely.

Yet, in my several male friends, the ones who had been in both Ian's and my lives seemingly forever, I found the same level of tenderness and support that came from my women friends. In our regular conversations and exchanges, they reminded me of who I was and who I am, and who I could trust. My situation might have changed but I had not.

All of this would take time. In the first year of widowhood, I acted in some crazy ways. I mean, I think I was crazy but I persuaded myself I was acting normally. The second week after the funeral, one of my grandsons suggested a trip to the theatre, something he and I had often done together. The following day he was due to return to London where he now lives; it seemed a nice way of saying goodbye. The play was *The Father*, which was later made into a remarkable movie, starring Anthony Hopkins. But the play was sombre, not the right one for the way I was feeling. In the middle of it a man fell off his chair and rolled down the stairs. I screamed loudly; the play faltered and carried on. The man, it turned out, had simply gone to sleep, for he got up and returned to his seat.

Not long after this, I booked a flight to Europe. I left seven months later. I came back, had a new book launched, toured New Zealand with it, talking all the while, bursting into sudden tears now and then. I expected other people to take care of my feelings. To echo Jennifer, one of several friends I interviewed for this essay, I tried to accept kindnesses from others, which is harder than it sounds.

It's been eleven years since Jennifer's husband, Allan Thomas, died from leukaemia. Jennifer is a dancer and a teacher of dance. Allan was a musician and taught music at the university. In the years and months between his diagnosis and his dying, he showed a quiet and unswerving courage. He had studied gamelan music in Amsterdam, then in Cirebon, Java. In the mid-1970s, he brought an ensemble of antique gamelan instruments to New Zealand, and taught courses using it for the next thirty-five years. That is what he kept on doing until the end. Jennifer kept on dancing.

I shared a good deal of time with Jennifer in the weeks and months after Allan's death, but her grief belonged to her. I remember that she got manuscripts Allan had left published that year, but I asked her to remind me of other things she had done. She told me that she:
    sat and stared out the window
    replied to the cards and letters
    bought a push mower to keep the grass down
    planted a tree
    survived an encounter with a bullying bank manager
    hugged the cat and sorted photos
    learned how to check the oil and water and windscreen wiper.
I did most of those things too, although the bank manager was kinder. I keep finding more photographs that have to be sorted. I am still a coward about the oil and water. But acquired helplessness doesn't get you anywhere.

I also kept a message Ian had left on our voicemail, until the phone company cancelled it a year or two later. Something about some shopping he was doing at the supermarket. I liked listening to this message.

———

The first time I went to London, nearly forty years ago, I stayed in a mean bedsit above Eccleston Square. I wrote about that experience in a story called 'The Tennis Player', and the character, so clearly myself, was called Ellen: 'In London she lugged her huge suitcase up five flights of stairs and found herself in a bedsit under the eaves of a building that looked elegant from the outside and was a dump inside. There was a fire escape out to the roof just like in *The Girls of Slender Means*.'

I was using that bedsit as a base while I researched *The Book of Secrets*, vacating it from time to time to make journeys to and from Scotland. I was dreaming that some day my work might be discovered further afield than New Zealand. Alone in that room, I drank German wine and ate imported avocados and fish and chips out of paper bundles. The woman in the next room banged on the wall at night when I turned over in bed. This was the nearest to being on my own that I had been in my entire life. I made collect calls home to my husband nearly every day, wrote letters, sent telegrams. That time remains with me.

And now here I was, back in a bedsit in London, only this one had every kind of creature comfort, and my dreams had long been realised. I knew people all over London. I had a publisher nearby. What I didn't have was a husband back in Wellington. I think it no great coincidence that I had chosen to flee to the other side of the world to relive that early experience of aloneness. In my beautiful apartment in Lower Sloane Street I lived it in a new way, one that no letters, or emails, or phone calls could reach. Two of my grandsons lived in London by then; they came and went, took me to concerts and art galleries and to clubs. They treated me like the invalid I was.

I came to live in Wellington when I was a young woman. In the suburb where we settled, there were several Greek families. On the street I saw widows dressed in black, their heads covered by scarves. I had been to tangihanga up north, where Māori women who had been widowed dressed in black, with green wreaths or pare kawakawa on their heads. But few committed their lives to wearing black as these Greek women did. The traditional period of mourning was forty days, but older women usually donned black for good. My friend Eirini remembers from her childhood her 'great-grandmother and her sister sitting side by side on old wooden chairs outside my great-aunt's house in Strathmore, dressed in that widow's black, knitting and crocheting. They always had a smile.'

At the time when I first came here, I remember thinking how lonely it must be, in a foreign country, to be without a husband, and to identify your solitariness in this way. I thought of Queen Victoria and her long solitude, the way she too wore black for forty years, from the time of Prince Albert's early death until her own. Eirini tells me that it is not the same now, that very few Greek women here wear black forever; they have moved into the new world. But, back then, this cultural distinction announcing their permanent bereavement struck me as profoundly sorrowful.

At the Cambodian Buddhist temple where Ian worshipped, and I frequently visited, I saw widows who wore either white with black scarves, or black with white scarves. Some shaved their heads. This period of mourning would last for around three months. But for older women it often went on for longer, even for life. Some of the women, who were collectively known as 'the old ladies', had come via the refugee camps after Pol Pot and the scourge of the Khmer Rouge; their husbands had died in the camps or soon after their arrival. They sat on the temple floor, intermittently pouring cups of tea for one another and for visitors, and praying. There was no going back, they were stranded by death in a community in which their identity and status was signified by their mourning garments. They must spend the rest of their days chanting in a land far away from home. They are comforted by the certainty that they will be reunited with those they have loved. Meanwhile, they have one another.

And in a different way, that is what I have too, that shared experience. Friendship is what has kept me going in recent years. My mother barely mentioned her bereavement after my father's death; her sister, my aunt, not at all, although her widowhood lasted forty years. It wasn't done to mourn publicly. But that wouldn't work for me. The partner of a close friend died a month almost to the day before Ian. Our intimate and seemingly endless conversations have sustained me, our experiences of grief and our interactions with the world outside often mirroring one another.

Beth Darroch, another friend, was fifty-nine when her husband
Paddy died after a short battle with acute leukaemia. He was a
policeman, a couple of years older than her. That was sixteen
years ago. She lives now in a beautiful restored villa, full of light
and charm. She is serene, the way I've always known her. When
we first met, she was the nurse at my doctor's surgery, where she
worked for years, a strong presence upon whom people in our
community depended. As it happens, and perhaps that is why
we turned instinctively to Beth, her life has been one of service.
Her mother died in a car crash when she was twenty-four and
already had two children of her own. Beth took on much of the
responsibility for her eight younger siblings. And then her sister-
in-law died of a sudden illness and left six young children, and
their lives merged into hers. All these children. But the church
supported and helped them, she told me. There was nothing they
wouldn't do to help.

I said to her at the surgery one day, not long after Paddy died,
how desperately sorry I was, how I had no words to express this.
She said, with customary stoicism, 'It's not the worst thing that
could happen.' I didn't then know about the earlier part of her
life. The back story. Thinking over that day, I see that it was as
bad as it gets, but carrying on, showing a brave face, was what
Beth had always done, how she survived.

Nor did I understand the strength of the faith she and Paddy
shared. Paddy went most days in his lunch hour to Mass at St
Mary of the Angels in central Wellington. Beth is still a regular
churchgoer.

'Do you believe you will see Paddy again?' I asked her recently.

She gave me a slightly puzzled look. 'Of course I will,' she said.

If some widows put their faith in what is to come, others assert their place in the present, perhaps even more firmly than when their husbands were alive. A friend reminded me of a film where the widow puts her wedding ring into her husband's coffin. She reckoned that was a brave acceptance of 'till death do us part', marking the start of a new existence. I couldn't have parted with my wedding ring like that. But the day would come when I did remove it. My wedding ring finger had swollen and I eased the ring off. At first, I couldn't think what to do with it. In fact, for a week I went back and forth to check that I hadn't lost it and attempted unsuccessfully to jam it back on. If I saw anyone, I tried to hide my hand, as if I was being unfaithful to the past. At that point, I began to ask myself if I wanted to have the ring enlarged so I could continue to wear it or, on the other hand, to wonder about the significance of leaving it off for good.

I had first received the ring when I was twenty, in a wedding ceremony in the Māori Anglican church of St Faith's beside Lake Rotorua. Steam rose outside from underground thermal streams, the rain pelted down, I wore a cream satin gown modelled on Princess Margaret's wedding dress (she had married Antony Armstrong-Jones three months earlier). I made my vows, promising to love, honour and cherish – but not obey: I was prescient about that – till death did us part. I accepted the ring, a thick gold band, surrounded on each rim by a milled pattern, expecting that I would never take it off. Rings for men were not fashionable then, and so Ian did not get one. It was later, when we had been married for several decades, and he was gravely ill, that he asked for one. I measured his finger and bought him a wide chunky ring that I gave him in hospital. He wore it until he died, years later.

The thing, of course, is that death *did* part us in the end. You don't think about that when you are twenty. It can't happen. Or so you believe.

At some point, widowhood becomes less about grieving and more about living. Living as well as you can, not just about survival. There is more to life than that. Nobody can tell you whether to wear your ring or not. There is no time frame for taking a ring off. But I did discover some interesting views on the subject. I was told that keeping it on implied one was unavailable for new relationships. This hadn't occurred to me. I did still feel as if I was married, even if my husband had died. When I thought about that, I asked myself if leaving it off might be a step towards my life as a single woman. Besides, the ring is so worn and thin, the milled rims long vanished, that I couldn't see how it could be successfully altered. Another option was to move it to my right hand, which is apparently a universal sign that you are a widow or widower. But my right hand is larger than my left. And, I'm told, it indicates that you may be interested in dating.

That hadn't occurred to me either. Some of my friends have turned to dating apps, looking for companionship. I can't tell you anything about this. I didn't think it would suit me, any more than a second marriage.

In the end, I chose to put my ring in a silver box inside the circle of my husband's wedding band. The weight and heft of that ring places mine inside a safe space.

Where my ring once sat on my finger there is a deep indentation, a permanent mark, almost like a scar.

Brigitte Blakemore said, 'Whatever you put in this story, tell people not to get married in a hurry.' It's hard to imagine her as anything but the dynamic person she is now, an easy talker, overflowing with energy. But, as she tells it, it becomes clear that the way has not always been easy since she became a young widow.

She was thirty-seven when Kevin, her builder husband, died of a degenerative illness. There had been a misdiagnosis, then two years of being in and out of hospital. Even though there were long warning signs, his death in a hospice came as a shock to her and her two children. Kevin was an incredibly hard worker, a man popular with their friends, an optimist; this wasn't supposed to happen to him. They had met when she was sixteen, barely out of school, teenage sweethearts – he was the great love of her life. When he died, she had cried for days on end, until her eleven-year-old son begged her to stop. You're torturing me, he said. She'd thought about ending things; nothing made sense to her any more.

Brigitte is a person with natural resilience and she did get a great deal of support. Besides, there were the two children who needed her. The opportunity for a new career presented itself; she took it with both hands and has succeeded ever since.

Some acquaintances had been dismissive, especially those who were divorced. You get all the flowers and the sympathy, they said, we get nothing. It shocked Brigitte at the time. But, looking back, she takes their point.

She has learned to question situations more closely. Her second marriage, four years after widowhood, lasted two years. It still troubles her, in the sense that she doesn't want to see other younger women in the same situation. 'My doctor told me at the beginning, whatever you do, don't rush into marriage. Take your time. My chemist said the same thing. Friends said it. But you know, there were men out there who were interested in me and I was lonely. I never sought them out, never did dating sites, nothing like that, and I thought the man I married was all right. But he wasn't.'

She learned from the experience and has found a rich life. These days, as I do, she lives in an intergenerational household. Hers includes her daughter, son-in-law, grandchildren. Her laughter is quick, her optimism bubbles; the next adventure is just around the corner.

———

In London, I often walked along Ebury Street to the offices of my publisher, Gallic Books, in Eccleston Street, with the bookshop Belgravia Books under the same roof. I had three books on the go that year, the one that was due to be released in New Zealand, which I had already started promoting from afar, an earlier title that had just appeared in London, and a still-earlier one that my Paris publisher had recently released. When I arrived over there, I would begin a French bookshop tour. There was plenty to occupy my thoughts. I liked to walk past No. 182 Ebury Street, the early home of the writer Vita Sackville-West and her diplomat husband, Harold Nicolson. Vita was also famously the lover of Virginia Woolf. The house has a deep-red door with a brass knocker, set in a white façade; black wrought-iron fences. It made me think of unusual marriages. I hadn't had one like theirs, a gay man and woman who somehow made their unconventional lifestyle succeed. But I had had a marriage that was different in its way, one in which we offered each other freedom to come and go when we needed. Now the freedom came without permission. I was responsible only to myself. I determined to make a trip to Sissinghurst to see Vita's famous white garden.

My grandsons took me there one day, driving in the older one's aged Mercedes. We got lost on the way, we laughed and FaceTimed with their brothers back in New Zealand, until we eventually made it through the sunlit Kent countryside to the most famous garden in England. If the grey, white and silver garden is Vita's creation, the whole vast garden is hers and Harold's. Irises nestled in the grasses, white tulips swayed between the paths. I climbed the stairs in the tower of Sissinghurst Castle to Vita's room, where she wrote her poems and plays and love letters to Harold and other people besides Harold. Her desk was covered with deep sultry red leather, books and paintings crowded the walls. Here was the world of a writer who had surrounded herself with beautiful things, but whose life was conducted in a way that contradicted all expectations of order. Had we, Ian and I, been as different in our way as these two were? Ian had said more than once that we were different. Is it the fate of the woman writer to be seen as different? I can't tell you that either. But people are curious about this. What I think now, is, that, in our life and in our marriage, it was the difference we made together.

On that early summer's day, the perfume of roses drifted up and around me. I remember gasping with pleasure. On the way out, my grandsons bought me a tiny white jug painted with violets; it's on my kitchen windowsill, one of those treasured precious bits of clutter that adorn my house and remind me of perfect days. This was one of them.

It was a revelation to me, that it was still possible to have one. There have been others since.

On the plane on the way back to New Zealand, I recorded, at last, what had befallen me over the previous months. It is all written down in a blue notebook.

———

As I have travelled over the years, the question of eating out alone has arisen. Often, there isn't much choice. I made the first leaps in Crete, decades ago. I remember eating fish, with side dishes of green beans tossed in olive oil and lemon, in a seaside taverna, stray cats moving between my feet waiting for scraps, drinking a small beaker of wine and, astonishingly, thinking I had never been more grown up or quite as happy. Joan Didion wrote somewhere that a woman who was afraid to dine alone still had a long way to go towards maturity, or words to that effect, and I agree. Whenever I go to Paris, on my first night in the city, I invariably race to the Café Neo in St Germain, to eat an omelette and drink a glass of wine, and watch the world go by and feel that I am part of it all.

But widowhood takes lone dining into a different dimension. It's not just about dining out, of course; it's what happens every day. The choice has been taken away. Every evening, Jennifer told me, she asked herself if making dinner for one was worth the effort: one schnitzel, one potato, one carrot, silver beet from the garden - his garden. My mother did it, she told me, I can do this.

———

Anne Else's husband, Harvey McQueen, a poet and educator, died on Christmas Day eleven years ago. I knew Anne and Harvey as a couple for many years. Ian and I went to their wedding in the eighties. It was a second marriage for both of them, a joyful occasion, surrounded by friends who stayed close to them, and to Anne after Harvey died. Just a week after their wedding, I found myself in the bedsit in Eccleston Square, on that first ever visit to London. I remember how I walked through Pimlico Station where, in a piece of strange synchronicity, I ran into one of the wedding guests with whom I had chatted days earlier in New Zealand. That mutual friend guided me through those first uneasy days away from home. These are the ties that bind, a close reminder of how I stepped late into the world beyond, Eccleston Square a lifetime away from family, friends and my house in Hataitai.

I sat and talked to Anne recently, in the large living room of the townhouse where she and Harvey were living when he died. I could still see him in his armchair, almost a presence in the room, which looks out onto trees and the birds he loved to watch. He and I would sit in there and talk about poetry and literary gossip of one kind or another, Anne and I about issues of the day. She is a forthright feminist writer and commentator.

One of her and Harvey's shared passions was cooking, until Harvey developed a rare degenerative condition that would slowly waste away his muscles and his power to coordinate them. Even so, his death came suddenly, during a trip to hospital following a fall. He was too weak to come home, but there was no hint that his life would end in the early hours of Christmas Day. Anne recalls sitting numbed in the afternoon, surrounded by friends who had planned to join them for their usual celebratory meal. They ate the ham she had bought before he died - her friends brought everything else.

Like me, Anne had never lived on her own. In a memoir she later wrote she said:

> On January 4 I went to the supermarket for the first
> time since Harvey died. Ever since I had started
> shopping and cooking when I married at nineteen,
> I'd had at least one other person to cook for and eat
> with. Now all that had vanished.
>
> There were so many things I no longer needed
> to buy, but when I tried to think what I should buy
> I had no idea. I wandered round slowly, trying to
> work out what to do.

She found herself engulfed by loneliness. 'My friends are wonderful and indispensable,' she wrote, 'yet no matter how close they are, or how much I enjoy their company, they can't fill the gap left by the loss of a man I not only loved but, perhaps more importantly, really liked and got on with so well for so long.'

As she drew on her inner resources, she convinced herself that she should not betray the tradition of cooking and eating good food that she and Harvey had built up together. 'People don't change because somebody's died,' she said, when we talked. And with that resolution in mind, she continued to serve delicious meals to friends, blogged about food, wrote her successful book on the subject, came to terms with her new life alone.

———

That is what most of us do. We come to terms with it. There are all kinds of widows whose experience is different from mine and that of the women I have talked to. Where are the ones living in poverty, you might ask, those who cannot support their children, the ones who have been abandoned with disability or sickness of their own? Those who do not have families, as I do. These are fair questions. I have talked to women whose husbands have died through suicide, and to those who have been partnered for most of their lives with men they have not formally married. We are equally bereaved. Only one of these women has remarried and that was ill-fated. Nor have I included any who have happily started over again, though it's not to say that none of these women have found new and satisfying relationships, without vows and commitments. We still have the capacity to love. If I identify with these particular women, perhaps it's because we have all made new lives with meaning and intent. We had large, significant lives with our husbands; those lives are complete in themselves. Now we must forge new ones that belong just to us. All of us have in common a belief that our husbands would have wanted us to make the best of things. As my mother and my aunts would have said.

Is it true that as a widow you no longer get invited to dinners? There is an element of that – being part of a couple fits into the jigsaw around a table. I suppose I get invited less to people's houses, but no less to restaurants where there are couples. What I do know is that there is a subtle shift in status. I said at the beginning of this piece that the word widow doesn't please me much. We are not the leftovers from a marriage, we are people in our own right, in the same way as divorced women or women who have never married. We do not need a label that sets us apart. I think of myself now as a single woman. I'm still here, still doing my life.

Granted, there are days when that life feels a bit flat. You never forget the other life. And sometimes the dead return. Our lives can fill with illusions and dreams. Who is to say what is true and what is not? Ian had a shed at the bottom of our garden where he made things, model aeroplanes in particular, but all sorts of other things too, like copper jewellery, small artworks. After he died, I had it fixed up so that I could let it as an artist's studio, but family have found other uses for it. Perhaps it was never a good idea to think about someone else in there. Anyway, one day, without thinking, I went to tell him that lunch was ready. It didn't occur to me that he wasn't there. And, for a moment, he was, his outline silhouetted in the shed window. I waited a moment or two to take his measure. I saw him move away, taking his time, the way he had not done when he died. Then he was gone.

And, here I am now.

So far, for now
(for Ian)

Hokianga's shy hills, the poet
wrote, and, Cilla, you got it right:
a skein of sand, a sleeve of trees
above the water beneath the dunes
a girl bringing a fish and chip
bundle, her cigarette, and
a stab of gold in her nose,

a baby under the black
dress, the hills diminishing
into the collapsed world
of evening. Oh, you know
that you are going, that
you have already gone
far along the journey
when you sit here, just the two
of you at a rough wooden
table in this dusk light,
eating with slow care, not talking
about anything much, having said
enough, sometimes more than enough
for as long as you can remember,
not needing to say it all again.
In the morning
there is mist, the hills
have taken fright.

Acknowledgements

Harriet Allan and Anna Rogers have been editing my work for more than thirty years. Without them there would have been no books. I can never thank them enough for their skills, patience and friendship. It has been a wonderful, life-affirming collaboration. I thank Louisa Kasza too for invaluable editorial advice and Carla Sy for her design work.

Thanks to Vannessa Kidman for technical support, dinners, and keeping me grounded during the writing of this book, and for listening to many of the stories. Other family members have contributed to the essays.

Many people have given freely of their time, advice and information over the past year. In particular, I am grateful to those women who have talked about our shared experiences of widowhood: Harriet Allan (again), Brigitte Blakemore, Lois Daish, Beth Darroch, Anne Else and Jennifer Shennan (Thomas), with added advice from Leaphy Moeung and Eirini Tudor (neither of whom are widows).

And then there are those who have provided hospitality,

journeys made in their company, and answered my questions. For these kindnesses and more, I thank Jennifer Beck, Lynn Belt, Justice Brendan Brown, the Caselburg Trust, Robert Cross, (the late) Richard Douglas, Alexandra Dumitrescu, Frances Edmond, Faran Foley, Pierre Furlan, Nelly Gillet, Michael Harlow, the Hawera Library, Heather Hourigan, Alison and James Kember, Justice Stephen Kos, Emer Lyons, Mary McCallum, Professor Liam McIlvanney, Niamh McMahon, Bernie and Kath Monk, Jill Nicholas, Tom Petterson, Maggie Rainey-Smith, H.E. Peter Ryan and Mrs Theresa Ryan and the Embassy of Ireland, Sarah Shieff, Bess Sutherland, Melody Sutherland, Professor Sonja Tiernan and CISS (Irish and Scottish Studies Department, Otago University), Dimitrios Vassiliadis, The Waipu 150 Trust, Sabine Wespieser and Redmer Yska.

Thank you also to Natalie Karaitiana for advice on Otago place names.

Thanks to the organisers of all the festivals they have invited me to, over the years.

Sources

So far, for now

—

Opening poem: 'Untitled' by Fiona Kidman, 2018.

About grandparents

—

Opening poem: 'Speaking with my grandmothers', *Where Your Left Hand Rests*, Godwit, 2010.

'a long journey to make just to see some rain': Helen Simpson, *The Women of New Zealand*, Paul's Book Arcade, 1962.

Finding home

—

An early version of 'Finding Home' was published in *Mātātuhi Taranaki: A Bilingual Journal of Literature*, Vol. 1, No. 1 (April 2021) ed. Trevor M. Landers.

'watching their cigarettes drift': 'How I saw her', 'Ten sonnets for my mother (3)', *This Change in the Light*, Godwit, 2016.

Ronald Hugh Morrieson: in Helen Martin and Sam Edwards (eds), *New Zealand Film 1912-1996*, Oxford University Press, 1997.

North River
—

A previous version of this chapter and all the Levack quotations in this essay are from Wynne Haysmith, Peter Couper, Hamish Levack, Jennifer Beck and Reuben Keeling (eds), *A Conscientious Bloody Clergyman: The Diaries Of Reverend William Levack 1952-1964*, Waipu 150 Trust, 2018.

'I believe it was brown top': Bev Brett (Translations by John Alick MacPherson, *Letters to Mac-Talla from John Munro A Cape Breton Gael in New Zealand 1894-1902*.

'After the farms' number 3 in 'Ten sonnets for my mother', *This Change in the Light*.

On writing memoir
—

A fuller version of the Palais Lutetia was previously published in 'I lay down in the Palais Lutetia' in Citrus Quartet, Imprim17 / Les petites allées, edited and translated by Nelly Gillet, 2021, and *Ngā Ripo Wai | Swirling Waters* (Pavlova Press) October 2021.

'Red Nightgown', Lauris Edmond, *Selected Poems 1975-2000*, Bridget Williams Books, 2002, with thanks to the Literary Estate of Lauris Edmond and Frances Edmond.

'No Time' from *Nine Horses: Poems* by Billy Collins, © 2008 by Billy Collins. Used by permission of Random House, an imprint and division of Penguin Random House LLC. All rights reserved; and reproduced with permission of the Licensor through PLSclear and Pan Macmillan.

'The Garden at Sainte-Agnès', *Where Your Left Hand Rests*.

Albert Black
—

This chapter has been developed from a public lecture given for the Centre for Irish and Scottish Studies, Otago University.

All long quotations in this essay are from Fiona Kidman, *This Mortal Boy*, Vintage, 2018.

Extract from 'Tate's Avenue' from District and Circle, by Seamus Heaney, reproduced with permission from Faber and Faber Limited, 2006.

Pure Duras
—

'It isn't the transition . . .': from 'Black Block', by Marguerite Duras, translated by Barbara Bray, in *Practicalities*, Grove Press, 1990.

'So we resorted to Pho Hàng Gai': 'Silks', *The Trouble with Fire*, Vintage, 2011, pp. 166, 167.

Quardling around Glover
—

This chapter was developed from a piece written for *Newsroom*, 2017, with thanks to Steve Braunias.

'You were these hills and the sea': 'In Memoriam H. C. Stimpson [Mick] Port Levy', *Towards Banks Peninsula*, Pegasus Press, 1979.

'He was such an intelligent man': Gordon Ogilvie, *Denis Glover: His Life*, Godwit, 1999, p. 19.

'The Harbour is a Laundry': Denis Glover, *Wellington Harbour*, Catspaw Press, 1974, reproduced with permission from the Glover Estate.

Some other girl: the case for Jean Batten
—

Radio broadcast, archive held by Sound Archives Nga Taonga Korero ID 31502.

Jean Batten: the Garbo of the Skies, Ian Mackersey, Macdonald, 1990.

Flying places
—

'What followed for me was a kind of dreamtime': *A Needle in the Heart*, Vintage, 2002.

'. . . it is another story': 'Peggy's Cove', *This Change in the Light*.

'Walking West', the Going West keynote address, 2000, since published in *Voices of Aotearoa: 25 Years of Going West Oratory*, The Going West Trust, Oratia Media, 2021.

'On small planes': *Where Your Left Hand Rests*.

On being massaged
—

'. . . a skinny girl': 'The First time', *This Change in the Light*.

'I raised the curtain': 'All the Way to Summer', *A Needle in the Heart*.

Playing with fire
—

An earlier version of this chapter appeared in *Women Now: The Legacy of Female Suffrage*, published by Te Papa Press, 2018, with thanks to Nicola Legat.

'The route we women took' from 'Malala Yousafzai: in tribute' in *This Change in the Light*.

In the time of Covid
—

This chapter was developed from a piece written for Deborah Shepard, ed, 'In the Time of Coronavirus: A Collection', https://www.deborahshepardbooks.com/, with thanks to Deborah Shepard.

At Pike River
—

Part 1 of this chapter was developed from a piece written for *The Spinoff*, 2016, with thanks to Toby Manhire.

The quotations in part 6 are from the joint statement of Mr Bernard Monk; Hon. Andrew Little, Minister Responsible for Pike River Re-entry; and the Attorney General of New Zealand, released on 16 September 2021.

99 Albany Street
—

The survey mapping the Irish in New Zealand/Aotearoa is *Irish in Aotearoa: Mapping the Irish Community and People of Irish Heritage in New Zealand,* by Sonja Tiernan, 2020.

Translations by Brian Friel was published by Faber & Faber, 1981.

The blue room

An earlier version of this chapter was first published by Canvas magazine, *NZ Herald,* 2020, with thanks to Sarah Daniell.

On widowhood

Two of the early paragraphs came from 'Letter from Europe', Academy of NZ Literature, 2018.

'On January 4 I went to the supermarket': Anne Else, *The Colour of Food*, Awa Press, 2014.

For more information about our titles
visit www.penguin.co.nz